GENDER, POWER,
and PROMISE ৪৩০৪

GENDER, POWER, and PROMISE ✺

The Subject of the Bible's First Story

Danna Nolan Fewell
& David M. Gunn

ABINGDON PRESS
NASHVILLE

GENDER, POWER, AND PROMISE:
THE SUBJECT OF THE BIBLE'S FIRST STORY

© 1993 Danna Nolan Fewell and David M. Gunn

Translations from the Bible are the authors' own except where indicated as follows:

NRSV is from the New Revised Standard Version Bible, Copyright © 1989 by the Division of Christian Education of the National
Council of the Churches of Christ in the USA. Used by permission.

REB is from the Revised English Bible. Copyright © Oxford University Press and Cambridge University Press. Used by permission.

TANAKH is from *The TANAKH: The New JPS Translation According
to the Traditional Hebrew Text.* Copyright © 1985 by the Jewish Publi-
cation Society. Used by permission.

Published by Abingdon Press
Nashville, Tennessee

Printed on acid-free paper

PRINTED IN THE UNITED STATES OF AMERICA
2 4 6 8 9 7 5 3 1

Library of Congress Cataloging-in-Publication Data

Fewell, Danna Nolan.
  Gender, power, and promise : the subject of the Bible's first story / Danna
Nolan Fewell & David M. Gunn.
      p.   cm.
  Includes bibliographical references and indexes.
  ISBN 0-687-14042-0
  1. Women in the Bible. 2. Sex in the Bible. 3. Kinship in the Bible.
4. Bible. O.T.—Criticism, interpretation, etc. I. Gunn, D. M. (David M.)
II. Title.
BS1199.W7F48 1993
222'.06'082—dc20   93-31666
                                                                  CIP

To

Elsie
Isabel
Jeanne
Kim
Marilyn
Mary Charlotte
and
Millie

I am the first and the last
I am the honored one and the scorned one
I am the whore and the holy one
I am the wife and the virgin
I am the barren one
   —and many are my daughters
I am the silence that you cannot understand
I am the utterance of my name

—from *Daughters of the Dust*
a film by Julie Dash (1991)

CONTENTS

Of No Account

Where were the children of Sodom
when the mighty destruction came?
How many cried,
how many died
midst the brimstone and the flame?

How many babies in Sodom
asleep at their mothers' breasts—
never to know
never to grow—
died with all the rest?

Of all those children in Sodom
not a daughter or a son
could raise divine pity
to save a lost city—
there wasn't a righteous one.

Such wicked children in Sodom
there surely must have been
for a whole town
to be burned to ground
and everyone within.

How many babies in Sodom
were lost in the show of might?
How many cried,
how many died
on a count of divine oversight?

—DNF

INTRODUCTION

Imagine a large blue painting on a wall at the far end of the room. Yes, just blue, nothing but blue. You try to suppress speculations about how much the gallery paid for it and who was the "artist" who laughed all the way to the bank. You walk toward it to examine it more closely. Actually, the blue is not just blue. It is textured and variously hued. But more than that. There are red dots on/in the painting. Mostly around the margins, but a few scattered through the center, randomly, it would appear. Your interest is suddenly piqued. You even begin to ponder this painting. How do you feel about it? What does it mean? Is it a picture about blue or red? Is it, perhaps, about the importance of blue? Or, there again, the subversion of the dominant blue by the apparently subordinate red? (So does that make the red more important—after all, isn't it the red that is lending the blue its meaning?) And who knows? Scrape the blue, and perhaps there are rivers of red beneath. You peer even more intently at the red dots against the blue. The edges of the red are sometimes less distinct than you had at first perceived. They slide into orange and then green before becoming blue. Indeed, perhaps there are some separate green dots. Very small. Yes, and orange ones. The question of meaning is becoming more complex than you thought . . .

Red dots. Let us explain a little further.

> "Say to the people of Israel," [said YHWH to Moses], "When a man makes a special vow of persons to YHWH at your valuation, then your valuation of a male from twenty years old up to sixty years old shall be fifty shekels of silver, by the sanctuary's shekel. If she is a female, your valuation shall be thirty shekels. If the person is from five to twenty years old, your valuation of a male should be twenty shekels, of a female, ten shekels. If the person is from a month to five years old, your valuation of a male should be five shekels of silver, of a female your valuation should be three shekels of silver. As for someone sixty years old or older, if a male your valuation should be fifteen shekels, if a female, ten shekels." (Lev. 27:1-7)

This appraisal table, Carol Meyers (1988) contends, reflects the relative economic value of individuals in an agrarian society. Each person's "value" is based upon his or her contribution to the family's economy. In other words, value is a matter of labor and productivity.

Anthropologist Peggy R. Sanday, whom Meyers is following, argues that, in terms of gender, the most balanced societies are those in which females contribute a maximum of 40 percent to the household economy. Conditions of pregnancy and childcare responsibilities would deter further contribution. Meyers points out that in three of the four age groups listed, females are worth around 40 percent of the combined values of males and females (actually 37.5 percent for two groups and 40 percent for the oldest group). The only category in which this is not the case, the five to twenty year range (33.3 percent), is an understandable exception since, during this age "men were coming into their own as productive workers and females were beginning childbearing with its attendant demands and mortality risks" (Meyers 1988:171). What would seem at first glance to be gross inequity between genders is, in Meyers's view, evidence for gender equality (at least in Israel's premonarchic farming society).

Yet, while the anthropological insight into such a system of valuing is illuminating for those of us who do not live in such a society, it hardly settles the matter of gender value. On the contrary, we could argue that it precisely opens up that question. How so?

Let us understand the biblical text as the blue painting. On first view it seems to mean that (blue) males are more valuable than (red) females, and indeed this meaning has been accepted by numerous commentators. Vitally interested in the place of women in the world of the biblical text, however, Meyers sees it differently. She argues that, despite an apparent disproportion between the females and the males (females valued from one half to two thirds the value of males), the text is really presenting equilibrium. The blue and the red are of equal importance, once it is appreciated that there is more to the red than meets the eye—that is, once the childbearing and child-rearing roles of women are taken into account. Yet to another observer, that may not seem an entirely satisfactory interpretation.

The issue of women's roles raises the question, Who has determined that childbearing and childrearing have no economic value? Can we imagine women devising a system in which the "production" of the economy's labor force is counted as worthless? (The question remains one of serious contemporary social and economic significance.) Here we have a schedule of valuation for persons being "redeemed" from dedication to God, that is, showing the value of a person to God. Can we imagine women originating such a schedule that places no value at all on the role that, in biblical literature, most gives women identity, worth, and security, namely the role of motherhood? A woman's personal risk in childbearing, her commitment to the care of her children, detracts from, rather than adds to, her worth, it would appear.

Motherhood, it turns out, is a catch-22. To have value in society, a woman must be a mother. But being a mother makes a woman less valuable than a man, even though childbearing is crucial to human survival and a feat that men are incapable of. Indeed, is that the point? Since men are incapable of childbearing, is that why it is not valued? For these are plainly male constructions, both the particular valuation schedule for the sanctuary and the underlying understanding of economic value upon which, as Meyers shows, it is based.[1]

Indeed, we could press our point a little further. In drawing attention to characteristics of the red dots that were not apparent to us at first sight, Meyers has sharpened our focus. On the other hand, in arguing that the red and blue are in fact equitably distributed, despite appearances to the contrary, she risks being understood as having accepted the underlying premise of the painting: in paintings of blue and red, blue is always to be accorded more space than red because a significant part of red's space is, by the rules of such paintings, invisible. Or, to put it back in terms of the text, males are always to be valued more than females because a significant part of the lives of females is, economically speaking, unrecognizable. But this is patently a male premise (as no doubt Meyers would agree). In that case, if we are to continue to talk about gender equality here we need to take Meyers's argument a step further and challenge the underlying premise of the valuation system. Then we might say: yes, we can agree that there is something like gender equality in the Leviticus text, but only on androcentric terms. Or, put another way: no, we do not accept that paintings of blue and red should always have blue predominate spatially.

To leave the underlying system unchallenged is to give patriarchy the last laugh. As we shall argue in the chapters to follow, those who hold dominant power are only too ready to cede some measure of freedom, equity, or what you will, as long as it is controllable and does not in fact disturb the status quo. For the undervalued to perceive their undervaluing as, all things considered, equity is an ideal arrangement. Nothing need change. Likewise, as we trace the biblical texts that are the concern of this present book, we may see apparently strong and influential women, generally working behind the scenes with guile and deception. But we find ourselves unable therefore to decide that, given a degree of restriction upon women's lives, they really are an "integral part" of the story, partners with men in their reception and direction of the promise, successful and strong "in the same sense that their husbands are . . . [and] not unusual because they are women" (Sharon Pace Jeansonne, 116; cf. 114-117). We do not see it that way. Michel Foucault (1978:86) makes the point well: "power is tolerable only on condition that it mask a substantial part of itself. Its success is proportional to its ability to hide its own mechanisms." Biblical patriarchy has mastered this rule.

We have called our book *Gender, Power, and Promise: The Subject of the Bible's First Story*. That is a mouthful of loaded terms and, deliberately, no little ambiguity. So let us introduce some of these terms—and others that are related and will be important as the book proceeds.

Our book is an interpretation, one of many possible, of *the first great story in the Bible*. This story extends from the creation (Genesis 1–3), through the deliverance from Egypt (Exodus 1–15), the giving of the Law and wandering in the wilderness (Exodus–Deuteronomy), the taking of the promised land (Joshua and Judges 1), the establishment of the monarchy (1 Samuel), the division of the kingdom into (northern) Israel and (southern) Judah (1 Kings 12), the deportation of Israel (2 Kings 17), and the fall of Jerusalem and exile of Judah (2 Kings 24–25).

We do not claim that this huge and meandering text is the first story to have been composed among all the component stories of the Bible, though it may well contain some of these earliest accounts. Despite sometimes large claims about the dating of biblical material, scholars actually know very little about the Bible's literary history. "First" in that sense is not our concern. Rather we offer a reading, or perhaps better, a set of readings, of a text which not only is placed first in the Bible (whether the Jewish or Christian scriptures),[2] but which is a primary text in the sense that the story it tells is foundational for much of the rest of the Bible. Prophets, psalms, and other "history" books (Chronicles, Ezra, Nehemiah) all appeal to main outlines, or specific parts, of this primary story.[3] When exactly it found its final form we do not know. Perhaps it was in the latter part of the sixth century BCE, during the Babylonian exile or at the time of Judah's restoration in the wake of the conquest of Babylon by Cyrus the Persian.

We read as *literary critics*,[4] not as historians (and we are certainly not trying to establish "what actually happened"). Our book belongs with a broad movement that has recently broken in decisive ways with the program of "historical criticism" that has dominated the European tradition of academic biblical scholarship for nearly two centuries. Instead of seeking meaning in the (reconstructed) origins or sources and compositional history of the Bible, we read the final form of the text (admittedly a notion not without its own problems) as we might read modern literature like a novel. Instead of attempting to reconstruct an ancient "history," we seek to construct, in the first instance, a story world in which questions of human values and belief find shape in relation to our own (and our likely readers') worlds. In so doing, we draw from current literary theory and practice—and sometimes from other related fields such as sociology and anthropology. At the same time we do not deny the possibility of reconstructing an ancient "history" using these texts as source materials. Indeed, in this present book we are attempting to describe a textually encoded ideology, part of what some social historians would call the "domain of notions" of an ancient society. Such an account, we trust, might prove useful to an historian of the ancient world.

Many commentators have seen in the story, or in its component parts, the theme of *promise*: promise to Noah regarding sustaining the creation, to Abraham regarding land and progeny, to Moses and the people of Israel regarding a covenant of law and security as a nation in exchange for exclusive allegiance, and to David regarding the maintenance of a royal dynasty. The counterpoint to the story is the failure, with dire consequences, of Israel and the nation's leaders to live up to the promise. If we think of Deuteronomy as its center we also see a story which offers to its (implied) audience in exile the chance to relive the promise anew. Like the people whom Moses addresses ("you, this day"), they stand on the "other side" of the river, in the wilderness, looking toward the promised land. The land from which they have been expelled (like the Canaanites!) is set as a possession before them, as YHWH swore to their fathers, to Abraham, to Isaac, and to Jacob, to give to them and their seed after them (Deut 1:8). Only they must take care not to forget their side of the promise—forget, that is, their sole allegiance to YHWH. "For YHWH your god is a devouring fire, a jealous god" (4:23-24). But if they seek YHWH with heart and soul, return to him, and obey his voice, then, says Moses to both audiences standing on the other side, both those within the story and those outside it, "YHWH will not fail you or destroy you or forget the covenant with your fathers which he swore to them" (4:30-31). Read thus, the challenge of the story is to grasp the promise and live it again—but differently this time!

Our own reading is also, though in a different sense, from the "other side." The audience Moses (or the narrator) addresses is nominally "the people," but in practice, as we shall show in the course of our discussion, it consists primarily of adult male heads of households. We read wondering what the story of promise might look like to those excluded people, in particular the women, who stand on the "other" side of a *gender* divide.

The primary concern we bring as contemporary readers of this ancient story is a commitment to see a radical reformation in gender relations in our own society. This, then, is a book about women in the Hebrew Bible, and (to a lesser extent) about the children who, in the social world of the Bible, are particularly bound up with the lives

of women. Issues of class and ethnicity (the place of the "alien") turn
out to belong intimately with the analysis and would each make a
primary focus as relevant for our time as the question of gender.
And since gender relations, at least as constructed in a patriarchal
world like ours and like that of ancient Israel, are power relations,
this is also a book about power.

We use the term "gender" to refer to the culturally defined
system of behavior deemed appropriate for biological females and
males in any given society. Gender is not a biological given (like a
person's "sex" inasmuch as that is determined by, for example, genital difference), but rather it is a performance or role. Or, as one of
Mark Twain's characters puts it in Huckleberry Finn, "Hellfire Hotch-
kiss [the girl] is the only genuwyne male man in this town and [the
boy] Thug Carpenter's the only genuwyne female girl, if you leave out
sex and just consider the business facts" (quoted by Jehlen 1990:272).
"Girl" and "boy," "woman" and "man," no less than "femininity"
and "masculinity" (or their adjectives "feminine" and "masculine")
have no independent or palpable reality apart from their function as
stereotypes embedded within cultural discourse.

> Neither social reality nor the 'natural' world has fixed intrinsic meanings
> which language reflects or expresses. Different languages and different
> discourses within the same language [e.g., the language of bio-chemistry
> as compared to that of psychology] divide up the world and give it mean-
> ing in different ways which cannot be reduced to one another through
> translation or by an appeal to universally shared concepts reflecting a fixed
> reality. For example, the meanings of femininity and masculinity vary
> from culture to culture and language to language. They even vary be-
> tween discourses within a particular language, between feminist dis-
> courses, for example, and are subject to historical change, from Victorian
> values to the suffrage movement, for example. (Weedon 1987:22)

Moreover, these concepts lend themselves to polarizing reality so
that biological males and females "learn to see reality as carved
naturally into polarized sex and gender categories, not carved—
whether naturally or unnaturally—into some other set of categories"
(Bem 1993:125). As a result, sex-determined biological difference,
gender difference, and difference in sexual orientation and/or sexual
practice become mainstays in the definition of society, and they do so
in polarized or binary terms. That is no accident in a patriarchal society where power lies in the hands of well-to-do heterosexual males.
In order to maintain power it is necessary for them to define themselves as the "norm" by marking all others as different. That is most
easily done when social reality is defined, in binary categories, as
"naturally" and "essentially" a matter of sex and gender difference.

It follows, of course, that for this system to be sustained not only must men endeavor to control women's sexual behavior (and indeed the social understanding of women's sexuality), but they must police and, preferably, prohibit all forms of sexual expression that fall outside the binary world of heterosexuality. The intimate connection between patriarchy's suppression of women and homophobia, particularly as directed against homosexual males, is today well recognized; we explore homophobia as an expression of patriarchy in our discussion of law (Chapter Five) and of the relationship between David and Jonathan (Chapter Seven).

We have begun to speak of *power*, and we need to say a little more here about how we understand that term. Power is often thought of as a substance, a kind of limited resource drawn from a reservoir in the exclusive control of the powerful. One either has power or lacks it. Rather we follow Michel Foucault (cf. 1978:92) in understanding power as a relational term. It describes the social relationships or structures by means of which people—whether individuals or groups —control and dominate, or inspire and sustain. We stress that power can be positive or productive as well as negative or repressive. It is not simply the province of the law or institutional authority, though it certainly inheres in those spheres of social life. People can have power without having authority, that is, they may still find ways of effecting change despite oppressive structures that militate against their interest. Power, then, exists on a continuum.

Perhaps for us the key point to make is that power relations are multiform and always in process—always, in short, unstable and subject to unending struggle.[5] Single explanations of power relations will always fall short, though they may be themselves powerful. That is because there is always a multiplicity of elements (or subjects or interests) involved in power relations, and because these do not necessarily form a single unity but, rather, are often in some degree of tension, disjunction, or contradiction with one another.

This understanding of power has implications for our understanding of the social order we are exploring in Genesis–Kings, which is often termed *patriarchy*. We use the term broadly, as Gerda Lerner has neatly put it (1986:239), to refer to

> the manifestation and institutionalization of male dominance over women and children in the family and the extension of male dominance over women in society in general. It implies that men hold power in all the important institutions of society and that women are deprived of access to such power. It does *not* imply that women are either totally powerless or totally deprived of rights, influence, and resources.

Nor, we would add, does the term imply that patriarchal society is everywhere and at every time the same.

Over the past decade or so, critical theory has been challenging us to consider that language itself is infinitely unstable and that *meaning*, therefore, is always deferable. It is not that words do not mean anything. But their meaning is always having to be established in relation to other words, other texts, whose meaning is always having to be established in relation to other words, other texts, and so on. Some critics are radically foregrounding the reader's values as determinative of interpretation; some are arguing that meaning is not anchored simply in fixed texts but is a production, at least in part, of fragile communities of interpreters; and some are recognizing that criticism is social construction, or persuasion, if you will.

One way such discussion has helped our own understanding of the business of critical reading is through the notion of *coherence*. (The link between what follows and our remarks about power should, we trust, become obvious.) We believe that most readers are driven to form interpretations that offer an encompassing, comprehensive, and coherent account of their text. Critical theory, in particular feminist and poststructuralist (particularly deconstructionist) discourse, helps us to see that this "totalizing" drive is hardly inevitable or innocent. It places a premium on sameness (unity) and univocality (one meaning), and it devalues difference (diversity) and multivocality (multiple meanings). It leads to our ignoring or suppressing the very tensions and fractures in texts that may offer us enlivening insight or, indeed, an escape from the tyranny of a given interpretive tradition.

Consequently we have learned to be more suspicious readers, with an eye for the subliminal construction of the norm and the different (or Subject and Other, on which more shortly). We have learned to seek out the different and the discordant, the puzzling element in the text that is usually bypassed or harmonized, and to build a reading around it. That is like seeking out the loose threads in a sweater and by pulling them carefully observing the garment's (de)construction. No persuading voice can make its case without acknowledging, even if only implicitly, the voices that speak against it. We listen for those voices, pull the threads, and look for red dots.

Another way of thinking through the text from Leviticus about the sanctuary valuations is to ask a question about its *subject*. By "subject" we do not mean its topic, the subject of the cultic (or economic) valuation of persons. We are not looking for an answer to the question, *What* is its subject? Rather we mean the governing consciousness (and unconsciousness), the point of view whose interest this text expresses, or better, constructs. That is, we are seeking to answer the question, *Who* is its subject? (Or, to avoid confusion, Subject.) This is a question about *subjectivity*, which we understand to be "the conscious and unconscious thoughts and emotions of the individual, her sense of herself and her ways of understanding her relation to the world" (Weedon 1987:32). Subjectivity is constructed, and constantly being reconstructed, out of the relation between the individual and the social. It is "not innate, not genetically determined, but socially produced . . . in a whole range of discursive practices (areas of discourse)—economic, social and political—the meanings of which are a constant site of struggle over power" (Weedon 1987:21).

Linked to the concept of the Subject is that of the Other. In feminist discourse (starting with Simone de Beauvoir in her pioneering book, *The Second Sex*, in 1953), this concept has been used to help understand how male subjectivity is constructed and maintained. Values associated with being a "man" (or "masculine," "male") are assumed to be a neutral standard or the norm, and are unmarked, while values associated with "woman" (or "feminine," "female") are negative, abnormal, inessential—in short, inferior—and are marked (see Humm 1990:156; Bem 1993:2). An important achievement of the women's movement over the past several decades has been its enabling of many women (and growing numbers of men) to recognize this "androcentric" value system and either reject the notion that woman is Other or reverse the negative evaluation of women's difference and instead celebrate it.

Language—and by the same token, the text—is the matrix within which subjectivity is formed and reformed. For example, the meaning of the term "woman" in English is produced within language rather than reflected by language, that is, it acquires its meaning(s) through its position in relation to (i.e., in its similarity to and difference from) other terms in the language system. And the meaning of "woman" will change depending on its specific social location and on what competing uses of the term are being advanced within competing discourses.

Because of this instability, the meanings of crucially important social terms like "feminine" and "masculine," "female" and "male," "woman" and "man" are always open to challenge and redefinition with shifts in the power relations within which this language functions. Likewise, texts which employ these terms are open to rereading and reinterpretation also. Readers come to a text with their own subjectivity, the construction of their own specific personal and social worlds. In the process of exposing the differences between the reader's understanding of "woman" and that of the text, the difference between the reader's subjectivity and that of the text may also emerge. Or, the process may work the other way round: in the process of exploring the difference between the subjectivity of the text and that of the reader, the differing conceptions/constructions of "woman" may surface.[6]

We have spoken of reading for the Subject as one of the ways we open up the consideration of women and children in the Bible, consideration which they have been denied in a male-dominated interpretive tradition. That means, in practice, several things.

First, no matter what the ostensible topic, or the ostensible addressee, of the text, we want to know about its Subject. Whose primary subjectivity governs this legal code, or this narrative? Whose interest does this text serve? We are clear about our bias. As already stated, we ask these questions out of a primary interest in gender relations, though we also pursue a closely related interest in the Subject's understanding of ethnicity as well as other kinds of "strangeness" (i.e., where the male Israelite is assumed to be the norm). As others have shown, and as will be apparent in this book, the male Subject of these biblical texts frequently finds his identity in opposition not only to the female, but to the *alien* female. The alien woman is the quintessential Other.

Second, we practice reading in defiance of the apparent disposition of the text. We go looking for women in our reading. We seek those with speaking parts, those with walk-on parts, those with no part at all but whose presence we miss. In order better to expose the subjectivity that predominates, we seek to assign primary subjectivity to the women of the text, to make woman the Subject, in other words, though that, of course, is impossible. Put simply, we deliberately read the text as a story of women. This is not to say that we think Genesis–Kings is best described as a story of women. On the contrary. But by consistently reading in this manner we have become much more radically aware of the potential power of this biblical text to engage (and shape) readers' understanding of gender. We need hardly remind our own readers: this is no ordinary text but a primary religious text, Scripture, whose connection with current social behavior is accepted and sought by large numbers of people throughout the world. This is a text already deeply enmeshed in the power relations of many persons and many societies.

Third, we take seriously God's function as a character in the story and are willing to explore to what extent, as a male character, he is a key manifestation of the male Subject. The notion that the figure God in the biblical text is actually God who is worshiped by Jewish and Christian believers seems to us to be, ironically, a form of idolatry such as biblical voices constantly warn against. Why a visual image should be qualitatively worse than a verbal one is not immediately apparent, though no doubt an erudite case can be made in support of crucial difference. Our point is that unless the character of God is subject to the same kind of critical scrutiny as all the other characters, we are not really reading the text. The history of biblical interpretation has a poor record here. Among interpreters within the scriptural traditions the figure of God (like the figure of Jesus in the Gospels) is largely sacrosanct. It is little different among professional academics in secular institutions, perhaps because few are genuinely free of the constraints of religious traditionalism in both their immediate and their wider social contexts. The deity can have a powerful symbolic function representing and assigning value to social norms. That male subjectivity should be constructed reciprocally with the divine Subject would hardly be surprising. We need to take that possibility seriously in our reading of the text. And that is why, too, we retain the male pronoun "he" for the divinity, whether YHWH, God, El, or whichever designation he goes by in the text. God as male (though without a genitally-marked body!) is part and parcel of this story.

Just because the Bible is susceptible to strongly held religious beliefs and commitments by many of our own readers, we have no doubt but that what we have to say will be disturbing to some, though liberating, we trust, to others. More, we imagine, will have mixed emotions. The fact is, that for readers within the Jewish or Christian faiths in north America, for example—which is where we locate ourselves—much of what we read in this text, is bound to be disturbing, given inherited traditions of understanding and using the Bible in religious and social life. It is disturbing to us, who have taught for some years in theological seminaries (Methodist and Presbyterian, respectively). Some readers, indeed, may feel that at times a tone of anger enters our writing, that our attitude becomes irreverent and our language bluntly explicit. But it is difficult to avoid anger and irreverence in the face of the violence against women which permeates these texts.

Neither of us is convinced that either Christianity or Judaism has yet seriously come to terms with the challenge of feminist thought and practice where the Bible is concerned, though many individuals have voiced eloquently the nature of the challenge. We can read to "redeem" the text, making it more palatable to a new world which is beginning to recognize a huge legacy of gender oppression (among the many oppressions to which patriarchal Western society has lent itself), yet we are left with a pervasive subjectivity that is constructed on the back of woman as Other. We can tinker with official translations, turn patently androcentric language into inclusive language as the New Revised Standard Version does, yet be doing no more than masking the extent of the problem.

Nor does it help to do what Christians have been prone to do over the centuries and claim that all is made well in the New Testament. All is not made well. Few Christian readers are prepared to read Paul's letters or the Pastoral Epistles the way we read Genesis–Kings, though the number is growing. Far fewer yet are willing to read the Gospels this way. But the New Testament is rife with the fruits of patriarchy no less than Genesis–Kings. That is hardly surprising, since these bodies of text were produced on a powerful social and literary continuum, and within powerfully patriarchal social contexts.

We do not know where our own reading takes us. The problems feminist criticism raises for traditional notions of revelation and biblical authority are immense. Sometimes they seem intractable. What we do see is the need for change. What we can do now is attempt to be honest, as professional biblical critics, about how deeply implicated in an oppressive ideology is the Scripture of our own religious communities. At the same time we have tried not to be overwhelmed by our sense of the negative in our reading.

We do see moments of great liveliness and hope, especially through the enlivening ironies of the text, and we have attempted to give expression to these. In our teaching we reach out to other biblical books which offer different visions. Ruth, for example, while no feminist tract, makes enlivening reading beside Judges, Samuel and Kings. The Song of Songs offers a superb counterpart not only to the other garden story, in Genesis, but also, in its celebration of erotic love that breaks boundaries, to the jealous husband metaphor that threads its way through Genesis–Kings as a whole. Our present book, however, has not made those connections and no doubt is the poorer for that, but a sustained reading of Genesis–Kings seemed to be enough of a task for now.

We tried hard, as we wrote this book, to be "balanced." But that has proved to be difficult. Most difficult is to conclude that this text is not deeply prejudicial to the interests of women. For it seems to us that it is. That is a hard thing to be "balanced" about. Or to put it another way, Do we really want our children to read this story? We wish at this point that we could more confidently answer, Yes. Of one thing we are very sure: we need to teach our daughters and sons to read the Bible differently.

Next, a word about the organization of the book. We devote a significant part of our discussion to the Book of Genesis, which remains one of the most read and most influential of biblical books. The first three chapters examine closely some of the component stories of Genesis 1–22: the account of creation and the first humans in the garden of Eden (Genesis 1–3; One), the story of Abraham, Sarah, and Isaac (Genesis 11–22; Two), and a short account embedded in that larger narrative, namely the story of Lot, his family, and the city Sodom (Genesis 18–19; Three). Thereby we hope to convey some sense of the key issues generated right at the beginning of the greater story (Genesis–Kings) and to demonstrate our reading method in detailed application.

Thereafter we use broader strokes, starting with a chapter (Four) that looks at other women of Genesis and then considers the story of deliverance from Egypt at the beginning of Exodus. There follows a chapter (Five) on Exodus–Deuteronomy, concentrating on the laws of the Exodus Decalogue and Book of the Covenant, and then Levitical texts detailing regulations of sexual control. The chapter closes with some other texts that deal with legal control over, and threats to, the body. Subsequent chapters explore (Six) possession and dispossession in Judges, with a preface on Rahab in Joshua and a postscript on Hannah in 1 Samuel; (Seven) the Books of Samuel and the beginning of 1 Kings, construing David's kingship though the subjectivity of the women upon whose lives he impinges; and (Eight) the remainder of the Books of Kings, taking as a point of departure the devouring of Jezebel's body.

We have no concluding chapter. We began to write one but could only conclude as we proceeded that we were reducing the multiple threads of our writing (and our own multiple subjectivities) to an unacceptable singleness. In the end we were unwilling to tame either the biblical text or our own simply in the service of the genre of the academic book. So we risk our readers' displeasure and opt for a measure of open-endedness.

Finally, we wish to acknowledge that many have lent us help along the way, as we have shaped and reshaped the material that has come to be fixed on these pages. Among them are our spouses, David and Margaret, who help make our collaboration possible. Perkins School of Theology provided a Lilly Faculty Outreach Scholarship to the same end. Once more we find ourselves thanking Tim Beal for valuable suggestions, practical advice, and encouragement when it was needed most—though he is not to blame! Tod Linafelt proofread at short notice. Rex Matthews at Abingdon trusted us, was patient, and blessedly flexible. And the women and men of the "Eve's Daughters" class at Columbia Theological Seminary in the Spring of 1992 were an inspiration, much treasured.

Chapter One

SHIFTING THE BLAME

And God created humankind in his own image, in the image of God he created it, male and female he created them. And God blessed them, and God said to them, "Be fruitful and multiply, and fill the earth and subdue it; and subjugate . . ." And God saw everything that he had done, and behold, it was very good. (Gen 1:27-28, 31)

Then Yhwh God said, "It is not good that the human should be alone; I will make it a helper, a counterpart for it." (2:18)

And the human said: "This at last is bone of my bones and flesh of my flesh; this shall be called 'woman,' because from man was this taken." (Hence a man forsakes his father and his mother and cleaves to his woman, so that they become one flesh.) (Gen 2:23-24)

And God said: "Have you eaten from the tree of which I said not to eat?" The man said, "The woman whom you gave to be with me, she gave me fruit of the tree, and I ate." And Yhwh God said to the woman, "What is this that you have done?" And the woman said, "The serpent beguiled me, and I ate." And Yhwh God said to the serpent . . . . (Gen 3:12-14)

For good and evil, Genesis 1–3, perhaps more than any other biblical text, has influenced the way men and women relate to one another in the Western world. For good and evil—because good and evil have a way of changing their spots, depending upon where we stand in society.

The story is about the origins of humankind. It is also a story about the divinity, God, or Yhwh God, as the narrator goes on to call him in chapter 2. Indeed we could say that God is the dominant character in this story of origins. Yet curiously, while commentators over the centuries have had an overabundance of observations to make about the character of the humans, and especially of Eve, whose failings have provided them with rich pickings, they have been remarkably reticent regarding the character of Yhwh and, in particular, notably reluctant to put the deity under the same kind of critical scrutiny as the humans.

As any family therapist worth her salt would want to ask, however, How can you understand the children without understanding something of the parents and the interrelational dynamics of all?

Families are systems. So here we have a story of what appears to be a single parent family, a family which, the narrator suggests, enjoys a measure of dysfunction (which some theologians have termed "The Fall"). Since we wish to understand the daughter, Eve, it makes sense to take a searching look at this curious figure, God, who seems to function as her father.

He is a talker. He talks the world into existence.

He appreciates the need for rest. Sabbath marks the culmination of creation.

He has a strong penchant for order. The story begins in Genesis 1 with a strong bias towards the binary. God divides up the world in clear categories: light and dark, day and night, wet and dry, plants and animals, heaven and earth. We see a desire to divide, differentiate, categorize and, in a word, name. Of course, differentiation could be said to be indispensable to creation. Certainly separation, division, difference is indispensable to meaning. Meaning *is* difference. A world that is no longer simply *tohu vabohu* ("a formless void," NEB) is a world of difference. Naming, the shaping of the world in language, is the manipulation of difference. Naming is the prerequisite of a meaningfully ordered world. Naming, as is often observed of this account, may also be an expression of control.

On the other hand, when the account reaches a climax with the creation of humankind, that is, the creature in the image of God (Gen 1:26-30), we see movement against that desire to differentiate. Blurring the binary poles, God desires to create likeness or sameness, to recreate self, a desire impossible to achieve.

Equally interesting are the sharp edges of God's naming. The binary impulse is there very clearly. Yet in all this careful defining, separating and opposing there is a curious slippage. God "himself" is unsure whether he is plural or singular, echoing the narrator's grammatical confusion of a plural name (*'elohim*, which may or may not be a proper noun!) and a singular verb (Gen 1:26-29):[1]

> Then God(s) [or "divinity"] said [sing.] "Let us make humankind in our image, after our likeness" . . . So God(s) created [sing.] humankind in his own image, in the image of God(s) he created him, male and female he created them . . . And God said, "Behold, I have given you . . . ."

Significantly the slippage extends from the God(s) to the human(s) created in his/their image. While humankind is one (him/it) it is also plural—male and female (them).

Thus, despite the appearance of a world ordered and sustained by exclusive and fixed definitions, God's own blurred and slipping self-definition suggests that things might be otherwise. This world might in fact be as inherently indeterminable as the identity that creates it.

Within this system of divisions and separations, God begins to institute a hierarchy of dominion: the greater light is to rule over the day, the lesser light over the night. At the creation of the human, however, the language of dominion grows stronger (1:26-28, 31):

> And God said, "Let us make humankind in our own image, after our likeness; and let them subjugate [*radah*: trample, put under foot] the fish of the sea and the birds of the air, and the cattle, and all the earth, and every creeping thing that creeps upon the earth." And God created humankind in his own image, in the image of God he created it, male and female he created them. And God blessed them, and God said to them, "Be fruitful and multiply, and fill the earth and subdue it [*kabash*: bring into bondage]; and subjugate all fish of the sea and birds of the air and every living thing that moves upon the earth." . . . And God saw everything that he had done, and behold, it was very good.

Rule, subjugate, subdue. The language is, disturbingly, the language of totalitarian power, as others have observed. It would be at home, for example, in the Assyrian imperial annals. Humankind's first mandate is to subdue the earth and subjugate every living thing that moves upon it. Not to cooperate with, be partners with, share with, but bring into bondage and subjugate. On the other hand, God seems to envision this subjugation as a blessing for the humans, along with being fruitful and multiplying and filling the earth, which lead to the instruction to subjugate.

"And God saw that it was good." That constant refrain speaks of discovery. This creator God is plainly not, as Christian theology would have it, omniscient. He does/says something new, observes it, and remarks upon his discovery: "it is good!" God is experimenting. God desires to explore. God desires something new and greets with enthusiasm each new discovery of his own handiwork. By the same token we suspect that there may come a point when he will exclaim "it is not good!" And indeed God does so in chapter 2: "It is not good," he finally admits, after trying out a single human being, "that the human [*ha'adam*] should be alone." This, too, is a discovery on God's part.

The very phrase, "not good," however, reminds us that meaning cannot simply be confined within binary terms. The true opposite of "good" is "evil." Intriguingly, the narrator manages in chapter 1 to insist repeatedly that God's creative differentiations are good without ever mentioning the term evil. That is kept out of sight until chapter 2. Some readers, on the other hand, may have already begun to wonder whether, in the face of such protestations of goodness, somewhere there must be evil, even if only in the imagination of God's heart (cf. the discussion within Jewish mysticism [Kabbalah]). They might also have begun to wonder whether evil is already latent in that ordered world as an expression of God's desire for himself to have dominion over the earth and for his viceroy, the creature made in his image, to subjugate all living things. The desire to subjugate is an ethically ambiguous one, for it may mean the desire to subjugate good (where subjugation is evil) or to subjugate evil (where subjugation is good).

> And YHWH God planted a garden in Eden, in the east, and put there the human whom he had formed. And he made grow from the ground every tree that is pleasant to look at and good to eat—and the tree of life was also in the midst of the garden, and the tree of the knowledge of good and evil. (Gen 2:8-9)

So the story confirms that this discriminating God does indeed know good and evil, though clearly his eagerness to proclaim his own work as "good" suggests that he desires good rather than evil.

In Genesis 1 (through 2:4a) the narrator has opened up a broad and highly schematized view of creation. From 2:4b, the account takes a different shape and the focus falls upon a particular category of creation: the human.[2]

> On the day that YHWH God made the earth and the heavens . . . YHWH God formed the human, dust of the ground, and blew into its [his] nostrils the breath of life, and the human became a living being . . . And YHWH God took the human and put it [him] in the garden of Eden to till it and tend it. (Gen 2:4, 7, 15)

Although the new episode goes on to present the human divided into its binaries, man and woman, it deals little with *biological* difference. In 1:26-30, the narrator has recounted the creation of the male and female of humankind in order to show how humankind as a species is to be fruitful and multiply—so as to fill the earth and subjugate it (cf. Bird 1981). In Genesis 2–3 it is gender that is under construction: here the *social* roles of man and woman are being defined. And what we shall discover is that, as usual, binaries are less equal than they at first appear. The apparent (biological) equity of Gen 1:27 ("in the image of God he created them; male and female he created them") dissolves under closer scrutiny. Simple binaries in fact lend themselves to hierarchies. One term becomes Subject and Norm, the other becomes Object and Other. And hierarchy has a cunning way of ordering, of putting and keeping things—and people—in their "proper" place.

Let us trace the story further as it tells of God and humankind in the garden.

Two trees grow at the center of the garden. The fruit from the tree of life is at first freely available (though it is not clear that the human knows of it). The other tree's fruit has not been put at the human's disposal. God's first words to the human, therefore, are characteristically authoritarian. He permits and prohibits (2:16-17).

> And YHWH God commanded the human, "You may certainly eat from any tree of the garden, but from the tree of the knowledge of good and evil you shall not eat, for the day you eat from it you shall certainly die."

The forbidden tree has been put before the human and named: the knowledge of good and evil. But to what purpose? This, after all, is a highly ambiguous gesture by God. Some have answered that the point is to instill trust. Perhaps so. But we could equally as well identify the action—as Francis Landy (1983:188) suggests in his wonderfully rich (and, for us, influential) reading between the texts of Genesis 2-3 and the Song of Songs—as temptation. "Do not seek this knowledge," God tantalizes, "trust me!" "Stay ignorant—or seek it at your own risk!"

Of course, one might argue that God has no well-conceived plan for either of the trees. The narrator seems reluctant to implicate God in their planting. While God plants every tree that is a delight to see and good to eat, the narrator says, somewhat remotely, "the tree of life was in the midst of the garden as well as the tree of the knowledge of good and evil." God himself says that the latter tree is *not* good for food—"if you eat of it you will die"—thus further distinguishing it from the trees God is said to have planted. Perhaps God's control of the design and contents of this garden is less than complete. Certainly the serpent's later behavior will suggest this to be the case.

For most commentators, however, the issue is not one of control but of authority. As Walter Brueggemann (1982:46) puts it:

> There is a *prohibition* (v. 17). Nothing is explained. The story has no interest in the character of the tree. What counts is the fact of the prohibition, the authority of the one who speaks and the unqualified expectation of obedience.

We are less sure than Brueggemann about the story's lack of interest in the tree. The tree is specifically labeled an intriguing name, by both the narrator (2:9) and God (2:17). Moreover, it turns out that to eat of it is not only to acquire the knowledge of good and evil but to "become *like God*, knowing good and evil" (3:22). Those characteristics are not incidentally mentioned, but proposed in due course by the serpent in a key speech (3:4) and confirmed by God (3:22). On the contrary, then, the character of the tree may be, for some readers, far from inconsequential. To block the question about the tree is to block a troubling question about God. Why does God put (or allow) this particular tree in the garden in the first place? We shall return to this question in due course.

After he has formed and placed the human in the garden, YHWH God then decides that

> It is not good that the human should be alone; I will make it [him] a helper, counterpart [*keneged*; "like-opposite"] for it [him]. (2:18)

Despite God's own presence, despite the fact that the human, made in God's image, is arguably the deity's counterpart (like-opposite him), the deity deems the human to be alone. The implication, of course, is that God is deeming himself to be still alone.[3]

God's sense of the creature in his own image is ambivalent. Is it like or unlike him? Is the human a suitable counterpart for God or not? Or, to put it the other way around, Is God a suitable counterpart for the human or not? Either way, God decides not. The sense of separation wins over the sense of sameness. Is that because the human is silent before God's commands? Does God seek response—or diversity in unity, like himself? (Of course, another reason why a helper is sought might be in order to produce fruitfulness and multiplication through division into male and female.)

God therefore forms the animals and parades them before the human, like gifts before a monarch, "to see what it [he] would call them." Confident that the human will replicate God's own desire to name, God is not disappointed. Yet the experiment fails in its main purpose, for a counterpart is not found. Perhaps the human is unwilling (or unable) to recognize the animals as counterparts because, like God, the human desires its own image. God reverts, therefore, to division. Man and woman are created. Likeness is conjured by separation. Male and female. Opposite and alike. Difference and sameness. Other and self.

> So YHWH God caused a deep sleep to fall upon the human [*ha'adam*], and while he slept took one of its [his] sides and closed up its place with flesh; and the side which YHWH God had taken from the human he made into a woman and brought her to the human. And the human said:
> "This at last is bone of my bones and flesh of my flesh;
> this shall be called 'woman' [*'ishshah*]
> because from man ['*ish*] was taken this." (Gen 2:21-23)

In other words, the effect of this new experiment is spectacular. The man formed from the human claims the woman, also formed from the human, as his own. Presumably he finds in her a suitable helper (partner?) because she is, as he puts it, bone of his bones and flesh of his flesh. On the other hand, as Landy wryly observes, this experiment, too, is a failure: though woman successfully supersedes the inadequate animals, she *is* the human. The human is thus still alone (Landy 1983:234)! The desire for relationship with a like-opposite is therefore both fulfilled and unfulfilled, fulfillable and unfulfillable, in the case of the human as in the case of God.

The passage invites us to ponder the character of God a little further. We may by this stage in the story have decided that the deity's uncertain self-perception about being singular or plural may have been settled when the narrator begins (from Gen 2:4 on) to use a name that pushes toward singularity: YHWH God. Yet identity slippage emerges again in connection with the differentiated human. Following God's point of view we see the human divided and a woman formed whom he brings to the human. But, of course, the one to whom he brings her is in fact the man, and it is the man, not the undifferentiated human, who then speaks. The narrator mirrors for us a striking confusion of categories. Is that because God has a problem recognizing singularity or plurality in his image? Or is it because he automatically assigns a hierarchy to his creation? He brings the newly formed woman before the man, as earlier he had brought the animals before the human. But he nevertheless nominates the man as still (or also?) the original inclusive being, the "Human." Thereby the human becomes *both* the human *and* the man. The woman is merely the woman.

The man is not slow to give human expression to the divine desire to name and control (if not subjugate). He moves a step beyond YHWH God and objectifies the woman. He does not address her as "you" or even refer to her as "she." Rather she is "this" (Landy 1983: 228). She is "this" in fact three times within a handful of words. Moreover, the man, like God in Genesis 1, is allowed the privilege of discovery. Though he does not pronounce her "good," he declares that she is appropriate. His standards, it seems, are likeness and lineage. He claims *her* as bone of *his* bones and flesh of *his* flesh. The direction of his claim for control is as clear as it is perverse: "wo-man" (*'ish-shah*) was taken out of "man" (*'ish*). Apart from his perverse interpretation of the wordplay (apparent to anyone who just listens to, or looks at, the words), there is the crowning perversity of his claim to be her progenitor. The woman (strictly the "side" from which she was formed) was taken out of the human, not the man. The man, however, claims the past (and Humanity) as his own dominion. And flying in the face of what every reader knows to be reality, he claims that woman comes out of man—claims for himself, that is, woman's biological function of childbearing. A breathtaking claim, indeed! In all this he asserts authority over the woman as a parent over a child. For this moment, at least, God and man form the same perceptions, make the same moves, desire the same ends.

But what may we say of the woman? Had she, rather than the residual man, been allowed the role of discoverer in her introductory scene, might we have heard a somewhat different perspective? Would she have recognized the man to be flesh of her flesh and bone of her bone? Would she have decided to call him "man" because he had once been part of "woman"? Upon meeting her new companion, would she have been impressed? Disappointed? Ambivalent? Her opinions are suppressed. We are being led to conclude that they do not matter—not to God, the man, or the narrator. Men can have opinions about women (women, after all, are the objects of male desire: Gen 2:24), but women's perceptions of men are not important.

In an explanatory aside, the narrator then maintains that, of all human relationships, the union of man and woman is the primary bond, stronger than the relationship between parents and children: "Therefore, a man shall leave his father and his mother and cleave to his woman and they shall become one flesh" (2:24). Implicit is a claim that the man's desire is the defining norm. He is the one leaving and cleaving. The woman is the point of gravity, the object to be acquired. She, by contrast, is allowed (at this point in the plot) no desire and no attachments to parents or children. As we shall see later of Sarai, the woman comes to us without past or future. She is simply there, waiting to be subsumed. Union with a man is her consummate purpose.

Implicit, too, is another claim. Just as relations with parents and children are diminished, so, too, are excluded relations between people of the same sex. The "helper corresponding to [like-opposite]" the human/man is a sexual "opposite." According to this claim, human sexuality is clearly monogamous exogamous heterosexuality: one partner, outside the family, of the opposite sex. Partnership, according to this agenda, demands sexual and familial difference.[4]

Returning to the story line, the narrator introduces a new character, the serpent, "shrewder than any other wild animal YHWH God had made" (3:1). The serpent speaks to the woman (3:1-5):

> "Did God really say, 'You shall not eat from any tree in the garden'?" The woman said to the serpent, "We may eat the fruit from the trees in the garden; but the fruit from the tree that is in the midst of the garden, God said, 'you shall not eat it, nor shall you touch it, or you shall die.'" But the serpent said to the woman, "You will not indeed die; for God knows that on the day you eat it your eyes will be opened, and you will be like God, knowing good and evil."

Like the tree in the center of the garden, the serpent's existence and character is both unexplained and deeply intriguing (cf. Landy 1983:188).

Why did God put the serpent in the garden? How does the serpent know so much about the tree of the knowledge of good and evil? Has the serpent eaten of it? Is God in control of this garden or not? If he is, is this all a test? Does God *want* to be defeated by his children? ("God loves to be defeated by his children"—Elie Wiesel.) Landy comments that the serpent "symbolizes a side of God (the tempter; good-and-evil) he refuses to recognize."

The narrator hurries us past such questions to the turning point.

> And the woman saw that the tree was good for food, and that it was a pleasure to the sight, and the tree was desirable for discernment. She took some of its fruit and ate, and she also gave some to her husband with her, and he ate. (3:6)

The woman reaches for sustenance, beauty, and wisdom. And for doing so she is blamed, both within the text and by countless generations of biblical interpreters in the text's afterlife. Particularly through the influence of Augustine, she has become known as the authoress of what Christian theology has come to know as "The Fall." Human sin is laid at her door. Why? Because she reaches for sustenance, beauty, and wisdom—and disobeys the divine command to eschew the knowledge of good and evil.

Yet like God, the woman is an explorer. She seeks the good, fruit that is good for food. She delights in beauty (God took care to create trees that were beautiful) and the fruit is a delight to the eyes. Furthermore, she seeks to learn, to discern. The commentators cry for her blind obedience, her trust. But mature trust grows out of experience. How can the woman discriminate between God's words and the serpent's words until she has the experience of failure or the discrimination she seeks? Why should she believe that one peremptory command is in her best interests and not another? She seeks, reasonably, to be in a position to make a choice. Or, alternatively, she merely responds to her programming: to eat the good food, and to be like God!

Indeed, she desires to be like God! We should not be surprised. God's own breath has transformed the human into a living *nephesh*, "a bundle of appetites/passions/desires" (as W. J. A. Power has pointed out to us; and cf. Landy 1983:242-43). That is to say, desire is part of the divinely inspired programming of the human. The woman can no more ignore her *nephesh* than she can refuse to breathe.

God had told the human not to eat the fruit for then the human would surely die. Does the woman even know what death is? (She has not even bothered to eat of the tree of life.) Until she has the knowledge she seeks she is unable to do anything but bend to every suggestion. In other words, the command is impossible for her to adhere to as long as God allows the possibility of alternative speech (the serpent's)—which he patently does until it is too late to make any difference. (Its suppression is then gratuitous.) By definition—God's definition—Eve is unable to know the difference between good and evil. How then can she be blamed for her actions?

On the contrary, the woman's adventurous spirit, analogous to God's need for discovery, exhibits courage. She is willing to take risks. She is comfortable with lack of closure. She does not know what is going to happen. Obviously, neither does God.

The process by which the Genesis text constructs the character of Eve has been shrewdly tracked recently by Mieke Bal (1987). In the course of her essay she not only shreds "Paul's" careless exegesis of Genesis 3 (in 1 Timothy 2) but also offers a more favorable interpretation of Eve than is usually found in male writing. Eve's decision to eat the fruit is the first act of human independence. This independence forces the human and the divine into a real relationship of give and take rather than an artificial relationship of puppet and puppeteer. Eve does not "sin"; she chooses reality over her naive, paradisiacal existence. Her choice marks the emergence of human character.

Despite her provocative reading of Eve, Bal is, nevertheless, unwilling to see here a "feminist, feminine, or female-oriented text." Rather, she sees a text serving an ideology (patriarchy, the mainstream biblical ideology) that is struggling to be monolithic—struggling, for the text inadvertently encodes some of the *problems* involved in man's priority and domination:

> The burden of domination is hard to bear. Dominators have, first, to establish their position, then to safeguard it. Subsequently, they must make both the dominated *and* themselves believe in it. Insecurity is not a prerogative exclusively of the dominated. The establishing of a justifying "myth of origin," which has to be sufficiently credible and realistic to account for common experience, is not that simple a performance. Traces of the painful process of gaining control can therefore be perceived in those very myths. They serve to limit repression to acceptable, viable proportions. (Bal 1987:110)

We find a similar position being taken by David Jobling (1986). Challenging Phyllis Trible's (1978) reading of an ideal equality between the sexes prior to the fall, he doubts that such a "feminist" story would have been composed, and wonders how it could have been received, in the "man's world" which Trible elsewhere sees as the Bible's matrix.

He also argues against Trible's interpretation of the 'adam as first a sexually undifferentiated "earth creature." While that interpretation is logical, since maleness is meaningless before sexual differentiation, the text nevertheless asserts the illogical, namely "the originality of maleness over femaleness" (1986:41-42).

As Jobling sees the text, the patriarchal tendency of the story is to subordinate the woman in the social order and to blame the woman for the misfortune that has befallen humankind in its struggle to till the earth, which Jobling sees as the main theme of the story. In tension with this agenda, however, are the undeniably positive characteristics of the woman in the text. How has such a conflicting depiction come about?

The incongruities are inevitable. To blame the woman for eating of the tree, continues Jobling (42-43), is to associate her with *knowledge*.

> Part of the price the male mindset pays is the admission that woman is more aware of the complexity of the world, more in touch with "all living." And finally, at the deepest level of the text, . . . the possibility is evoked that the human transformation in which the woman took powerful initiative was positive, rather than negative, that the complex human world is to be preferred over any male ideal.
>
> But these "positive" features are not the direct expression of a feminist consciousness . . . Rather, they are the effects of the patriarchal mindset tying itself in knots trying to account for woman and femaleness in a way which *both* makes sense *and* supports patriarchal assumptions.

Another striking instance of patriarchal knot-tying may be found in the account of the aftermath of eating the fruit from the tree. The man and woman know nakedness and shame (Gen 3:7, 10-11; cf. 2:25). The knowledge of sexual difference brings shame in its train.

Sex and shame. That association, however, primarily serves the interest of the party wanting sexual control—that is, men who want to control women's sexuality. For example, the history of patriarchy is replete with societies where a sexually violated woman is conditioned to be ashamed. As we write, many raped Bosnian Muslim women are unable to return to their homes (if they still have a home) because of the shame that society places upon them. Thus patriarchal sexual mores lend their aid to the horrors of "ethnic cleansing." The double standard in the sex and shame ethic is amply evidenced in the biblical story: rapist Amnon is not described as knowing shame. That is reserved for Tamar, his sister, whom he rapes (2 Samuel 13)! Shame is a mechanism for passing the blame. Amnon does something evil but it is really Tamar's fault. Why else should she be ashamed?

So the story of Genesis 1–3 embodies a splendid contradiction. Sex, it proclaims, is good, part of the divine creative design: procreate (multiply)! Sex, it proclaims, is bad, the result of disobedience: cover yourself, be ashamed! And to reinforce the latter point, sexual relationships are drawn into the sphere of disobedience's conse-quences, the "punishments" of 2:14-19.

Jobling has suggested that one function of the garden story is (to use Pamela Milne's paraphrase [1989:30]) to "shift guilt or fault for the fall away from God (since the idea that God is ultimately respon-sible for evil is intolerable) and away from man (since it is no less intolerable for the male mindset that all the guilt should pass to man)." It seems that man and God are aligned when blame is to be shifted. That is interesting because, at first sight, the blame is all laid, so to speak, at the feet (with apologies to the serpent) of everyone else but God—that is, the man, the woman, and the serpent.

> And God said [to the man], "Have you eaten from the tree of which I said not to eat?" The man said, "The woman whom you gave to be with me, she gave me fruit of the tree, and I ate." And YHWH God said to the woman, "What is this that you have done?" And the woman said, "The serpent beguiled me, and I ate." And YHWH God said to the serpent,
>
> "Because you have done this,
> cursed are you above all cattle,
> and above all wild animals . . . ." (3:12-14)

Indeed, Gerhard von Rad sees the narrative as being concerned with

> the great disorders of our present life—shame, fear, the dissonances in the life of the woman and the man—and ascribing them to human sin. And this, of course, is the chief concern of the entire narrative . . . For it is concerned to acquit God and his creation of all the suffering and misery that has come into the world. (1972:101)

If we look again, however, we may decide that God, too, is implicated. The man insinuates as much when he speaks of "The woman whom *you* gave to be with me . . . ."

Attention to the rhetoric of blame-shifting can also open up the question of God's involvement. When God asks the man about the eating of the fruit of the forbidden tree, the man blames the woman, and when God asks the woman, "What is this that you have done?" the woman blames the serpent. A reader might notice that though God readily redirects his question from the man to the woman, the serpent's mouth he stops first with words and then with dust.

As cunning as the serpent, God moves to stop the sequence of blame from becoming a cycle of blame. For to the question, "What is this that you have done?" might not the serpent have said, "You didn't tell them the whole truth, so I gave them the chance to choose for themselves"? Or perhaps the serpent might have asked the counter question, "What is this that *you* have done? Why did you put that tree in the garden?" Or "Why did you allow me, serpent, to have an alternate voice?" Or simply, "Why can you not stand for anyone to be like you?" Instead God moves to stop the cycle of blame from coming to rest on himself. Or, to put it another way, he, like the humans, rushes to shift and fix the blame.

What is at the center of all this blame? Tradition, as we have observed already, blames the woman. The woman reaches for sustenance, beauty, and wisdom—and disregards the divine prohibition. But what is the nature, or better yet, the point, of this prohibition?

Does God put this particular tree in the garden in order to test the human? Is it there so that God can see whether the human will recognize God's authority, abide by the prohibition, and accept unquestioning subordination as humankind's ordained place in life? But if so, why would God want to prove that this status pertains? Could God be anxious, or perhaps even insecure, about the docility of his creatures? In the process of challenging that ordained subordination, would the human not become like God? Would this not surely threaten, even provoke from a God, jealous of his power, an anxious response?

> "Behold, the human has become like one of us, knowing good and evil; and now, lest he put forth his hand and take also of the tree of life, and live for ever—"and YHWH God put him out from the garden of Eden . . . He drove out the human; and . . . he placed the cherubim and a flaming sword . . . to guard the way to the tree of life. (3:22-24)

The issue on this reading, then, would be God's need to guard jealously his privileged position, to dominate (or transcend, if you will). Bal (1987:125) words it this way:

> It was the likeness to God that the serpent presented to [the woman] as the main charm of the tree. This likeness included the free will to act, which was implied in the interdiction itself. Jealousy about the possible equivalence is alleged [by the serpent] as Yahweh's motive for the interdiction. Yahweh's later reaction proves the serpent was right. (1987:125)

Or is the tree (and accompanying prohibition) there to provoke the human to do just what the human does? That it is a potentially provocative action on God's part (i.e., from the human's point of view) is hard to deny.[5] What would eating from it achieve? Nothing short of a measure of independence (cf. Bal 1987). Why should God want a humankind that is wholly dependent, blandly agreeable, and slavishly conformist? Perhaps that is why God is so conspicuously absent in the crucial central scene, where the serpent is allowed free rein by this otherwise ever-present God.

But why, then, the "punishments" of verses 14-19?

To the woman [God] said:
"I will multiply indeed your toil and your pregnancies;
with travail you shall bear children,
but towards your man [husband] shall be your desire
and he shall rule over you."
And to Adam [Human] he said:
"Because you obeyed your woman [wife]
and ate from the tree about which I commanded you,
'You shall not eat from it,'
cursed is the ground ['ᵃdamah] on your account.
With labor you shall eat from it
all the days of your life . . .
until you return to the ground,
for out of it you were taken;
you are dust, and to dust you shall return.

The first question to ask is, Are they punishments? Some, (e.g., Phyllis Trible and Carol Meyers) have argued that they are rather consequences of knowing good and evil. Let us pursue that suggestion. Would not knowing good and evil inevitably have to include the good and bad of what sustains human beings? Procreation involves children to love but also physical and emotional pain, not to mention infant and female mortality (a major risk in the ancient world as in many parts of today's world). Passion allows for love and intimacy, but also the possibility of domination (even violence); it can be the excuse for estrangement and the cause of unwanted pregnancy. In work one may find the satisfaction of accomplishment as well as the weariness of labor and the frustration of failure.

Is this the kind of knowledge of good and evil that God knows? Does God somehow benefit from humans knowing these things too? Yes, we could reply. Just as God claims that it is not good for the human to be alone, neither is it good for God to be alone; and God will always be alone if there is no one to share some part of his experience. Good and evil is part of divine experience, and a relationship with humans who know nothing of life's labor, pain and dissonance could only be a facile and impoverished relationship.

At the same time, having pushed the human to open the Pandora's Box of reality and independence, the deity still wants to assert control. So he simply claims control for himself: "I will put enmity . . . I will greatly increase . . ." God's rhetoric turns natural consequences into divinely controlled repercussions. In other words, from the human point of view, they become punishments.

Whether viewed as punishments or predictions, God's words further define the gender roles of the man and the woman who now know good and evil. The woman is defined in relation to the man, as a toiling mother (indeed, the man goes on to reinforce this identity as mother, by naming her Eve, the mother of all living; 2:20), desiring (sexually) her husband but facing the danger of numerous pregnancies (cf. Meyers 1988:109-117). The man is defined in relation to the ground, with which he must struggle in order to eat. The basic drives of sex and eating are paralleled in these definitions (cf. eating as a common metaphor for sex; e.g., Proverbs 1–9 and Song of Songs), the one ascribed to the woman and the other to the man. But control of her sexuality is denied the woman: the man shall rule over her. Thus both sex and eating end up in the domain of the man. The woman becomes subordinate, the man subjugator.

An air of unreality has descended on the text. It is women's sexual desire for men that is named, not men's for women, and it is this desire that will subordinate women. Because she sexually desires her man so greatly, she will put aside her concern for the risks of childbearing and will be unable to resist her man's (unnamed) sexual advances (Meyers 1988:116). His (unnamed) desire will predominate because her (named) desire is so predominant! (So when she says "no" she really means "yes"?) Hence, because she really wants him to do so, the man will rightly rule over her. But how curious, in a story where the man is passive and compliant and the woman active and assertive, for such a man to rule over such a woman's sexuality!

Eve's primary characterization in this divine speech carries over to most of the other women in Genesis–Kings. Eve's literary daughters are commonly inscribed in the text in the first instance as mothers, mothers of sons who are crucial either to lineage or plot. Yet secondarily they are often inscribed as objects of men's sexual desire, a characterization at odds with the tenor of the speech: only Potiphar's wife (Genesis 39) quite fits that bill. Of course, such discrepancy is to be expected, for the narrative cannot sustain the odd logic of the divine rhetoric. This is again patriarchy tying itself in knots.

Ironically, Adam's sons are not so limited in their vocations. Despite the fact that Adam is charged to work the earth by the sweat of his brow, his successors are hardly confined to farming. The men of Genesis–Kings become herders, musicians, city builders, wealthy landowners, administrators, deliverers, law-givers, judges, warriors, kings, sages, prophets, and priests, to name some of the more obvious professions. Men are much more likely than women to be featured in their own stories, whether brief or extended. The few women who do make inroads into these professions may assure us that ability is not at issue, but they also accent the majority who are confined to maternity or who are omitted altogether.

Thus the woman's punishment turns out to be a confirmation of what the man has already claimed and God has already approved, namely, the hierarchical priority of the man. God thus plays to the man. Hierarchies have a way of spawning favorites. God's hierarchies in this story are no exception.[6]

To mediate the "punishment" God extends gracious clemency: "And YHWH God made for Human and for his wife garments of skins, and clothed them" (3:21). On the one hand, the gesture may be seen positively as one of guidance—the deity shows the humans how to care for themselves. After all, from this point on they are responsible for their own (food and) clothing. Clothing becomes a symbol of autonomy and vulnerability, both protecting and revealing that one needs to be protected. Clothing is also a symbol of knowing good and evil. Only humans (who know good and evil) need clothes. This separates them from the other animals and it separates them from each other. On the other hand, one can also read this act as the gesture of the beneficent lord, offering handouts (see Kennedy 1990). The gift creates obligation and is therefore a means of continuing control.

The expulsion, too, slides between consequence and control. We have already observed one obvious dimension of control: expulsion prevents the humans from closing the difference between them and God by eating from the tree of life. Without difference there can be no hierarchy and hierarchy facilitates control. The expulsion is also a natural consequence of knowing good and evil. To know good *and* *evil* in paradise would hardly be possible. And for the humans to eat from the tree of life and live forever would exclude them from knowing a whole dimension of evil, namely experience related to death. The humans must leave the garden.

But do we not find God exiled as well, following his human creations in their wanderings? The human beings may have chosen their own plot, but God is there to enforce the continuation of the story they have begun. In a sense the humans have led God out of paradise. Why does God follow? Out of a concern for his creatures? Out of his need for relationship? Out of curiosity? Out of a desire to maintain dominion over his creatures and, through them, over his newly created world? However complex the reason, God ventures out and the gate to paradise is closed. The story moves on. There is no return to simplicity, for human beings or for God.

Between human desire and the desire of God in this story there is a creative tension of separation and sameness. Good and evil are not separate elements in simple opposition. They turn out to be shifting, sliding terms, like most of the story's discriminations. Humankind cannot simply "trust" God and vacate its responsibility for its own well-being (even when looking to providence). Women and men need to seek food, beauty, and discernment, and, indeed, be prepared to sweat for them. We can blame the woman for human vulnerability and culpability, yet we then need also to recognize God's vulnerability and culpability. God, too, bears responsibility and God is not capable of simply fixing up the mess.

God's desire for dominion is both corrosive and creative in this story. While it is one of the desires that drives the creation of the world, it is also a desire that complicates and so creates the plot. The complication has an uneasy resolution. The desire to have dominion is coupled with a desire to create meaning through difference, while simultaneously replicating self through likeness. But too much likeness threatens the separation that guarantees dominion. Be like me, but not too much like me! On the other hand, Why are you so different, when I made you to be like me? God in the garden wrestles with dilemmas of sameness and difference, power and equity, in creative relationship. These dilemmas we shall meet again in Genesis–Kings.

An entire social world is constructed by a simple story about a tree in a garden, a world which underlies the remainder of Genesis–Kings, a world in which humans are valued on the basis of gender, a world in which women are subdued and the needs of children are suppressed in deference to those of adult men, a world in which human sexuality has only one legitimate expression, and that is too often described in terms of domination and subjugation.

Cutting through the constraint of social construction is, however, some glimmer in the construction of character. Though Eve's behavior is condemned by God and berated by centuries of readers, she emerges as a character with initiative and courage. Too innocent to be evil, too guileless to be seductive, she is a child testing her boundaries, weighing her options, making her choices. She makes her decision independent of those who claim authority over her. From time to time, in the larger story that follows, we shall glimpse Eve's daughters following in her footsteps. They will show initiative, courage, and independence despite societal constraints. Yet just as Eve is eventually cast into the shadow of the Adam, not to speak of the tree, women in Genesis–Kings will often shade into invisibility. And when we see them most starkly, it will often be to witness the patriarchal "punishment" inscribed on and in their bodies because they have dared to usurp men's (divine?) authority.

Chapter Two

KEEPING THE PROMISE

Many readers have come to understand God's friendship with Abraham to mark a new beginning for humankind, one which promises to unloose the tangled skein created by the earlier beginning. For things have not improved since Genesis 3. On the contrary, this new event comes in the wake of a deteriorating relationship recounted in Genesis 4–11, including the stories of Cain and Abel, the Flood, and the Tower of Babel.

> Primeval history [Genesis 1–11] had shown an increasing disturbance in the relationship between humanity and God and had culminated in God's judgment on the nations . . . Here [in Gen 12:1-3] in the promise that is given concerning Abraham something is again said about God's saving will and indeed about a salvation extending far beyond the limits of the covenant people to "all the families of the earth" . . . All at once and precipitously the universal field of vision narrows; world and humanity, the entire ecumenical fullness, are submerged, and all interest is concentrated upon a single man. (von Rad 1972:153-54)

> The one who calls the worlds into being now makes a second call . . . The purpose of the call is to fashion an alternative community in creation gone awry, to embody in human history the power of the blessing. (Brueggemann 1982:105)

A plot that has spiraled downward since the expulsion from the garden, that has included escalating violence, evil, and hubris, now takes a more hopeful turn as God invests in a new relationship with his creation. Replace the old characters and begin again, from scratch—and trust that this time there will be no Eve to blame for a new fiasco.

The linchpin for this new relationship is to be Abraham, a man with little to recommend him except, ironically, a willingness to wander. We meet him, called at this time Abram, at the end of an extensive list of sons and fathers in Genesis 11. We meet, too, his wife Sarai, though she comes to us without family or lineage. Her barrenness, moreover, marks the end of Abram's line and sets up Sarai as a woman without past or future (Trible 1991:183). In more than one sense, then, she has no place from the beginning.

As part of his father's house, Abram migrates with his father toward Canaan (11:31-32):

Terah took Abram his son and Lot the son of Haran, his grandson, and
Sarai his daughter-in-law, his son Abram's wife, and they went forth
together from Ur of the Chaldeans to go into the land of Canaan; but when
they came to Haran, they stayed there . . . and Terah died in Haran.

It is here, on the way to Canaan, but after his father's death, that
Abram receives a call and promise from God (12:1-4):

Now YHWH said to Abram, "Go from your country and your birthplace
and your father's house to the land that I will show you. And I will
make of you a great nation, and I will bless you, and make your name
great, and you will be a blessing. I will bless those who bless you; I will
curse whoever curses [trifles with? makes light of?] you; and by you all
the families of the earth shall be blessed."
And Abram went, as YHWH had told him . . .

For many readers this compliant response has shown Abram to
be a man of faith and obedience.

Abraham obeys blindly and without objection. The one word *wayyelek*
("and he set out") is more effective than any psychological description
could be, and in its majestic simplicity does greater justice to the importance of this event. Abraham remains dumb, "a wonderful trait of absolute obedience when compared with a promise the full importance of
which he could scarcely surmise" [Procksch]. Here is one of the passages
where Abraham becomes a kind of model. (von Rad 1972:161)

Abram the obedient. Abram the courageous. Abram, a man willing
to take risks for the sake of his god. And yet, we might wonder,
how remarkable is such obedience and courage when one is clearly
in limbo between a home left behind and a home on the horizon?

The first dimension of the promise, suggests Brueggemann (1982:
118), is a call to relinquish, "a call for a dangerous departure from the
presumed world of norms and security." But what exactly characterizes
Abram's departure? Context suggests that it is less than "dangerous."
Abram is to leave his native land, which he has already done, and his
father's house, of which there is nothing left, to go to the land which
is already the destination of his migration. God's call is hardly
inopportune. A convenient arrangement, we might surmise.[1]

Moreover, should this not be sufficiently advantageous, God
offers a promise of reward and protection to further motivate Abram:
"I will make of you a great nation, and I will bless you, and make
your name great . . . I will bless those who bless you; I will curse
whoever curses you." As Brueggemann (119) points out, the gifts of
the promise "are an index of what we crave: well-being, security,
prosperity, prominence." What more could Abram ask? The risks are
now minimal, the benefits substantial—if, of course, this YHWH god
can be believed or trusted.

So what prompts Abram to comply? Faith? Trust? Ambition, perhaps? Or could it be a sense of responsibility to other people? Surely he has not forgotten that part commissioning him to be a blessing to other families of the earth. What might that mean?

Whatever it means, it is not clear that it includes sharing the blessing with his own family. If we were to take the text's silences seriously, we might notice that Abram does not tell his wife Sarai of God's call, nor does he consult her concerning the move. She is not privy to, nor seemingly included in, God's plan. And yet, as a member of her husband's house, she is expected to follow his lead wherever it takes her, doing dutifully whatever is necessary in order that he might prosper.

When Abram brings his family into Canaan, he passes through the land, less than eager to linger. He camps in Shechem where God tells him, "To your descendants I will give this land" (12:7). But, as von Rad (1972:166) wryly observes,

> the gates of salvation do not swing open at all with the solemn disclosure that God would give this land to Abraham. Rather, this promise is strangely contiguous to the statement that at that time the Canaanites were dwelling in the land [12:6]. Abraham is therefore brought by God into a completely unexplained relationship with the Canaanites, and Yahweh does not hurry about solving and explaining this opaque status of ownership as one expects the director of history to do.

But the problem is more profound than a simple quirk in the plot (expressed in the question, How will Abram come to own land obviously owned by others?). Not only do we become aware that the "giving" implies a "taking" but, in this uneasy tension between the promised gift and the notice of the Canaanites, we witness a conflict between call and promise. The gift of the land collides with the commission to be a blessing to other families of the earth. How can one be a blessing and yet also supplant?

Is it such an incongruity that leads Abram further south, the realization that this promise is much more complicated than it first had seemed? Whatever the reason, Abram is seemingly unimpressed with "this land" and tarries only long enough to build an altar before he heads toward the Negeb desert. (We see a similar detachment from the land of promise when he separates from Lot [Gen 13:5-13], allowing Lot to choose whatever portion he desires.)

Famine strikes and Abram turns toward Egypt (Gen 12:10-20). The detour to Egypt suggests that we might now see an example of how other families of the earth will, through Abram, receive a blessing. Abram, however, sees no such responsibility here. Upon entering Egypt, he says to Sarai (12:12-13),

> Look here, I know you are a beautiful woman. The Egyptians will see you and they will say, "This is his wife." Then they will murder me, but they will let you live. Say you are my sister, that it may go well with me because of you, and that my life may be spared on your account.

Can we accept Abram's speech at face value (cf. Miscall 1983:40)? Does he truly think Sarai's exceptional beauty will put him at risk? If indeed all Egyptian men desire her, would not all this unwanted attention put her at risk as well? (And, recalling Gen 3:16, is this talk of sexual desire not the wrong way round? Are not women supposed to be the ones who do the desiring?)

Abram's priorities are clear. Sarai should avail herself sexually to the male population of Egypt "that it may go well" for him. Have we perhaps come to the heart of the matter?[2] As the story progresses, things go *very* well with Abram on account of Sarai because he, in essence, sells her to the Pharaoh for a handsome profit: "And for [Sarai's] sake [Pharaoh] dealt well with Abram—he had sheep, oxen, male donkeys, male and female slaves, female donkeys, and camels" (12:16). Later we are told that, when Abram went up from Egypt, he "was very rich in livestock, in silver, and in gold" (13:2).

Does Abram truly fear for his life? Or does he see in Sarai the opportunity to increase his economic worth? He certainly uses his life as a means of persuading Sarai to go along with the ruse. How much is genuine anxiety? How much is rhetoric?

In the course of his appeal to Sarai, he subtly mixes flattery (Trible 1991:183) and guilt, shifting blame and responsibility onto his wife. First the flattery: "Look here, you are a beautiful woman." Then he constructs a hypothetical scenario of danger. The danger, it soon becomes clear, is the woman's fault. Her beauty will drive men to murder him, but she, he claims, would be spared. How could she live with that sort of guilt, knowing that she thrived while he lay dead on her account? She must take responsibility for his safety: "Say you are my sister, that it may go well with me and my life may be spared on your account." As Miscall notes (1983:32), "[Abram] mentions nothing of Sarah's fate, particularly the situation she could be in if she masquerades as his sister." Does she comprehend the ramifications of this ruse? Or does she comprehend them too late? Doubtless Abram knows the score—it is, after all, his composition. But a little unwanted sex, according to Abram, is a small price to pay for a husband's survival.

If truthful, his speech is merely ironic. We are given no indication that his life would have been in danger. We soon learn from the Pharaoh himself that Egyptian men know to respect other men's property.

The Egyptians show themselves to have more integrity than he. If, however, Abram means to deceive Sarai as he does the Pharaoh, his speech unveils him as both liar and panderer. In either case, his disregard for Sarai is clear and powerfully foreshadows his later treatment of both Sarai and Hagar (Miscall 1983:32).

Once Sarai is taken into Pharaoh's harem, the man Abram grows increasingly wealthy due to Pharaoh's good favor. How does Abram intend to break free of this situation? Or does he plan to do so?

The terms of the exchange do not appear to be temporary. Sarai is hardly being "borrowed"—Pharaoh himself later claims that he took her for his wife (12:19). Abram can hardly expect to get Sarai back. But then, perhaps he is not presuming to get her back. Certainly he values her beauty (though a liability as well as an asset) and (we presume) their previous years together, but her chief value now lies in his safety and his wealth. Besides, she is barren. Fidelity to her would certainly mean the end of his line. If he is giving any thought at all to God's promise that *he* will be a great nation, that *he* will be blessed, that *his* name will be great, that *his* descendants will have land, he realizes that Sarai is hardly likely to be of help. Another woman—a younger, fertile woman—will be necessary if his family is to increase.

Thus Abram sacrifices his wife, for his safety perhaps, but assuredly for economic gain. As for God's call and promise, it is clear that he sees himself as the sole subject. If God is interested in blessing *him*, then he must be the one to succeed. Sarai is expendable.

And conveniently for Abram, Sarai is silent. No pleading or protesting voice deters him from his callous barter. Some commentators have regarded her silence to mean complicity (e.g., Westermann 1985:163; Niditch 1987:57); others have suggested it is but a sign of her powerlessness (e.g., Jeansonne 1990:17; Rashkow 1992:65). True, she does not protest to Abram. But neither does she voice his lie as he had asked her to do. As Pharaoh reveals in later speech (12:19), it is Abram who lies to Pharaoh.

Abram has made her believe that she is responsible for his safety. In her silence she bears that responsibility. Nevertheless, her refusal to lie directly gestures to the injustice being done to her. Her silence is the silence of a survivor.

God, nevertheless, hears her silence. In God's point of view, Sarai is not responsible for Abram and she is not expendable.

> But YHWH afflicted Pharaoh and his house with great plagues on account of Sarai, Abram's wife. So Pharaoh summoned Abram, and said, "What is this you have done to me? Why did you not tell me that she was your wife? Why did you say, 'She is my sister,' so that I took her for my own

wife? Here now is your wife. Take her and leave!" And Pharaoh gave his men orders concerning him and they sent him off, with his wife and all that he had. (12:17-20)

So Abram leaves, blessed with wealth, but hardly having been a blessing to other families of the earth. While he had survived and prospered, his sense of exclusivity had endangered all other parties. His distrust of God's protection interferes with God's envisioned plan (which, as already noticed, is not without its own problems). God soon discovers that, as long as he deals with Abram, it can never be a simple matter of blessing those who bless and cursing those who curse. Pharaoh, in his innocence, "blessed" Abram but, because of Abram's deception, Pharaoh's house is cursed. The imbalance of the situation is striking. In order to rescue Sarai, God must compromise his principles. In order to protect Abram's family, other innocent families must suffer. Such compromise is hardly likely to teach Abram any worthwhile lessons on responsibility.

As it transpires, despite God's pointed restoration of Sarai, Abram seems to have learned nothing of her value. Though God continues to reassure Abram that he will become a great nation (13:14-18; 15:1-21), ten years pass and Abram has yet to share with Sarai any mention of YHWH's call and promise. (Of course, YHWH has not yet mentioned it to her either.) In the meantime, Abram's actions, by contrast to the events in Egypt, further devalue Sarai's worth. When his nephew Lot is kidnapped by the enemies of Sodom (Genesis 14), Abram wastes no time mustering the men of his household in order to save him. The reader might ask why the capture of Lot inspired such courage and risk on the part of Abram when the taking of Sarai by Pharaoh did not.[3]

Furthermore, when he brings back the people and their possessions to Sodom, he spurns the king of Sodom's offer of wealth (14:21-23):

> Then the king of Sodom said to Abram, "Give me the persons, but take the possessions for yourself." But Abram said to the king of Sodom, "I have sworn to YHWH, God Most High, maker of heaven and earth, that I would not take a thread or a sandal strap or anything belonging to you, lest you should say, 'I have made Abram rich.'"

Where was such self-reliance when Abram was in Egypt? He certainly had no qualms about Pharaoh's sandal straps.

In the meantime YHWH continues to nuance the promise. Abram's descendants are to be incalculable, as the dust of the earth. Their homeland will extend as far the eye can see (13:14-18). But, after awhile, Abram is doubtful: "My lord YHWH what will you give me? I continue childless . . . My household servant will be my heir"

(15:2-3). Abram's persistence meets with reassurance: "This man will not inherit. Your very own issue shall be your heir." And, says the narrator, Abram believed YHWH, "and [YHWH] counted it to him as righteousness."

As von Rad (1972:185) is quick to point out,

[Abram's] righteousness is not the result of any accomplishments, whether of sacrifice or acts of obedience. Rather, it is stated programmatically that belief alone has brought Abraham into a proper relationship to God. God has indicated his plan for history, namely, to make of Abraham a great people; Abraham "has firmly assented" to that, i.e., he took it seriously and adjusted to it.

One should also note, however, that this promise is something Abram desperately *wants* to believe. He can "firmly assent" to God's plan because God's plan and his own desires are one and the same.

Despite belief and righteousness, Abram wants more answers. "My lord YHWH, how am I to know that I shall inherit [this land]?" (15:8). YHWH responds yet again, but this time the promise takes a darker tone. YHWH's description is filled with talk of aliens and slavery and oppression and judgment (15:13-21). Does Abram fully understand this revelation? We are not told. One thing is certain, however: the gift of the land, it seems, is not without its price.

Sarai then takes center stage in Genesis 16. She, too, would like to have children. Her sense of self-worth, shaped and sustained by the patriarchy, depends upon her ability to bear children. So frustrated is she by her infertility that she offers to Abram her young Egyptian maid Hagar as a surrogate. She does this not for Abram's sake, but for her own:[4] "Look, YHWH has prevented me from bearing children. Go in to my maid. Perhaps I shall be built up through her" (16:2).

Joel Rosenberg (1986:94-95) aptly describes her situation:

Her age is well past childbearing, by any normal reckoning, so her subterfuge is perhaps an honest bid for a qualified motherhood, courageous in its swallowing of pride, yet prideful in its legal and class hubris. For it is a highly problematic action she proposes, a questionable and exploitative legal fiction, predicated on the availability of a servant whose own parental rights will be severely circumscribed.

Sarai finds her voice and moves to ensure her own well-being. We find her mode of operation to be not unlike Abram's. As Abram traded the sexuality of a woman in his possession for the sake of his security, so too Sarai trades the sexuality of a woman in her possession for the sake of her own security. Hagar, like Sarai in Egypt, is confined to powerless silence.

Abram accepts the proposition without hesitation. Sarai's desire for a child coalesces with his own desire to attain God's promise of a mighty lineage. He eagerly takes the young Egyptian woman into his bed.

Hagar conceives, but Sarai's plan backfires. For when the young woman learns that she is pregnant, she makes the most of her newly elevated status as Abram's second wife. Young, fertile, and the object of Abram's embrace, Hagar begins to take Sarai's position and authority less seriously.

Finding herself further devalued, Sarai proceeds to blame Abram:

> My violence be upon you! I gave my maid to your embrace and, when she saw that she had conceived, she belittled me! May YHWH judge between me and you! (16:5)

Understandably, Sarai feels violated. The triangle, designed to exploit her maid and bolster her own position in the household, has collapsed, making her the outsider. Hagar has become the object of Abram's embrace. She is the mother of his child and Sarai can see that no fictive surrogacy will change the facts.

Yet, the ambiguity of her outcry—"My violence be upon you!"— reveals the extent of her frustration as well as her sense of injustice. She is angry to the point of doing violence. And Abram, she claims, is accountable for whatever violence she commits.

Abram, surely pleased about the pregnancy but obviously unconcerned about the young woman Hagar, leaves her to Sarai's harsh treatment. "Your maid is in your hand," he says, washing his own hands of the matter. "Do with her whatever you see fit." Sarai "sees fit" to abuse ('nh) her, to humble her, to put her back in her place—as the true outsider. (After all, she is a woman, a foreigner, and a servant.)

Hagar, having caught a glimpse of self-autonomy, is not willing to return her former status. She runs away into the wilderness. Just as she had threatened Sarai's importance in the family, Hagar now temporarily usurps her place in the narrative's spotlight (cf. Hackett 1989). We follow Hagar to a spring of water where an angel of YHWH finds her and instructs her to return. YHWH's message is both good and evil: "Hagar, maid servant of Sarai," he calls her, in seeming collusion to put her in her place, "go back and suffer further abuse ('nh) under the hand of your mistress." (YHWH has much to learn about liberation!)

But although she is told to return to an oppressive mistress and an indifferent master, she is also given a promise. Abram is not the only one destined to have a mighty lineage. God has heard of her humiliation and she will be recompensed for it. She will bear a son and name him "God hears." Indeed when the time comes, she does bear a son to Abram, who names him Ishmael, "God hears."

The promise to Hagar is an ambivalent one: "The divine promise of Ishmael means life at the boundary of consolation and desolation" (Trible 1984:17). On the one hand, Hagar is to become the mother of a multitude. On the other hand, as he does with the woman in the garden, YHWH entraps her in her own initiative. "Your desires are of no consequence," he in effect tells her. "In addition to your labor, you shall give birth to a son, a free-spirited but contentious man who will give you no rest. In the meantime you will remain a slave in another's household and your mistress will rule over you."

From this point on we learn nothing more of Hagar's life in the household of Abram and Sarai. Did she indeed suffer further abuse? Was she accorded any special privilege? Or was she confined to the margins, ignored in favor of her son? She loses her place in the story, as she is soon to lose her place in the household.

Thirteen years go by and God appears to Abram in order to establish a covenant (Genesis 17). God renames him Abraham, father of a multitude, and promises that his lineage will produce nations and kings. Abraham, now a proud father who sees the future in his son Ishmael, listens with reverence, acceptance, and no doubt pleasure, to the promise of greatness and to the call to covenant.

Even the command to circumcise himself and the men in his household does not assuage his pious anticipation of his family's future. And how fitting that circumcision should be the mark of the covenant, this agreement between a male deity and a human father and son.[5]

When, however, God announces that Sarai is also to receive a new name (Sarah, "princess") and that she, too, is to be included in this promise of descendants and land, Abraham loses his composure.

> God said to Abraham, "As for Sarah your wife, you shall no longer call her Sarai, but Sarah shall be her name. I will bless her, and moreover I will give you a son by her. I will bless her, and she shall become nations. Kings of peoples shall come from her." Abraham fell on his face and laughed and said to himself, "Can a child be born to a man of a hundred years? Can Sarah, a woman of ninety years, give birth?" And Abraham said to God, "May Ishmael live before you!" (17:15-18)

This time Abraham does not believe. He does not "firmly assent" to God's plan, as von Rad would have it. He does not "take it seriously" or "adjust to it." God cannot be serious, thinks Abraham. Sarah is neither capable nor necessary. I already have a son. May Ishmael live in your sight!

God, however, is resolute. The promise includes Sarah. It is not enough that the child is Abraham's. The child of promise must be

Sarah's, a child to be named Isaac, "he laughs," to remind Abraham perpetually of his skepticism. As for Ishmael, he is also to be blessed, but it is Sarah's son Isaac with whom God will renew the covenant.

Abraham falls silent before God. We might think this symbolizes acquiescence if not for the fact that Abraham is also silent before Sarah. Even after hearing directly from God of Sarah's importance to the promise, even after her name has been changed to symbolize that importance, even after being informed that her pregnancy is imminent (17:21), Abraham says nothing to her of her role in God's plan (cf. Miscall 1983:32).

Consequently, God returns with two messengers to reiterate Sarah's part in the promise (Genesis 18). Taking no chances on Abraham's mediation, the three ask for Sarah. Assured of her presence God goes on to speak to Abram: "I will surely return to you in the time of life and Sarah, your wife, will have a son" (18:10). Sarah, having been pulled in and then left out of the conversation, stands in her marginal place at the entrance to the tent, listening to the announcement. She cannot believe what she hears. She laughs. It is a small wonder. This is the first she has heard of any divine plan, the first time she has considered that she might have a part in God's promise. Years of living with Abraham have conditioned her response to be much the same as his: "After I am withered, shall I have pleasure—and with my husband so old?" Abraham, so protective of his own special standing with God, shows no confidence in Sarah, and Sarah, unaware of her own importance and potential, shows no confidence in herself (or in him either in some matters!).[6]

The woman's knowledge makes her laugh. As these men, both divine and human, make reproductive plans for her body, she stands on the sidelines, knowing intimate details that render these plans highly unlikely. She is withered, worn out—post menopausal in our vernacular. Her husband is too old to give her pleasure. The ideas of sexual intimacy and parenthood make her laugh, but it is an intrigued laugh nonetheless.

YHWH, whether temperamentally or teasingly one can only guess, chides Sarah for her laughter. "Why did Sarah laugh and say, 'Shall I indeed bear a child, now that I am old?' Is anything too extraordinary for YHWH? I will return to you in the time of life and Sarah will have a son" (18:13-14). YHWH, it seems, understands only part of Sarah's amusement. The act leading to conception is, at Sarah and Abraham's age, every bit as extraordinary as having a child. YHWH, however, misses this point, but what can one expect from a god who, seemingly, has no sexuality!

Her humor turned to fear, Sarah recants. She has been told she has no right to laugh. Her emotions are denied her. Her knowledge is irrelevant. She is reduced to silence once more.

The connection between YHWH's treatment of Sarah and his treatment of Hagar is striking. Sarah's womanly knowledge and its accompanying humor, like Hagar's need to protect herself, is renounced by God. The self-expressions of both women are trivialized in light of God's important plan, a plan that is, for the women, both good and evil. On the one hand it imparts to them a value (motherhood) that they themselves deem desirable; on the other it patriarchally confines their worth to that very function.

God's move to include Sarah is left hanging without closure, while her husband debates with YHWH over the fate of the city of Sodom (Lot's new home), whose sin is profound and whose destruction appears imminent. Abraham presses YHWH concerning the lives of possible "righteous men" (*tsaddiqim*) in the city and YHWH concedes that should even as few as ten such men be found there, Sodom will not be destroyed (18:16-33). Abraham's rhetoric, however, is in vain. Ten righteous men are not found. Nevertheless, as God effects judgment on Sodom, he recalls Abraham's conversation; and he delivers Abraham's nephew and his nephew's daughters from the midst of the overthrow (19:24-29). But that is a story for another chapter (Three).

In chapter 20 the narrator draws us back to Abraham and Sarah. If we expect God's last visit finally to have made an impact on their vision of themselves and each other, we are to be disappointed.

> From there Abraham journeyed toward the territory of the Negeb, and dwelt between Kadesh and Shur; and he sojourned in Gerar. And Abraham said of Sarah his wife, "She is my sister." And Abimelech, king of Gerar, sent and took Sarah. (20:1-2)

Although God again intervenes and Sarah is returned to her husband, the episode clearly tells us that, for Abraham and Sarah, the lesson never seems to end. The nephew Lot may be worth a show of courage on Abraham's part, but Sarah still is not. Abraham will give her to any powerful man who might fancy her—and he no longer bothers to explain to her the reason. In this case she is more at risk than ever before. Due to have a child within the year, she faces certain danger if found, while in Abimelech's harem, to be pregnant with another man's child (Rashkow 1992:66).

And as for Sarah, she allows herself to be sacrificed for the safety of the "chosen one." According to Abimelech (20:5) she even corroborates Abraham's story. Her self-worth diminished, she plays the role of traded goods.

Abraham, the man to bring a blessing to all the other families of the earth, fails again. Though he desperately defends his behavior to Abimelech, we have no reason to believe him (10:11-13):

> [I did this] because I thought, There is no fear of God in this place, and they will murder me on account of my wife. Besides, she truly is my sister, the daughter of my father but not the daughter of my mother. She became my wife. When God caused me to wander from my father's house, I said to her, "This is your loyal act that you must do for me: At every place we stop, say of me, He is my brother."

The narrator does not confirm Abraham's story though there has been ample space to do so. There is no mention of Abraham and Sarah being siblings. We know for certain that Abraham's wanderings started long before he heard from God, that there was little left of his father's house when he started for Canaan, that he was hardly forced to drift abroad without destination. We also know that only upon their entry into Egypt did he instruct Sarah to lie (cf. Miscall 1983:14).

As in Egypt, his deceit brings affliction on the innocent. The only one to receive a "blessing" is Abraham himself:

> And Abimelech took sheep and oxen, and male and female slaves, and gave them to Abraham, and restored his wife Sarah to him . . . And to Sarah he said, "Look, I have given your 'brother' a thousand pieces of silver; it is compensation for you before all who are with you. With all, you are set right." (20:14, 16)

But while her "brother" continues to acquire more wealth, in the larger scheme of things, Sarah is not exactly "set right." Being returned to Abraham is no guarantee that she will not be wronged again by a husband who views her as expendable.

It is not until she herself is visited by God that Sarah can finally view herself as a rightful participant in God's call and promise. She bears the child she thought she was incapable of bearing. For Sarah there is laughter: "God has made laughter for me; everyone who hears will laugh over me!" Having accomplished the seemingly impossible, she begins to see her own value. She has a special place in her family and in God's plan. "Who would have said to Abraham that Sarah would nurse children? Yet I have borne him a child in his old age."

From Sarah, however, laughter is not the last sound we hear. Comfort and privilege breed a narrower vision. Security becomes a thing to be guarded. She, like Abraham before her, sets limits on who is to be included in the promise (21:8-10).

> Abraham made a great feast on the day that Isaac was weaned. But Sarah saw the son of Hagar the Egyptian, whom she had borne to Abraham, playing. So she said to Abraham, "Cast out this slave woman with her son; for the son of this slave woman shall not inherit along with my son Isaac."

"This slave woman" and "her son" are conceded no names. Sarah's labels keep them in their place, a place without identity, worth, or privilege.

Abraham is unhappy with Sarah's demand, but God's response, surprisingly, indulges Sarah's exclusivity (21:12):

> Do not consider this to be evil on account of the boy and on account of your slave woman. Listen to whatever Sarah tells you, for it is through Isaac that offspring will be named to you.

For the ethically sensitive reader such response is troubling: a god who shows arbitrary favoritism is a god who cannot be trusted.

> Is Yahweh immune from moral judgment? Should not Yahweh be judged by the ethical standards of the period? Abraham . . . appears to have more immediate concern for Hagar and his son than God does. Sarah's request that Hagar and Ishmael be "cast out" is in opposition to Near Eastern law, yet it is God who provides permission for Abraham to execute the plan. Would it not be in the best interest of God to have Abraham demonstrate some humane treatment to Hagar and his son? It is inexcusable to put this mother and her son out with so little (21:14). As a wealthy man, Abraham could at least have provided some means of transportation and some financial assistance to them. (Waters 1991:200)

Again God shows himself to be a god of good and evil. On the one hand, God is rather limited by the cast of human characters. The jealousy and competition between these two women spells inevitable strife. The gesture surely averts more tragic hostility between these women and their sons in the future. On the other hand, God is clearly biased in favor of an ungenerous family, willing to send the innocent into the wilderness, willing to have Hagar and her son suffer for their redemption. God is fully implicated in this dispossession.

This uncanny god circumvents Abraham's weaknesses as well. The patriarchal penchant for the firstborn son might also bias Abraham in years to come, thus thwarting God's whimsical desire to use and bless unlikely candidates. The thing was "exceedingly evil" to Abraham, says the narrator, "on account of *his son*." God nudges him to see that the woman as well as the boy should be of concern: "Do not consider this to be evil on account of the boy *and on account of your slave woman*." God knows better, however, than to push the point. For Abraham, the woman was merely the means to an end; he is unlikely to change his thinking now. And even to God, the woman is without name or personhood, merely the possession of Abraham. God continues to address what is, for Abraham, the major concern: "As for the slave woman's son, I will make a nation of him also, because he is your offspring."

While God panders to Abraham and Sarah's constricted vision,

and perhaps reveals his own prejudices, God also acts to prevent
human frailty from gaining the better ground. Moreover, as the rest
of the story soon reveals, God attempts to make up for human fail-
ing. As Abraham and Sarah circumscribe their divinely blessed family, God envelops Hagar and her son in blessing and promise as well.

For one final brief moment, the narrative spotlight returns to
Hagar as she, coerced by Abraham and Sarah, takes her child, a loaf
of bread, and a skin of water and trudges into the wilderness. Time
and circumstances have subdued Hagar. No longer the spirited
woman reaching for self-worth and grasping at freedom, she is now
an object acted upon, completely humiliated, submitting to the
cruelty of Sarah, Abraham, and God, and submitting to the certain
death of her child and herself.

It is only when her physical and emotional resources are completely
exhausted that God re-enters the picture to save the day (21:15-18):

> When the water from the skin was depleted, she put the child under
> one of the bushes and she went and sat down by herself some distance
> away, about a bowshot, thinking "I cannot bear to see the death of the
> child." She sat opposite him and raised her voice and wept. God heard
> the boy's voice and a messenger of God called to Hagar from out of the
> blue and he said to her, "What is the matter, Hagar? Do not fear, for
> God has heard the boy's voice where he is. Get up. Pick up the boy and
> hold him securely with your hand for I will make of him a great nation."

Despite a mother's despair, it is the boy's cry that catches God's
attention. And it is the boy's future that piques God's interest. In
that moment God discloses to Hagar a source of water. She resusci-
tates the boy, replenishes their water skin and, we assume, continues
on her way. Their journey, their story, is not told—at least not by
this narrator. We only know its ending (21:21-21):

> God was with the boy. He grew up and lived in the wilderness. He
> became a great archer. He lived in the wilderness of Paran. His mother
> took a wife for him from the land of Egypt.

Hagar and Ishmael. Another example of Abraham and Sarah's
blessing of the other families of the earth? Banished to the wilderness, expelled from the garden of Canaan, they inhabit only the
margins of the text.

The fact that Abraham has sacrificed his first wife Sarah to
strangers on two occasions, has sacrificed his second wife Hagar first
to affliction and then to ostracism, and has sacrificed his firstborn
son Ishmael to the savagery of the wilderness, casts an ambiguous
shadow on the testing of Abraham in Genesis 22. Commentators,
trying to reconcile this episode with those preceding, often suggest

that, in Genesis 22, the man of unfaith has reached a pinnacle of ultimate faith, that here he has severed the final attachment limiting his relationship with God. A reading attentive to consistency of character, however, might conclude otherwise. This man has shown no difficulties sacrificing members of his family. As Phyllis Trible (1991) has also observed, undue attachment has never been Abraham's problem. Granted, he has not volunteered nor has he been called upon to do violence personally to any of his family. He has, nevertheless, given their bodies over to certain suffering.

With that in mind we read that "It was after these things that God tested Abraham." The test, we discover, hinges on God's command to Abraham to offer up his son Isaac as a burnt offering. We are not told what God wanted or expected to find in Abraham's performance. Most readings assume that what Abraham did met with God's approval. Abraham, on account of his radical obedience, becomes an exemplary character. Unfortunately, such a reading leaves the character of God in a more uncanny light than usual. At the very best one might reason that God is simply unfathomable; at the worst, God is deranged and sadistic. On the other hand, perhaps he is, as earlier in Genesis 1–3, simply curious.

Suppose, however, that God is well aware of Abraham's tendency to forfeit his family to danger and uncertainty. What if the test is really designed to see just how far Abraham will go?

To begin with, we might ask, what is the unspoken alternative? If Abraham refuses to do this thing, what will happen to him? Disobedience usually results in punishment. Might not Abraham hear in the silence a threat, an unstated "or else . . ."? As Westermann (1985:152) states in relation to Gen 12:4, "he would be putting himself at risk were he not to go." Abraham, as we have seen, is rather sensitive when it comes to his personal safety.

How far will Abraham go when self-preservation is at issue? Perhaps God needs to see if there is *ever* a point where Abraham is willing to sacrifice himself rather than his family. He has sacrificed the other members of his household; will he go so far as to sacrifice this son of promise? Will he go so far as to implicate himself in the violence?

What might we have heard from an exemplary Abraham? "Take me! I am old. The boy has his whole life in front of him." We might even have heard the Abraham of old, who pleaded with God before Sodom (Gen 18:25), saying, "Far be it from you to expect such a thing, to want to bring death upon the innocent . . . as if he were guilty. Far be that from you! Shall not the Judge of all the earth do what is just?" But whereas the Abraham of old would dare to challenge God concerning people he did not even know, this Abraham says nothing on behalf of his own son. Whereas the Abraham of old argued for the deliverance of what was reputed to be an irredeemably violent and perverse city, this Abraham risks nothing for this innocent boy.

Instead, we get nothing but silent obedience, with commentators through the ages injecting profundity into each mute movement. Abraham makes every effort to go through with the sacrifice of his son. Only God's intervention keeps him from murder. Here we have a rather sudden revelation of character. God is not willing to have the boy killed. But Abraham is. In the final analysis, God says no. Why doesn't Abraham?

Perhaps it is because God has been sending Abraham the wrong signals all this time. Every act of familial sacrifice performed by Abraham has been met with God's intervention and, on one occasion, approval (Genesis 21). God has restored Sarah twice and saved the lives of Hagar and Ishmael when Abraham had sent them to wander in the desert. And in the midst of all this, God continues to renew his call and promise to Abraham. God keeps trying to set right what Abraham causes to go wrong, but the final outcome of this is that Abraham is relieved of responsibility. Abraham is always the one who wins. Abraham has been conditioned to bank on his chosen status.

God's response to Abraham is impossible to decipher with certainty. "Now I know that you fear God." For most commentators, this spells triumph for Abraham: he reveres God for God's sake. Tone, however, is an elusive thing, and "fear" can mean more than reverence. God could be saying that, at the very least, Abraham has shown that he fears God (as Sarah feared God's reprisal for her laughter in 18:15), indeed for his very life. He may not have much backbone or compassion, but at least he fears God. Or perhaps God is saying, "Now I know that you fear God as much as you do other human beings. You have given in to your fear of me in the same way that you have given in to your fear of others—the Egyptians [ch. 12], the men of Gerar [ch. 20], even Sarah [chs. 16 and 21]."

Abraham, ironically, names the place "YHWH will see." YHWH has, in Abraham's point of view, "seen" to the sacrifice, substituting a ram for a son. But what does YHWH actually see? On the mountain, YHWH perhaps sees a man who fears, a man in need of grace.

> A messenger of YHWH called to Abraham a second time from the heavens. "By myself I have sworn," declares YHWH, "that, because you have done this thing, you have not spared your son, your only one, indeed, I will bless you and I will make your offspring as numerous as the stars of the heavens and as the sands of the seashore. Your offspring shall possess the gate of their enemies. Through your offspring all the nations of the earth will be blessed because you have listened to my voice." (22:15-18)

Whether or not Abraham has passed the test, we do not know. It all depends on how one reads this god of good and evil. What we do know is that God chooses to bless Abraham anyway. Although Abraham has been busy reducing his family, YHWH will work even harder to expand it, to make his descendants as numerous as the stars of the skies and the sands of the shores. And because Abraham has listened to God's voice, the voice that said "Do not raise your hand against the boy or do anything to him," Abraham's offspring (at least this particular offspring) will be given the chance to multiply and to do what Abraham has been unable to do—namely, be a blessing to the others.

The blessing, however, is no longer as seemingly benign as it was in the beginning. Its loose threads are beginning to show. Difference and division leave their imprint. The "families of the earth" (*mishpᵉhot ha'ᵃdamah*) in the original blessing (12:3) are replaced by "the nations of the land" (*goyey ha'arets*). Kinship gives way to politics; likeness gives way to difference; connection with the other gives way to violence against the other. How Abraham's descendants are to be a blessing to others is obscured by the allusion to war. No longer a peaceable source of blessing, Abraham's children will *possess the gates of their enemies*. Division and conquest, possession and dispossession, mark the future of the promise, as it grows ever more bellicose (e.g., Exod 23:25-33; 33:1-3). Fitting perhaps that the episode ends here, the violence against a child leading to the violence of a nation.

Chapter Three

ASSAULT AT SODOM

Who will weep for this woman?
Isn't her death the least significant?
But my heart will never forget the one
Who gave her life for a single glance.
—Anna Akhmatova[1]

Abraham's dialogue with YHWH over the fate of Sodom is famous.
"Will you really sweep away the righteous [*tsaddiq*] along with
the wicked [*rasha'*]?" he demands of God in Genesis 18, having
gained the distinct impression that God is indeed about to bring
Sodom's existence to an abrupt end.

> Perhaps [he continues] there are fifty righteous within the city. Will you
> really sweep them away and not spare the place for the sake of the fifty
> righteous who are in its midst? Far be it from you to do such a thing, to
> put to death someone righteous so that it would be the same for righteous
> and wicked. Far be it from you. Should not the judge of all the earth do
> justice? (Gen 18:24-25)

YHWH concedes the point, and as Abraham nervously reduces the
numbers—what about forty-five or forty or thirty or twenty or ten?—
YHWH's concession grows. To Abraham the achievement has generally been reckoned as righteousness. Abraham trades words with God,
risking wrath, to save the righteous few.

Of course, the argument proves otiose, since God proceeds nonetheless to rain brimstone and fire on Sodom and its sister cities of the
plain, leaving only the column of smoke rising from the furnace of
their undoing—and a pillar of salt. Of the righteous the only glimpse
we appear to have is the remnant family of Lot, saved from destruction—except for Lot's wife, that pillar of salt. And if Lot and his
daughters are saved, are they saved because they are righteous?
There's the rub. Our tight-mouthed narrator neglects to tell us so, at
least in as many words. The commentators are generally less reticent.
Lot usually comes out looking bad, a buffoon, foil to hero Abraham.
And the daughters whose story ends with them sleeping with their
father? Well, righteousness and the commission of incest do make
uneasy bedfellows. The daughters are more often quickly condemned
or passed over in awkward silence. And their mother, Lot's wife?
She did look back, didn't she? Wasn't that forbidden?

The categories of righteousness and wickedness (good and evil?) thus frame this story and the history of its interpretation. But for the reader interested in loose threads, there is an abundance here waiting to be pulled. And to the reader interested in red dots, there is a pillar of salt.

The Sodom story grows out of the story of God's visit to Abraham to announce that Sarah will have a child. The angelic visitors leave and head for Sodom. YHWH, however, has something to say and lingers behind to converse with Abraham. We overhear him deliberating with himself whether he should hide from Abraham what he is doing or let him know in order to teach him and his descendants something important. "How many," he remarks now to Abraham, "are Sodom and Gomorrah's cries of distress [or cries for help], and how very serious their sins! Let me go down and see whether they have done everything their cries suggest—and if not, I need to know" (18:21).

At face value the remark implies simply a fact-finding mission. Abraham, however, takes the words as a thinly veiled threat to execute judgment on the cities, to destroy them no less. So he confronts God with the question of righteousness. At this point we may be inclined to conclude that the lesson YHWH has in mind for Abraham concerns his (YHWH's) way of doing righteousness (*ts^edaqah*) and justice (*mishpat*).

Why precisely does Abraham raise this question? Although the obvious answer is that he simply wants to rescue the righteous of Sodom, there are some less altruistic possibilities that we need to consider. He could be interested in his own position as a righteous man—would God rescue *him* if he were caught in such a situation? Remember, this is a man who has shown himself very quick to consider his own safety. Moreover, the terms righteous and foreigner hardly go together in Abraham's vocabulary: foreigners in Abraham's book have no fear of God and are willing to commit even murder to satisfy their desires. That he even imagines there to be some righteous Sodomites severely stretches probability. Remember, this is the man who told his wife, "I know what a beautiful woman you are. If the Egyptians see you, and think, 'She is his wife,' they will kill me, and you will they let live!" Or is it that he is trying to save only one person, his nephew Lot, as some critics suppose?

Why Lot? We need to remember for a start that it was to the cities of the plain, and Sodom in particular, that Lot moved when, at Abraham's urging, he separated from his uncle earlier in the larger story (chapter 13). Some commentators assume, moreover, that Abraham still considers Lot his heir—though we find this argument strained. They observe, too, that Abraham has already mounted a major rescue operation for his nephew after Lot was carried off from Sodom in a war soon after he settled there (Genesis 14); perhaps this, then, is Abraham's second rescue mission. Perhaps. But Abraham never pleads for Lot, as we might expect if Lot were central to Abraham's concerns. What precisely is in Abraham's mind remains tantalizingly uncertain.

Following Abraham's discussion with God, the narrator switches our attention to Lot. Confronted by visitors to the city, he offers them hospitality in his own home. They decline. He insists. They finally relent. Then the complication arises. "But before they lay down, the men of the city, the men of Sodom, closed around the house, both young and old, all the people, to the last one [or 'on all sides']" (19:4). The men demand that Lot produce the visitors: "Bring them out to us that we may know [i.e., sexually know] them."

Perhaps premonitions about such assaults upon strangers led Lot to insist in the first place that the visitors not stay in the street overnight. Perhaps he knew something of the violence awaiting visitors to Sodom from his own experience. At any rate his response suggests that his desire to sustain his hospitality now drives his action. He goes outside in an attempt to appease the mob (19:7-8).

> Please, my brothers, do not do evil. Please, look—I have two daughters who have not known a man. Please let me bring them out to you, and do to them whatever is good in your sight. Only do not do a thing to these men, for this reason: they have come under the shelter of my roof.

The proposition is, to put it mildly, disgusting. Two young women, his own daughters (and sexually pristine, he stresses, by way of invitation), for two grown men. Two young women, captive to their father's will, dragged from what they might have supposed was the security of their home, in exchange for two grown men who arrive uninvited, of their own accord, at night in a strange city. In disbelief we may scramble around for an explanation. Could it possibly be that his offer is not in fact sincere but a desperate attempt to shock the assailants into a realization of the enormity of their demand, so that they desist altogether? Is he hoping that his sons-in-law who, according to the text's logic, are evidently part of the crowd, would protest his offer and so move the other men to listen to reason?

But these are desperate explanations. The simpler reading is that this is patriarchy caricaturing itself. The values are crystal clear: male over female, age over youth, with the father's power over the daughter epitomizing the social order. Lot is willing to sacrifice his daughters in order to uphold his honor as a provider of male hospitality.

Assuredly he has not offered *himself* in place of the strangers!

Lot's gambit, however, fails and his personal predicament becomes more acute. The men of the city are bent on violence, not sex. "Come on, get closer!" they mock. "This one came to sojourn and he's busy being a judge! Now we'll do you more evil than them." The narrator adds: "So they pressed at the man, at Lot, hard, and came close to breaking the door" (19:9). A glance at the imagery of locking, latches, and doors in the Song of Songs (e.g., 4:9–5:8) is enough to suggest a perverse double entendre here. Rapidly Lot himself has become the rape object. With the next sentence the narrator mischievously maintains our focus on the rapists and their new victim—"And the men put out their hands and brought Lot to them"—before adding words which completely redefine the sense—"(in)to the house, and shut the door." The "men," therefore, become the visitors, the reaching out a rescue instead of the inflicting of more abuse, and the door is again literally a door (though its closing against the attackers is also figuratively the closing of the door to Lot's body).

Now the visitors take charge. They pull Lot inside and disable the assailants, "both small and large." They ask whether Lot has any others with him—"son(s)-in-law, or your sons and daughters, and all who belong to you in the city"—in order to take them out of the place, "for," they explain, "we are destroying this place."

Lot goes out to do the visitors' bidding, but fails to convince his sons-in-law that YHWH is destroying the city. In their eyes he is just fooling around. (The word *mᵉtsaḥeq* means "laughing," "jesting," "playing the fool"; perhaps there is a play on *mᵉtsaʿeq*, "crying in distress.") Indeed, he hardly seems convinced himself, for at dawn he is still at home. The visitors (now called "messengers" or "angels") urge him, "Arise, take your wife and your two daughters who are found [here], lest you be swept away [cf. 18:23, 24] in the iniquity of the city." Yet still he lingers.

Why the delay? He is obviously loathe to leave this community in which he resides. It has become his home. His father's house no longer exists. His uncle Abraham has not pressed him to stay with his family. Despite the provocations of the night, Lot seems deeply reluctant to begin again the aimless moving that has begun to mark his life. Perhaps that is why the angels speak first to him of his sons-in-law, not his sons or daughters, for they recognize where his heart is. Sons-in-law represent his primary connection to his new home, Sodom. Sons-in-law represent the possibility of permanent belonging.

The visitors, however, are not deterred. "So the men seized his hand and his wife's hand and his two daughters' hands, through

YHWH's pity on him, and they brought him out and set him outside
the city" (19:16). "Flee for your life!" they urge him again. "Do not
pay attention behind you, and stop nowhere in the plain! Flee to the
hills, lest you be swept away!" But Lot takes charge, and again stalls,
though this time his reluctance begins to give shape to a new desire
on his part:

> No, my lords, if you please. Look here, your [sing.] servant has found fa-
> vor in your [sing.] eyes, and you have made a great commitment [*hesed*] to
> me in saving my life [lit., causing my life (*nephesh*) to live]. But I cannot
> flee to the hills, lest [the] evil cling to me and I die. Look now, this city
> is close to escape to, and it is tiny; please let me flee there—it is tiny, is
> it not?—and my life [*nephesh*] will be saved [lit., will live]. (19:19-20)

Is he saying that he does not trust that the visitors can guarantee his
survival if he travels to the hills? But why should a city offer him any
more protection? What evil is going to cling to him? The evil prac-
ticed in Sodom or the evil (destruction) that is to befall Sodom? Or
is he speaking of the fate likely to be his, a townsperson living
without support in the hill country? Evil can mean many things.
What *is* clear is that, if he must flee at all, it must be to this little
town of Zoar. And so it happens: the divine visitor grants him his
wish; Zoar is reprieved and Lot is urged to escape there. Lot's
appeal appears to make a difference: it would seem that, for whatever
motive, he has actually modified the divinity's intention to destroy
all the cities of the plain.

With Lot safely at Zoar, YHWH rains brimstone and fire on Sodom
and Gomorrah, "and he overturned those cities and all the plain and
all dwelling in the cities, and the vegetation of the ground" (19:25).
Lot's wife, "behind him, gazed back, and she became a pillar of
salt." And, for his part, Abraham went at dawn "to the place where
he had stood before YHWH" and, looking down, beheld "the smoke
of the land going up like the smoke of a furnace" (19:27-28).

What has Abraham learned? What has he accomplished? No
word reaches him that his nephew is safe. For all he knows, Lot and
his family have gone up in smoke with the rest. What is he to
conclude? That there were no righteous in Sodom? Or that once
YHWH has made up his mind there is no changing it? That YHWH is
not a god to be taken lightly? As far as he himself is aware, Abraham
fails to save anyone, righteous or not.

And *has* Lot been spared because of Abraham's intercession, whether or not Abraham knows it? Commentators are apt to leap at the
sentence that follows in support of an affirmative answer: "So it was,
when God destroyed the cities of the plain God remembered Abraham and sent Lot away from the overthrow" (19:29). The sentence as

it continues, however, quickly overturns certainty. We may then read two separate statements about God: "So it was, when God overturned the cities of the plain, that God remembered [his conversation with] Abraham. And [so it was, too, that] he sent Lot out of the midst of the overturning, when he overturned the cities where Lot dwelt" (19:29). As he destroys the cities God recalls Abraham's words on the matter. At the same time he rescues Lot.

Does God send Lot away because of what Abraham had said about the righteous or despite it? Abraham could have mentioned Lot but did not; he talked impersonally about the righteous. He could have asked about saving some individuals but did not; he talked about saving the whole city. Perhaps God rescues Lot just because he was, from the beginning, part of this family that had journeyed on God's journey of promise. Perhaps God is once again simply being partial in his dealings with humankind. Perhaps his recollection of Abraham prodded him to extend to Lot a measure of the favoritism that he had shown (and would continue to show) Abraham. Nothing to do with intercession for the righteous. On the contrary, the issue of righteousness only complicated matters. In short, why YHWH saves Lot remains up to the reader's construal.

The divine plan completed and Abraham's knowledge at an impasse, Lot's story continues. Without indicating any significant lapse of time, the narrator tells us that "Lot went up from Zoar and dwelt in the hills, and his two daughters with him, for he was afraid to dwell in Zoar. So he dwelt in a cave, he and his two daughters" (19:30). In other words, after all his delaying and prevaricating, he ends up where the visitors told him to go in the first place.

Why did he say he wanted to go to Zoar if he was afraid to dwell there? Lot's behavior is paradoxical, yet therein perhaps lies a way of understanding him. For Lot, cities are home, yet he has good reason (unlike Abraham) to believe that they are also to be feared, especially by strangers. He presses to go to Zoar, nonetheless, because he thinks thereby to save it, whether for itself or more likely himself, as a new home. The reality proves otherwise: the fear wins out and the resident alien finds himself simply an alien.

But his effort is instructive, especially when we read him alongside Abraham. Plainly unable to prevent the destruction of Sodom and Gomorrah despite his repeated stalling, Lot tries for what he thinks is possible. Zoar is so tiny, a trifle, he insists. Surely God can overlook a trifle for Lot's sake? Sensing his visitors' impatience to get on with the destruction and at the same time counting on their obvious sense of responsibility for his own safety, Lot plays his cards well. On this reading, then, his delays are tactical in the interests of a larger strategy. Ironically, Lot saves a city where Abraham fails. Abraham's challenge hangs on the simple binary categories of righteousness and evil. Lot's challenge is more subtle. It is based on his own personal involvement with his visitors: he capitalizes on what he sees (and makes sure they see he sees), namely the *hesed* (faithfulness, commitment) they have shown him.

Lot's sons-in-law think that he is playing the fool. Perhaps they are closer to the mark than they imagine. Does he fool God? At any rate, in this world of divine-human interaction once more a self-serving man gains his own ends. And he saves for himself a whole city, tiny though it be.

What resurrected Lot's fear at Zoar? One answer might be that Zoar is the place of his wife's bizarre demise. They have reached the city when she regards Sodom and is turned to salt. In a sense, the evil (i.e., the destruction) clings to Lot even as he tries to escape it. How can one continue to ignore death and destruction when it is clearly within easy view? Zoar turns out to be a place of both life and death, an ominous place of safety. Perhaps, for Lot, Zoar becomes a pillar of salt.

Though his desire to belong is frustrated, his story is not quite finished. If we jump to its end we find him belonging more than he might have wished, to his daughters, as both father of them and father of their children. Instead of finding, in a city, a larger community beyond his immediate family, he finds himself, in a cave, turned inward. The irony in that inward turn, for the man who would give up his daughters to the crowd outside, is sharp. Yet he is also named as father of two nations. His belonging to a larger community lies in the future.

What of the fate of Zoar? Might God have destroyed Zoar, after all? Despite the visitor's assurance, the narrator does not explicitly except Zoar from the destruction (vss. 25 or 29), and later Lot's elder daughter seems not to know of any remnant anywhere. We have no certain way of settling the matter, though commentators as early as Ibn Ezra have argued that Deut 29:22 (which fails to mention Zoar in its list of four destroyed cities) does so. In the end any reading of our story must reckon, too, with this uncertainty.

We have talked of God, Abraham, and Lot. In the hillside cave we meet, apparently, another consciousness. Here Lot's daughters take charge of the story, assume a measure of subjectivity, if only briefly. The firstborn convinces her sister that, as sole survivors "in all the land," if they are to "make seed live" they must do so by their father. Over the next two nights they make their father drunk, and they go in and lie with him, first the elder, then the younger:

> Thus they were pregnant, the two daughters of Lot, by their father. And
> the firstborn bore a son and she called his name Moab—he is the father
> of Moab to this day. And the younger, she also bore a son and she
> called his name Ben-Ammi—he is the father of the Bene-Ammon (Am-
> monites) to this day. (19:36-38)

Thus Lot's hold on the narrative becomes tenuous. His older daughter (literally) "lays" him; he is (claims the narrator) oblivious to this
carnal knowledge; and the children of his ignorance are named not
by him but by his daughters. The sons, not Lot, are called the fathers
of their people. Thus Lot fades from the story, displaced by his
daughters and by the sons he must have thought he would never have.

The daughters are concerned "to make seed live" (not "have
children"). Whence this desire? Of course, we could say that it stems
from their social construction as women in patriarchy, where men's
seed is a central theme of control and inheritance.

We could also look back into their story and glimpse them on
their father's lips as exchange for two unknown men. His rhetoric
displays their disposability. They are marginal. The men, the visitors,
ask Lot whether he has someone else with him: "Son-in-law, sons,
daughters . . ." (19:12). We suggested that the order corresponds
perhaps to Lot's emotional connection to the city. A son-in-law
becomes more important than a son for he signifies the community's
acceptance of the father. Daughters are only a means to an end.
Lot's sons-in-law (vs. 14) are "takers of his daughters," an unusual
phrase suggesting both Lot's marginal situation and the daughters'
vulnerability in the power stakes of sojourning and citizenship.
These are tenuous sons-in-law: they have apparently not yet
"known" Lot's daughters and do not yet live with them.

Given such marginality, we are hardly surprised to find them, in
extremity, constructing their remaining value in terms of their ability
to bring (men's) seed to life, even if that has to be the seed of their
own father. As though complicit with these values the narrator
reports that the daughters bore sons—not daughters. (So, of course,
Sarah, Rebekah, Rachel, Tamar, Hannah, and Ruth, to name a few,
bear sons—not daughters.) Thus, given that they are the most marginal of all the story's characters, it is ironic that Lot's daughters'
story finally supplants all the others. While YHWH rains down brimstone and fire, overturns cities and wipes out whole populations, the
most vulnerable and subordinated characters in the story take charge
of their own lives, as they have been led to understand them, by
doing what must be done to bring seed to life.

Yet even as we read them into a commanding position in the
story we risk propagating a subliminal message that once again

subordinates them and all other daughters as well. For in the real world it is not daughters but fathers who initiate incest. Turn this text ever so little and praise becomes blame: it is the daughters who are to blame, it proclaims in a world of sexual abuse, not the fathers. (The apparent subjectivity of the daughters in this section of the story turns out to be but a projection of the father-narrator's subjectivity after all.) Surreptitiously, the father's offer of the daughter to sexual abuse is canceled out.

When the daughters were thrust out of Sodom, their mother was with them. We may have noted her palpable absence earlier in the chapter, at the visitors' arrival. Lot, we are told, "made them a feast, and baked unleavened bread, and they ate" (19:3). But just as in the scene of hospitality in the previous chapter, where Abraham is credited with preparing the visitors' food, despite the narrator's having already detailed the preparation as essentially the work of Sarah and the servant, so here we may decide that Lot is no more likely to have made the feast and baked the bread than Abraham. The narrator, in patriarchal fashion, is recounting a man's story: the host offers the visiting men hospitality. Lot's wife is visible only by inference.

We glimpse her next seized and expelled from home and city. Then she looks behind Lot and becomes a pillar of salt. Why? Why does she gaze behind and why is she turned to salt?

Commentators have little difficulty on the latter score. Why turned to salt? Because, they say, she disobeyed the angel's command. Few ask whether the command was heard by her, let alone addressed to her. In fact, having told us that the visitors had brought *them* out—Lot, wife and daughters—the narrator continues with the visitor's command: "Flee [masc. sing.] for your [masc. sing.] life; do not look back [masc. sing.] . . ." (19:17). The divine visitors are only concerned to talk to Lot, but the woman as subsumed in her husband is expected to obey.

On the other hand, the narrator is not at all specific about the agency by which she becomes salt. Given the emphatic way in which the destruction unfolding before the woman is ascribed to YHWH— "And YHWH rained on Sodom and Gomorrah brimstone and fire from YHWH in heaven"—coyness over her fate is curious. Is the narrator just a little nervous about signalling divine responsibility? Sandwiched between the big players, YHWH and Abraham, Lot's "pillaried" wife may make for disturbing reading. As any journalist knows, an account of devastation in general (as in cities and inhabitants), no matter how massive the scale, may shock less than an account of devastation in particular (as in Lot's wife). Thus in the middle of YHWH's concern to silence the outcry and Abraham's concern for justice stands a pillar of salt. A disturbance? A distraction? A seasoning? For salt surely makes a difference. We need to look further into this matter.

Why does Lot's wife turn her attention to what is behind Lot? Biblical commentators (mostly men) have rarely asked the question. When they have ventured an answer, they have stereotyped her as a Pandora, a curious, disobedient female entrenched in the tradition of Eve. Usually her plight is ignored; sights are set firmly on the men's story. But other readers have asked and found a different answer.

For the great Russian poet, Anna Akhmatova, the woman looks back to her town's towers, to the square where she used to sing and the courtyard where she would sit at her spinning; she gazes at the windows, now empty, of the room where she gave birth to her daughters. She looks back in anguish to her home, to where the threads of her life have been spun, not in the mighty acts of God, but in the everyday things.

Developing the same theme, Kristine Batey understands her looking back as her choice to be human.[2] She is the one who cooked the meals in Sodom ("whoever is god— / the bread must still be made"), raised her daughters in Sodom ("The Lord may kill the children tomorrow, but today they must be bathed and fed"), and visited her women neighbors in Sodom ("weren't they there / when the baby was born, / and when the well collapsed?"). Her final gesture is, like her life, mundane and profoundly human. "On the breast of the hill," she turns, "in farewell."

However, our reader may say, that is all very well, but in the story world of Genesis, Sodom is evil in its totality. These are fictions, these neighborly, child-rearing, family-nurturing women; they are fictions invented against the plain sense of the text. To which we reply that reading this text is not quite so simple.

When God speaks first it is of the myriad "cry of distress" or "cry for help" ($z^e'aqah$) of Sodom and Gomorrah and of their grave "sin" (18:20-21). Implied by the term "cry for help" are many who are oppressed. Are they all at the same time and equally oppressors deserving destruction? Neither the narrator nor God makes any attempt to clarify the matter. The term "cry for help" remains, disturbing the notion of total depravity. On the other hand, when Abraham (not the narrator or YHWH) introduces the terms "righteous" and "wicked" to define the fate of the cities, he forces the issue into a rigid choice between exclusive categories. For Abraham it is a matter of either/or: people are either righteous or wicked. Yet we might wonder where he would place himself on this grid.

Indeed, both Abraham and Lot have deeply problematic attitudes towards their families. Lot's offer of his daughters lies between Abraham's prostitution of Sarah at the beginning and his repeated attempt to do the same thing, despite YHWH's insistence that Sarah is to bear the promised seed, in the chapter that immediately follows the Sodom account (Genesis 20). By the same token Lot's offer may remind us of Abraham's preparedness to sacrifice Hagar and Ishmael (Genesis 16, 21) and, in due course, Isaac (Genesis 22). Lot can save (evil) Zoar, but speak of giving his (innocent) daughters to the ravening mob. Abraham can plead for (evil) Sodom but say not a word in defense of his (innocent) son. In short, however we look at this discussion of prospective corporate judgment its terms are fraught with unclarity if not contradiction.

A simple verbal echo also points to the text's inability to sustain a notion of total evil. Having heard Abraham persist in asking what YHWH will do if forty righteous, or thirty or twenty or ten, "are found [there]" (*matsa'*; Gen 18:29, 30, 31, 32), we may be struck by the way the angels speak of Lot's daughters: "Arise, take your wife and your two daughters who are found [here] [*matsa'*], lest you be swept away in the iniquity of the city" (19:15). The daughters who are "found" recall the righteous who may be "found."

Abraham, of course, does not have daughters in mind; he is talking of "righteous men" (*tsaddiqim*, masc. pl.), adult men like himself, the proper subjects of moral and religious discourse. But what if we were to suggest, no doubt perversely from Abraham's perspective, that instead of translating *tsaddiq* as "righteous" we chose the term "innocent" instead? That is, after all, a meaning within the regular semantic range of the Hebrew term. And let us take the masculine plural, *tsaddiqim*, as inclusive of feminine as well as masculine, as androcentric grammar would have it when convenient. What will God do if any innocents are found in the city? Are there any daughters to be found in the city? And, if so, might some of them not be innocent? Of the persons involved in the assault recounted in chapter 19, who are innocent, if not the daughters? So do the daughters signal the presence of "innocence" in Sodom?

The angels, however, no matter what their actions might suggest, signally fail to include the daughters in their spoken concern. "Arise," they say to Lot, "take your wife and your daughters . . . lest *you* [masc. sing.] be swept away . . ." Likewise the narrator's account of the angels seizing by the hand Lot, his wife, and his daughter is punctuated by a parenthesis about YHWH's compassion for *him*.

It becomes clear, therefore, that just as the narrator has rhetorically excluded Lot's wife from her work space and her table so too the angels exclude wife and daughters from their own moral space as persons. Lot's offer of his daughters to the crowd gives us sufficient clue to the identity of at least some of the oppressed in Sodom, whose cries have reached heaven. How many daughters have already been raped? How many young men? And if the men gather to rape other men (19:4), are they all there by choice in this violent city? But now we have another way of reading this story, for the excluded are beginning to appear and the included are beginning to look different.

Turn back to the crowd gathered around Lot's house and read again. "The *men* of the city, the *men* of Sodom, both young and old, all the people to the last *man*, surrounded the house . . ." (19:4). These are the *men* of the city. So where are the *women*? Where are the young, not the young men but the *children*—the daughters and sons. Where are the *babies*? Where are all these in this facile talk of the righteous and the wicked? This language is inappropriate, even more so in traditional translation: choose "righteous" instead of "innocent" for *tsaddiq* and the translator has semantically excluded the children.

We come back to the pillar of salt. Salt is seasoning for the food the woman prepares (Job 6:6), seasoning for the cereal offerings she makes ready for her man to take to the shrine (Lev 2:13). Salt is for purifying when she finds the drinking water to be bad (2 Kgs 2:20-21). The woman uses salt for preserving food. Her menfolk—and her god, YHWH—use it to prevent food from being grown (Judg 9:45; Deut 29:23). Salt preserves Lot's wife as a monument which cries out in distress to heaven. For salt is tears, anguish for the women and children of Sodom.

Why look back? Because Sodom has been *home*—Lot's wife's belonging. So who will weep for this woman, demands Anna Akhmatova, this woman who gave her life for a single glance? Is her death perhaps, after all, *not* the least significant?

Where have we come to in this story? The simple terms of YHWH's plan turn out to be simplistic, unless YHWH was not interested in the question of innocence at all. YHWH's action is deeply compromised. Abraham may be satisfied that absolute justice has been done, but some readers may be far from satisfied. Divine judgment, understood in terms of this story, turns out to be messy, rather like human judgment. Hiroshima, Dresden, and the cities of Iraq come to mind. This is rough "justice" indeed. Where YHWH, the judge of all the earth, might fit on the grid of innocent and evil is no less problematic a question than it is in respect of Abraham the family sacrificer. Put another way, theology built on binary terms is found wanting.

Chapter Four

THE WAY OF WOMEN

While Genesis 12–50 has often been called "sacred" or "patri-archal" history (i.e., the history of the "patriarchs," Abraham, Isaac, and Jacob), one might just as easily identify this material as stories of "family" life (and family strife). Granted, the stories focus on a particular family, for whom the divine promise of blessing, land, and nationhood is central. Yet, special or not, the family is, in many ways, typical and prototypical of "family" in Genesis–Kings. Indeed, to bring together the terms "patriarchal" and "family" is obviously appropriate for our present discussion, even if by "patri-archal" we mean more than what pertains to a few select characters in an ancient story. For the way the family, or household economy, is structured is a key part of the larger system of control and domina-tion exercised by men in a patriarchal society. In other words, the stories construct certain images of family that indelibly stamp the reader's understanding of the literary (and social) worldview of Genesis–Kings.

One of the most obvious structural features of the biblical patriar-chal family is its location of women within the role of motherhood. A woman is a childbearer. This role is marked out as the primary, if not the only, legitimate place for women. It is the place where women gain social identity and approval. It is a place where men can risk (cannot prevent?) women having some freedom, power even, but still within the formal constraints of male authority—male head-ship of the household and male control of the larger social structures of which the family is part (institutional religion, politics, etc.). Not surprisingly, despite many other dimensions of women's lives that could frame their stories, this narrow focus on woman as mother far and away predominates. Nevertheless, as the stories demonstrate, the power of authority is not the only kind of power that can be exercised in this patriarchal world. Despite attempts to monopolize power systemically, the ability to effect change does not wholly lie within the grasp of men.

The story of Abraham and Sarah is, for much of its course, a story of an incomplete family. They both, for complex reasons, desire children, seeing in children meaning and fulfillment. The valuing of children passes from generation to generation in Genesis. Integral to

God's promise to Abraham and indeed to the divine plan of creation (see Genesis 1), children come to represent blessing, enriching the household and providing a link to the future.

In a sense, the multiple pregnancies, encoded in the woman's "curse" in Genesis 3, have been transformed from punishment to boon. Is this a patriarchal reconstruction? Not completely, but at least in part. On the one hand giving birth is a miraculous experience that often changes a woman's view of herself forever. Though Sarah rejoices when she gives birth to a son in her old age, her sense of wonder is not all due to age. Even Eve, on the birth of Cain, marvels at her participation in the creative process: "I have had a man by [the help of] YHWH" (Gen 4:1). (Though, in more cynical vein, might we say that this exclamation is rather a celebration of having a male instead of a female child?) The attachment of mothers to their children appears to be too much of a biological given to say easily that eagerness to bear children is due solely to cultural construction.

On the other hand, from the viewpoint of men who want big families for the sake of productivity (more hands to work the farm), protection (safety in numbers), and prestige (as a sign of virility and prosperity and thus power), motherhood is an easily exploited role. To convince a woman that many children are a sign of blessing, and that her self-importance lies in her bearing of them, is to counteract a woman's disinclination to risk her life repeatedly in pregnancy and childbirth (cf. Meyers 1988).

In support of this program, many of the experiences and much of the pain of motherhood is passed over in biblical texts. The numerous miscarriages (at least one in four pregnancies would have ended this way), the frequent fatality of both mother and infant (the infant mortality rate was about 30 percent in the ancient world), even mothers mourning for older children, are rarely recognized in the word-world of biblical narrative and law. (Rizpah in 2 Sam 21 is a notable exception to this last point.)

Even when maternal suffering finds its way into the text, there is a pointed attempt to write over it, to reinterpret it. For example, when Rachel is dying, giving birth to her second and last son, she names her baby "Son of my sorrow." His father, however, renames the boy and so renames her experience. He becomes "Son of the south" and Rachel's sorrow is remembered only under erasure. When Eli's daughter-in-law goes into labor, traumatized by the news of the deaths of her husband and father-in-law (1 Sam 4:19-22), she, too, slowly dies giving birth. The women attending her attempt to console her. "Fear not," they say, "for you have given birth to a son." Her only response is to name the child Ichabod, "Where is the honor?" Her personal loss and despair are reinvented, however, as a concern for Israel's loss of its primary cult object, the ark of God, into the hands of the Philistines. Her hopelessness for herself and for her child is refocused on national events.

The primary experiences of motherhood inscribed and celebrated in the Hebrew Bible are conception and childbirth. Whether or not a woman can conceive is a common problem in plots involving women and is repeatedly used to feature divine power, providence, and of course potency. Childbirth, when the child is a boy, and particularly when the child is born against great odds, is often a strategic beginning or transition in stories that focus on family lineage (as do the stories in Genesis) or on the need for a hero (as in the stories of Moses, Samson, and Samuel). The actual work of "mothering," that is, the caring for and the guidance, education of children rarely comes to light in biblical narrative. The devaluing of "mothering" is clearly seen in the story of Hannah (1 Samuel 1-2). The narrative reports, without condemnation or misgiving, that she sends Samuel to Eli (who has done a fairly lousy job of raising his own sons) as soon as he is weaned. For this narrator, "mothering" is nothing much that Samuel should miss. (Though an ironic reading might argue that Samuel's loss of mothering was precisely why he turned into such an obnoxious adult!)

Mothers in biblical literature become defined by their ability to conceive and give birth. Adoptive mothers, of which there were presumably many, considering the number of women (30-35 percent) dying in childbirth, rate little mention. Pharaoh's daughter in Exodus 2 is the notable exception. Even the institution of surrogacy, in which a servant is called upon to bear a child for her mistress, is a clear fiction in biblical narrative. The child is always identified with, and obviously cared for by, his natural birth mother.

Consequently, while motherhood is almost exclusively defined (by men) as a role of honor and a source of great happiness, it is at the same time condensed into two, relatively brief, bodily events—conception and childbirth—over which women have little or no autonomy. We may glimpse in biblical narrative some of the joys and accomplishments of motherhood, but most often we witness women's values being constrained and manipulated to suit men's interests in large families, many sons, and remembered names.

What constitutes "family" in biblical literature? Families, in the biblical view, are incomplete without children, in particular, sons. For, in spite of the matrilocal paradigm established in Genesis 2, in reality, sons are the ones who stay with and contribute to the father's household. Daughters are "given" (though in actuality "sold") to other families. They invest in other fathers' families as the wives of other sons. Because a daughter will eventually be lost to the family anyway, the lack of daughters is never viewed with the same disappointment as the lack of sons. Understood this way, daughters-in-law assume an interesting priority over actual daughters. (As was clear in the last chapter, sons-in-law may also sometimes take priority, when there are no sons.) Sons must have wives for the family to grow and the line to continue, wives who will fit well into the family. Hence the concern to secure the "right" wife for Isaac (Genesis 24) and the bitterness created for Isaac and Rebekah when Esau chooses inappropriate wives (Gen 26:34 and 28:6-9).

Fathers, certainly, are essential to families, for without fathers, families disintegrate into widows and orphans, unconnected and marginalized citizens at best. What about mothers? They are essential to families—temporarily. They are needed to bear children, but once the children are born, mothers often disappear from the narrative picture. Once Isaac is weaned, for example, Sarah is no longer necessary to the story and, for the most part, disappears. Father Abraham has no difficulty in acquiring another woman and having another family. It is common in Genesis–Kings to read of families with absent mothers. We know nothing, for example, of Saul's mother. The same holds true for David's mother. Fathers, however, are usually somewhere in the picture, if even in the background. Everyone who is anyone has a father. One's father is the source of one's identity.

The stories in Genesis both mine and undermine this understanding of family. Fathers are primary, but they are often ineffective. Mothers lack the authority of fathers, yet they play prominent roles in the structuring of the family. Mothers often shape the family authority of the next generation by determining (by strategy or identity) which son will inherit or be favored. Sons find themselves, by nature of the patriarchal system of primogeniture, in competition and conflict. Daughters, when present at all, are for the most part ignored or are used as pawns in men's business dealings (a graphic description of which we have seen in the story of Lot). Daughters-in-law, as wives and mothers, exert much more influence in the family, usually in efforts to secure their own economic and societal position. As women who have given up the security of their own kin to join a different family, daughters-in-law must actively make inroads into the family power structure, which they can do most easily by giving birth to male children who will assume the leadership of the family.

Rebekah is the quintessential daughter-in-law who becomes a mother. She leaves her own family to join a family she has never seen before. Geography forms a permanent barrier to her family of origin. She is indeed on her own. It is imperative that she establish and safeguard for herself a respected place in her new household.

Of all the women in Genesis, Rebekah is most clearly the daughter of Eve. Although an understudy in this patriarchal production (as Eve was derivative of Adam), Rebekah, like Eve, quickly moves to the center of the action. She is a woman of initiative, a woman of knowledge, and a woman whose story takes a bittersweet turn. But she is also a woman who upsets the status quo—even that assigned to Eve.

We meet Rebekah in Genesis 24. Abraham is old; Sarah is dead. The next generation must take its turn upon the stage. The son of promise is ready to take his place. Daughters neither exist, nor are they missed. It is a daughter-in-law who will make all the difference in this family's story. The patriarch's heir Isaac must be matched by a matriarchal successor. Enter Rebekah.

The story is structured as a patriarch's commission and a servant's quest. The objective of the venture is to find a wife for Isaac— a suitable wife. Not just any woman will do, especially not a Canaanite. A woman from Abraham's own family is the goal. Not only does this move communicate the (temporary) security of endogamy, it also underscores the latent power of daughters-in-law to shape the family's sense of well-being.

The servant departs with ten camels loaded with gifts to secure his prize. The story is well-known. The servant meets Rebekah at a well. She offers him a drink and volunteers to water his camels. Her timely generosity and her lineage convince the servant that she is the woman for Isaac.

Rebekah enters the scene in a swirl of activity. In the course of fetching water for her household, she shares with a stranger. She moves with intention and haste. She "quickly" lowers her jar; she "quickly" empties it into the trough; she "runs" to draw water for the camels; and she "runs" to tell her family of the visitor.

One would be hard pressed to find a woman in greater contrast to her suitor, Isaac, the boy who had obediently followed his father up a mountain, who had remained passive while his father tried to kill him, and who was so engulfed by his father's shadow to be rendered completely invisible by him (Gen 22:19; see Crenshaw 1984). What we know thus far of Isaac the man is that he is content to let someone else go and seek his bride. Rebekah, we might imagine, would have never stood by, allowing someone else to make such decisions for her.

When broached with the decision to return with the visitor, she determines to go. Whatever her motivation—whether she is touched by the visitor's tale of divine guidance or whether she is enticed by the loaded camels and the report of Isaac's wealth or whether she is eager to leave the control of her (we later learn) greedy and conniving brother—she, like Abraham before her, makes the decision to leave her country and her kindred to go to a land she has not seen before.

It is she, not Isaac, who follows in Abraham's footsteps, leaving the familiar for the unknown. It is she, not Isaac, who receives the blessing given to Abraham (22:17). "May your offspring possess the gates of their enemies!" (24:60). And, as we shall soon discover, it is she, not Isaac, who determines the next recipient of the promise and blessing.

Consequently, Isaac's absence from this episode is a foretelling of the role he will play as the story progresses. As Adam was a passive bystander while Eve was engaging the snake in theological discussion and making a decision that would mightily affect their future, so Isaac treads in the wake of Rebekah's vigor. Isaac as family patriarch may have *authority*, the right to make decisions and to command obedience, but Rebekah, nevertheless, does have *power*, the capacity to effect change.[1]

Rebekah travels; Isaac waits. When they meet, she dismounts her camel without assistance to greet him. Once he has heard the servant's story, he takes her to his mother's tent where they consummate the marriage. Isaac loved Rebekah, we are told, "and he was comforted after his mother['s death]" (Gen 24:67).

The repeated mention of Isaac's mother here is noteworthy. Rebekah's family had wished upon her great fecundity: "May you become thousands of myriads," or as the REB puts it, "May you be the mother of many children" (24:60). How was she to know that her first mothering would be to her new husband Isaac? For his actions belie that Rebekah is, among other things, a replacement for his mother. She physically takes Sarah's place in her tent and emotionally eases Isaac's loss of her.

As far as actual mothering goes, Rebekah gets off to a slow start. Twenty years pass without children. But unlike Sarah before her and Rachel after her, Rebekah does not seem too bothered by her barrenness. She indulges in no schemes to have children (cf. Genesis 16; 30:1-24); she gives no evidence of desperation or frustration (cf. 16:2,5; 30:1). She does not pray about her childless condition, though we see later (25:22) that she shows no timidity in approaching YHWH when she feels the need to. The text gives no indication that mothering is the center of Rebekah's self-worth or her reason to be.

It is Isaac who prays that Rebekah might conceive (25:21). The frequency of his prayers is not revealed. While it is possible that he prays incessantly for twenty years, the narrator gives no indication that this is reiterative behavior. The wording suggests that he prayed only once, perhaps along about the eighteenth or nineteenth year of marriage. YHWH responds immediately, it seems, to Isaac's entreaty with Rebekah's conception (vs. 21). Why might Isaac have waited so long to bring the matter to YHWH's attention? Was he loathe to share his mothering Rebekah with anyone else? (We might find such anxiety confirmed as we watch Rebekah's later allegiances shift from husband to son.)

Just as Eve was the "mother of all living," Rebekah is to become the mother of all Israel (and Edom, too, for that matter). Moreover, if we are influenced by the traditional rendering of Gen 3:16 (e.g., "I will greatly increase your pangs in childbearing; in pain you shall bring forth children," NRSV),[2] we see Rebekah even more firmly entrenched in Eve's legacy. Rebekah is the first woman in the Hebrew Bible reported to have a difficult pregnancy. Troubled by her pain, she seeks an explanation from God. Obviously, she sees no need for Isaac's mediation in this matter. She inquires, and YHWH responds to her directly.

Two nations are in her womb, explains God, divided against each other. One is to be stronger than the other, and the older is to serve the younger (25:23). Rebekah keeps this knowledge of good and evil to herself—good in that there are two children rather than just one, evil in that the two are destined for strife.

Privy to this oracle, it is hardly surprising that, of her twin sons, Rebekah favors the younger Jacob. The dispositions of the two young men do nothing to alleviate the impartiality. The older, Esau, is a man of the wild, a hunter who caters to his father, a man who marries foreign women creating great bitterness in the household, and a man with little concern for his rights and responsibilities as firstborn in the family. Jacob, on the other hand, stays close to home, valuing family life and propriety (in particular, the birthright), caring for the herds and, no doubt, his mother. He is, in her eyes, "perfect" ('ish tam).

When the time comes for Isaac to pass on his blessing (Genesis 27), disparity of characterization, favor, and knowledge reaches a climax. Isaac, like Adam, has the *authority* to name, in this case, his successor. He is intent on blessing Esau, his firstborn, his favorite, the one who puts meat in his mouth. Rebekah, however, has other ideas, in particular one that has been planted by YHWH: the younger son shall prevail. It is in Rebekah's interests that God's plan be brought to fruition. Jacob represents the future—her future. He is the

son most likely to care for her in her old age. He is the most dependable, the one who values domestic life.

Rebekah cannot allow the blessing to pass to Esau. Isaac is old
and blind and confined to his bed. Rebekah is still young, alert, and
energetic. Unlike Isaac, she knows what God has in store and she
knows what is going on around her (27:5, 42). In David Jobling's
words (concerning Eve), she is "more aware of the complexity of the
world, more in touch with 'all living'" (1986:42). She has the *power* of
her knowledge. Unlike Isaac, she knows that Esau is an inappropriate choice. He has repeatedly shown himself negligent in family
matters (Gen 25:29-34; 26:34-35). She knows that God has chosen
Jacob. Rebekah may not be able to bless her son herself, but she can
manipulate Isaac's authority for her (and God's) purposes.

Like Eve, whose man stands passively by while she decides and
risks, Rebekah is no slave to the safety and security of the status
quo. Not only does she hatch a plan to foil her husband's will, she
takes upon herself all of the inherent danger. "Upon me be the
curse, my son," she tells Jacob when he, out of fear, protests her
strategy.

Nothing better illustrates the contrast between Isaac's authority
and Rebekah's power than the story of the usurped blessing. The
scene in which Isaac commissions Esau to hunt and cook for him so
that he might bless him (Gen 27:1-4) is precisely mirrored in Rebekah's commissioning of Jacob to undertake Esau's role. With
Rebekah's senses alert (27:5), and Isaac's dimmed (27:1) and easily
deceived (27:21-27), Isaac's authority capitulates to Rebekah's power.
The family underdogs, the mother and younger son, capsize the traditional power structure, namely the link between patriarch and
firstborn.

The upset is not without its repercussions, however. Esau seeks
revenge against his brother Jacob. But Rebekah, ever aware of the
goings-on in her household, maneuvers again to protect the interests
of her favored son. She commands Jacob to flee to her brother Laban
in order to escape Esau's wrath. But lacking the authority to give
him a proper send-off and unwilling to let him go without it (and
obviously reluctant to reveal to sickly Isaac the impending violence in
his household), she manages again to manipulate Isaac's authority.
"I am sick to death of Hittite women," she tells Isaac. "If Jacob
marries one of these Hittite women, I can't bear to go on living!" Or,
in modern idiom, "I think I'll kill myself!"

Of course, Rebekah has hit a sore spot with Isaac. We have
already been told that Esau's Hittite wives "made life miserable for
Isaac and Rebekah" (26:35). He hardly longs to have more Hittite

women join his household. Rebekah's lament is a threat to his own peace. He wastes no time in summoning Jacob and sending him off to find a wife from his mother's family in Paddan-aram. Isaac may have the authority, but Rebekah has orchestrated the events. Jacob leaves, twice blessed, because of his mother's foresight and initiative.

Genesis 2 had suggested that a woman's allegiance to her husband was primary, taking priority over other familial ties. Rebekah flatly overturns this notion. Rebekah's love for her child Jacob supersedes all other loyalties, revealing again the complexity of the world. Her actions might be regarded as treachery to some, but, unlike Eve, she faces no divine rebuke. In fact, one might easily surmise that she acts with God's sanction.

Eve gained knowledge but lost paradise and self-autonomy. Rebekah gains a blessing and a better life for her son, but in the end she loses him. Once she sends him to seek asylum with her brother, she never sees him again. The son who was to be her security in her old age does not return in her lifetime. If she had known the price of her initiative, would she have settled for less? Who can say?

Just as she never again sees Jacob, we as readers never again see her. We hear of Isaac being buried by his sons some seventy years hence, but we know nothing of the rest of Rebekah's life. We can safely surmise, however, that, Jacob or no Jacob, she continued to take care of herself and her dim-sighted husband, that she would have never retired permanently to her bed in mid-life as Isaac had done, that she would have never spent eighty years trying to die. No, death would have had to *hurry* to overtake Rebekah.

Rebekah and Jacob launch a sequence of events fraught with struggles concerning the internal and external definition of family. Jacob's conflicts with his brother Esau and his father-in-law Laban not only expose the internal family problems surrounding primogeniture and residence with the wife's family (matrilocal marriage), but they also grapple with the issue of family boundaries.

Esau the brother becomes Edom, both through Jacob's chicanery surrounding birthright and blessing and through a series of characterizations that portray him as a man oblivious to the family's values. The likeness of Jacob and Esau as twins is gradually chiseled away as contrasts emerge: Esau the hunter versus Jacob the herdsman; Esau the man of the wild versus the domestic Jacob; Esau the inarticulate (see 25:30) versus the smooth talker Jacob (27:20); Esau who marries a foreign woman versus Jacob who marries family; Esau the man of the present versus Jacob who looks to the future.

Jacob is not above taking advantage of these differences. His domestic interests, cooking (25:29-34) and herding (27:8-17), allow him to take the offensive against Esau, and Esau, by virtue of who he is, is slow to realize what has hit him. By the end of the story Esau retires to Seir in Edom, while Jacob resides in the land of promise.

Laban, the uncle and father-in-law, is also moved to the edge of the family through a series of episodes revealing that trust between the two men, Jacob and Laban, will never be forthcoming. When Laban meets Jacob, he greets him, "Surely you are my bone and my flesh!" The identification is solidified not only by maternal kinship, but also by similarity of character: they are both incorrigible tricksters. But Jacob, in danger of being subsumed by Laban, foments subtle rebellion. Just as he had tricked Esau (Edom = "Red") into selling him his birthright for a bowl of "red stuff" (25:30: ha-'adom ha-'adom), so he confiscates the best of Laban's (Laban = "white") flocks with magical white rods (30:37: libneh, l^ebanot, hallaban). Indeed at the heart of Jacob's story is his struggle to divorce himself from his flesh (red) and his bone (white), that is, his kin, and to claim his own identity. His last meeting with Laban is one in which Laban's claim on "his [i.e., Laban's] daughters and his sons" (31:26-28) is dismissed and a boundary is established between the two men. The physical marker, a heap of stones, witnesses to the fact that likeness has given over to difference, family to foreign. From this point on, Laban is clearly Aramean while Jacob is to become Israel (32:28).

At the apex of Jacob's story—sandwiched between his conflicts first with Esau (25:19-34; 27-28), then twice with Laban (29:1-30; 30:25-31:55), and then with Esau (32-33)—is a conflict between Rachel and Leah. Commentators (in particular Fokkelman 1975) have seen the literary parallels between Rachel and Leah and Jacob and Esau: the two sisters match the two brothers, the issue of who is firstborn is again crucial, favoritism creates a problem, and Rachel, in stealing her father's teraphim (31:19, 34-35), has even been described as a female Jacob stealing family blessing.

The stories are, in many respects, mirrors. But while the conflicts involving Jacob and Esau, and Jacob and Laban, center upon the issue of dominance (i.e., who is or will become the patriarch?), Rachel and Leah have their own problem to work out. They, through a cruel ruse of the patriarchy, indeed as a result of Jacob and Laban's struggle for dominance, have been pitted against each other in a denial of their separate lives. A good laugh among men around a campfire at the expense of a duped new son-in-law loses its humor when considered from the women's point of view. Rachel must share the husband who loves her. Leah, forever the outsider, must endure the resentment of both husband and sister.

Bound together in their marriage to Jacob, the women are like two prisoners chained together. Neither is able to escape the other. Used by their father to procure Jacob's labor, they are allowed no right to speak, no right to choose their mate or their future. They both live, wedded to Jacob, and therefore to each other in "unwholly" matrimony.

The problem for Rachel and Leah is indeed one of un-wholeness. Neither are allowed to be whole persons. From the beginning they are introduced to us only as parts, as though neither were complete in herself (29:16-17):

> Now Laban had two daughters. The name of the older one was Leah; the name of the younger was Rachel. Leah's eyes were tender and Rachel was shapely and beautiful.

The insinuation is that each woman possesses something the other does not. Rachel has beauty of form and face. By implication Leah is not so stunning. Leah, on the other hand, has "tender" eyes, affective, responsive eyes. In contrast, there seems to be nothing noteworthy about Rachel's eyes. Leah looks; Rachel is looked at. One woman, on account of the way men look at her, inspires love (indeed, from the moment he sees her, Jacob loves Rachel), but the other woman, on account of the way she looks at others, may actually be more capable of returning love.

Once married they become caricatures of the roles assigned to married women. Rachel is the wife, the lover, the one desired by her husband. Leah is the mother, the "other," and fertile to a fault, it seems. They each want to be the other.

Rachel may have her husband's love, but what she really wants is children. "Give me children or I shall die!" she demands of Jacob. In desperation she, like Sarah before her, uses her handmaid to acquire offspring. She struggles to see in these children signs of justice and victory.

Leah, on the other hand, has plenty of children, sons, in fact, who should secure her a place of honor. What Leah wants, however, is her husband's love. With every son born, she hopes for Jacob's love: "surely now my husband will love me" (29:32), "surely now my husband will be joined to me" (29:34), "surely now my husband will honor me" (30:20). She, like Rachel, is caught in a vain attempt to change her life, even to the point of bargaining with Rachel for Jacob's sexual attention. She trades to Rachel mandrakes, a fertility drug, for a night of love with Jacob. But instead of finding a place as wife and lover, her role as mother is reinscribed: she conceives and bears more sons.

Rachel, in the short run, makes better progress. She eventually conceives and bears a son, Joseph. She sees in his birth her restoration to wholeness ("God has taken away my reproach" [30:23]), yet, at the same time, recognizes that one son is not enough to satisfy her need to be a mother ("May YHWH add to me another son" [30:24]). Like Leah's comments in naming her sons, Rachel's speech at the naming of Joseph betrays her wishful thinking rather than her confidence in her status or her future.

It may indeed be her mothering interests that motivate her to steal her father's household gods (*teraphim*). Whether she sees the household gods representing a legal claim to the property Jacob had acquired from Laban, whether she understands the household gods to symbolize patriarchal authority, or whether the household gods simply, in her mind, "confer protection and blessing" (Westermann 1985:493), in all likelihood, her theft is prompted by a concern for her new son and any other sons she might someday have (see 31:16). Her devotion to her children causes her to risk death (31:32) and far outweighs any allegiance she might feel toward her father or her husband. She deceives them both: Jacob through her silence and Laban through her highly ironic remark, "Please don't be angry that I cannot rise before you, for the way of women is upon me" (31:35). Her plea is not only ingenious, since menstruation is not something a man is going to argue about, but the utterance is pregnant with double meaning. She can no longer show deference to her father because other loyalties are now more important. Has the patriarchy not constructed motherhood to be "the way of women"? Should she not (to subvert another famous biblical text) be about her children's business? Should the patriarchy be dismayed and offended when she fulfills the role she has been assigned?

Rachel's prayer for another son is answered toward the end of Jacob's story (35:16-21) in a cruel twist of her earlier demand of Jacob. "Give me children or I shall die," she had said. "Am I in the place of God?" he had answered. In route to the land promised to her children, children and death are once again linked. She dies giving birth to a son she names Ben-oni, "Son of my sorrow." Jacob, unwilling to be reminded of her suffering, renames the child Benjamin.

Here lies the poignant trap of patriarchal motherhood: women face social death without children and physical death to bear children. The risks and the sorrows, the ambiguities and the ironies, are all but passed over in the rush to tell a man's story.

While Jacob "struggles with beings both divine and human and yet prevails" (32:28), Rachel and Leah merely struggle with each other. While Jacob confronts God face to face, Rachel and Leah can only confront each other. Which is the more profound struggle? Rachel says, "Struggles of God I have struggled with my sister and I have prevailed" (30:8). Indeed God has been there, opening and closing wombs, taking the side of the oppressed, but at the same time sanctioning their oppression. Just as Jacob declares to Esau, "Seeing your face is like seeing the face of God" (33:10), so soon after his turbulent encounter with "the face of God" (32:30), we must wonder, is there much difference between struggling with God and struggling with one's sister?

Rachel and Leah, Jacob and Esau, struggling against God, struggling against each other, struggling against a system that constrains and forces competition. Has Rachel prevailed as she has claimed? Does anyone prevail in a system that pits brother against brother, sister against sister, a system blithely sanctioned alternately by God's silence and God's arbitrary participation? The God of good and evil, who both blesses and cripples Jacob, also blesses and curses these women, on the one hand granting them renown as the two women who "together built up the house of Israel" (Ruth 4:11), but on the other forever marring their hopes of life and love with fragmentation, alienation, even death.

The problems surrounding wives and mothers in the patriarchal family naturally carry over to daughters, daughters who live in and learn the system, the cultural definition of who they, as women, should become. This is their "subjection."

Dinah's story begins in silence (30:21). As the last child born to Leah, eclipsed by the arrival of Rachel's firstborn, Joseph (30:22-24), Dinah's entrance into the narrative world is anticlimactic. She is an afterthought in the patriarchal scheme of things. Her brothers have been born in the midst of great joy and hope, each symbolically named as a testimony of or a prayer for happiness, love, and honor. Dinah is born without a word, save her very name: Dinah, "Judgment." In what sense is the birth of Dinah a judgment? Does she represent a judgment for or against Leah's cause, that is, Leah's desire to be loved by her husband? Does she represent the end of Leah's bid for love? After all, her arrival heralds the fact that Leah cannot bear sons forever. As far as Leah is concerned, sons hold her only possible key to Jacob's heart. Dinah marks the end of Leah's sons.

Dinah is born into a world where daughters matter little. She is not even counted among Jacob's children as he makes his way back to Canaan from Paddan-aram (33:22). It is a small wonder that when

Jacob's family settles in the land of promise, Dinah seeks company elsewhere, among the women of the land, literally, among the "daughters" of the land. Her search for connection, and perhaps for worth, however, meets a tragic end.

> Dinah, the daughter of Leah whom she had borne to Jacob, went out to see the women of the land. Shechem, the son of Hamor the Hivite, the chief of the land, saw her, and he took her and lay with her and raped her. (34:1-2)

However we might respond to this account of brutal violation, the narrator immediately moves to complicate our response by capping the account of rape with an extraordinary sequel (34:3):

> And [Shechem's] soul clung to Dinah, daughter of Jacob, and he loved the young woman, and he spoke to the young woman's heart.

The verbs in verse 2, "he took . . . he lay with . . . he raped" (*laqaḥ, shakab, 'innah*), are overtaken in verse 3 by clinging, loving, and speaking to the young woman's heart (*dabaq, 'ahab, dibber 'al leb*). Verbs of violation merge with terms of affection, commitment, courtship, and marriage. Moreover, the last expression—"to speak to the heart of"—may move us beyond the account of Shechem's affections to those of Dinah. That "he spoke to [her] heart," indicates both Shechem's action and Dinah's positive response.[3]

Shechem's changed attitude to Dinah appears also in another feature of the language. In verse 2, the woman is an object: Shechem sees *her*, takes *her*, lies with *her*, and rapes *her*. In verse 3, the woman becomes for Shechem a real person: his soul clings to *Dinah*, he loves *the young woman*, and he speaks to the heart of *the young woman*.

He determines to marry her, insisting that his father make the necessary arrangements.

In a few short verses the narrator creates a complicated ethical and emotional situation. A man rapes a woman and then falls in love with her. A woman is raped, but then is won over by her rapist. What are we being told? Is it straightforward? Is it even reliable?

Let us first consider the man. However one views the rape, one must acknowledge that, in the story, the narrator tips the balance in Shechem's favor: Shechem moves from raping an object to loving a woman and seeking to make restitution for the wrong he has done her. If we were to accept the narrator's account at face value, we might even feel relief for Dinah as we view Shechem's resolve to take care of her.

Of course, therein lies the rub. Can we accept the (male) narrator's perspective? Can we listen to an account of rape then love and nod assent to its credibility? Can we believe that abusive men can change so suddenly and completely? Women's experience tells us, no. Rape has naught to do with love, not even unambiguously with sexual desire, but with misogyny and control. We have here yet another instance where women's experience has been rewritten—fictionalized and idealized from an androcentric point of view. We may follow the narrator's lead, but not without regard for his limited viewpoint. On the subject of rape, this narrator can never be wholly reliable.

What about Dinah? Why does she listen to Shechem? Why does she allow Shechem to touch her heart? Why does she return with him to his home (see 34:26)? In part, we may have yet another bit of male fantasy exposed. Men want to be so easily forgiven by the women they victimize. They want to believe that women really "want it," that women love to be abused by men.

Within the world of the story, however, Dinah's response has some degree of credibility. Ignored and devalued by her family, Dinah, we can safely surmise, wants to be loved. She wants friendship. Why else would she go seeking out other daughters in the land? Moreover, her victimization by Shechem may not notably surpass the neglect she has experienced within her own family. What would be different, however, is Shechem's expression of affection. Would she not consider this a rare commodity? Had she not witnessed from her infancy her mother Leah desiring love and never receiving it?

Is Dinah's trust of Shechem ill-placed? Has he indeed altered his basis for relating, or is the abuser destined to raise again a violent hand? The answer to this we will never know, because Dinah's decision to stay with Shechem is not allowed to stand. Her future becomes a matter for the men of her family to decide, namely her brothers who are so valued in contrast to her.

Dinah's brothers, upon hearing the news, are visibly angry (34:7). Their sense of injury to themselves is clear, but their emotional attachment to their sister is not. The narrator offers us a reason for their anger and seemingly couches it in their point of view: "The men were vexed and very angry because he had done a reckless thing against Israel by lying with Jacob's daughter." Their anger stems from the reckless act against Israel. The reckless act is qualified by "lying with Jacob's daughter." Some other "reckless act" could have produced the same anger. And note that the issue is not that their sister has been raped, but that she has been "lain with." The fact that she has been forced seems immaterial.

Despite Shechem's father's invitation to an "open trade agreement," and despite Shechem's vulnerable offer of an open bride-price, the brothers are unmoved.

> The sons of Jacob answered Shechem and his father Hamor with deceit, and spoke [because] he had defiled their sister Dinah. And they said to them, "We cannot do this thing, to give our sister to an uncircumcised man, for that would be a disgrace to us. Only on this condition will we give you our consent: that you become as we are, all your males circumcised. Then we will give you our daughters and we will take your daughters for ourselves, and we will settle down with you and become one people. But if you will not listen to us and be circumcised, we will take our daughter and go." (34:13-17)

Lest we become too impressed with the brothers' national and religious scruples, the reader has been forewarned that the brothers speech is deceitful. In fact, "deceit" frames the whole of the brothers' speech, so that the reader is unable confidently to posit sincerity in any of it, whether in the specific proposal or in its ostensible socio-religious motivation.

What the speech does do, however, is give us a clue as to what might lie behind the brothers' response. To have their sister marry an uncircumcised man would be a "disgrace" to them, they say. Perhaps their honor is at stake—*their* honor.

"Their words sounded good to Hamor and Hamor's son Shechem" (34:18). The Hivites' perception of and response to the brothers' speech will turn out to be heavily ironic. The irony of the "good" words that bring evil upon the Hivites invites the reader's response also. Are the brothers' words (*d^ebarim*) good? More to the point, are their deeds (*d^ebarim*) good? Might the narrator's irony touch not only Hivites but implicate the brothers also? This little phrase reminds us that our narrative world is also a world of moral discourse.

> And so it was, on the third day, when they were in pain, two of Jacob's sons, Simeon and Levi each took his sword and came upon the city in stealth. They murdered every male. They murdered Hamor and Shechem by sword and took Dinah from Shechem's house and left. The sons of Jacob came upon the slain and they plundered the city which had defiled their sister. Their flocks and their herds and their asses and what was in the city and what was in the field, they took. All their wealth and all their little ones and their women, they captured and plundered, and everything that was in their houses. (34:25-29)

Although Meir Sternberg (1986:445-81) attempts to separate the actions of Simeon and Levi from that of the other brothers (thereby keeping the two of them above materialist concerns), a reader could equally choose an inclusive understanding. Two people who are willing to kill so many for the sake of one are hardly likely to be above plundering the possessions and raping the families as well. Indeed, their sense of poetic justice, exemplified in the circumcision trick, might well demand the defilement of the Hivite women in return for the defilement of their sister.[4]

In the end, however, whether or not Simeon and Levi are implicated in the pillaging matters little. Their grossly disproportionate response remains just that. And their appeal to principle finds no confirmation, but simply hangs, questioning, without closure.

> Jacob said to Simeon and Levi, "You have made trouble for me by making me odious to the inhabitants of the land, the Canaanites and the Perizzites. My numbers are few; and if they muster against me and attack me, I shall be destroyed, I and my house." And they said, "Is he to treat our sister like a prostitute?" (34:30-31)

The issue, for the brothers, is family honor. Their sense of injury is of injury to themselves, not to Dinah. There is no concern for Dinah's restitution. Why did they not allow Shechem to redress the wrong as he had attempted to do? The brothers are proud; they are not to be trifled with. Shechem has tampered with their property. Their use of the term "defiled" to describe their sister lends support to this understanding. The term represents a male point of view: "defile" is not, in this instance, a synonym for "rape." She is not defiled because she has been raped, but because she is no longer a virgin.[5]

Shechem has taken what was theirs. Their indignant outburst against Jacob—"Is [Shechem] to treat our sister as a prostitute?"—betrays their attitude. Their words, their point of view, not the actions of Shechem, turn their sister into a prostitute. What they really mean is that their honor cannot be bought—which means that no restitution to Dinah herself is satisfactory. The injury is an injury to them, and they seek revenge.[6]

What of Dinah? For some commentators, Dinah is but a function of the plot (e.g., Sternberg 1986:537). She is needed to create the complication that drives the rest of the story. But if she has no voice, she has considerable narrative presence through naming: we are constantly being reminded of Jacob's daughter and the brothers' sister. As we read, therefore, of the responses to Shechem's "defiling" of her, and as we attempt to gauge the criteria governing those responses, we may also seek to fill the gap where her own voice ought to be.

What options does Dinah have? As a woman of ancient Israel, what are her alternatives? Once she has been raped, what are her rights? According to Deut 22:28-29:

> If a man meets a virgin who is not engaged and he seizes her and lies with her and they are discovered, the man who lay with her shall pay the young woman's father fifty shekels of silver and she shall be his wife. Because he has violated her he can never have the right to divorce her.

By this standard, at least, Shechem gives her her right to be married and more than makes the required restitution to the father.

Shechem also offers Dinah probably the best way for her to handle her life, given both the particular circumstances and the larger context of a patriarchal society. Except to Shechem, marriage would appear to be effectively denied her since she is now a "defiled" woman. And even if, by some chance, some other man were willing to marry her, she would remain highly vulnerable to being "put away" by him when it suited him (Deut 22:13-21). In short, her best interest within the narrow limits of this society is to marry Shechem, the man who loves her and takes delight in her.

That to stay in Shechem's house is the best thing for Dinah is further made clear by the analogous story in 2 Samuel 13 (cf. Bar-Efrat 1989:267). After raping her, Amnon demands that Tamar leave his house. Her reply is, "No, my brother, for this wrong in sending me away is greater than the other which you did to me" (13:16). Tamar is cast out to "carry [her] shame" (13:13). A desolate woman, she disappears into her brother's house, forever dependent upon his favor.[7]

As a literary construct in a male-conditioned narrative, Dinah's options are limited indeed. As long as rape is seen as a simple extension of sexual desire or as a breach of male honor, as long as restitution means marrying one's rapist, women's experiences, women's rights, like the daughter Dinah, will never have a voice. Justice can never be served, safety can never be assured in a society where men, men's rights, men's honor, and men's texts control women's lives.

As the story of Dinah (and, to some extent, the story of Tamar in 2 Samuel 13) makes brutally clear, daughters still living in their father's households could rely on the protection of the men in their family of origin. Even though that "protection" might not take the young woman's wishes into consideration, even though it might stem more from a concern for male honor (or ambition as in the case of Absalom) than for basic issues of social justice, an unmarried daughter would have had, ideally, some measure of physical support for her wellbeing.

Once a young woman married, however, she ceased to be the responsibility of her father's household. She passed from the authority of her father (or brothers) to that of her husband or father-in-law. However much affection her family of origin might feel for her, she was neither legally nor pragmatically their concern. No longer an economic asset, a virgin who might fetch a bride-price to her father, she would offer less of an incentive for the men of her family of origin to be anxious for her. Furthermore, as in the case of Rebekah, distance could often become a barrier to communication with one's family. Even a few miles could separate family members for long stretches of time. Daughters, having become daughters-in-law, were, for the most part, on their own as far as blood kin were concerned, reliant instead upon the good will of their family of marriage and, to be sure, their ability to bear sons. Marriage into a foreign family could, of course, bring its own special uncertainties for the daughter-in-law.

One of the surface messages of the story of Dinah's rape is the disdain of intermarriage with the Canaanites (see Sternberg). This disdain, however, is revealed to be somewhat pretentious in light of the circumstances that pertain to Jacob's family. Who, after all, are his children going to marry? They can no longer go back to Paddan-aram for suitable mates, because that part of the family has become foreign (Genesis 31). The same holds true with the clans of Ishmael and Esau. Whoever Jacob's children marry, they will, of necessity, be foreigners. As each son takes a bride from among the daughters of Canaan and Egypt (so Joseph), the "purity" of the family of origin (a brother and sister Abraham would have claimed!) is further diluted, blurring the boundaries between family and foreigner, between "us" and "them," and forever problematizing the exclusive promise of nationhood and the holy war rhetoric of Moses, Joshua, and YHWH.

For the next few generations of Israelites, women coming into the family are doubly Other: they are women and they are foreign. Having cast their lots with Israelites (or more likely, having had their lots cast for them), they must create for themselves places of security in the families into which they have married.

As far as the text is concerned, most of these women are completely invisible. They are, literally, veiled by the *toldoth*, the family stories of Jacob (37:2), in an attempt, whether conscious or unconscious, to maintain two fictions: that this family is comprised almost exclusively of men and that this male family, in its essence, is unaffected by foreign women.

Dinah's story had begun with a venture away from her family, a "seeing" and a "taking." Judah's story (Genesis 38, one of the "family stories" of Jacob) begins much the same way: Judah leaves his brothers to settle elsewhere.[8] He "sees" the daughter of a Canaanite, he "takes" her, and he "goes into" her. While his actions are not revealed to be as violent as those of Shechem, they are described in abrupt language nevertheless, suggesting that, where women are concerned, there may be little difference in the attitudes of Israelite and Canaanite men. They see, they desire, and they take.

Shechem had at least (though belatedly) recognized Dinah as a named person. The woman of Judah's choice is merely called, first, the daughter of Shua, and, then, Judah's woman. She is a woman veiled by the text, hardly a prominent subject in Judah's consciousness. The nameless woman joins the ranks of the numerous invisible daughters-in-law of Jacob. She is the one who stands for the many who are never mentioned at all. Her presence is required only by the logic of propagation: someone must bear the next generation of sons (though, as far as the text is concerned, the vast majority of Jacob's sons might have bred, conceived, and delivered children all by themselves!). Shua's daughter bears Judah's sons with all the submissiveness of a nameless, faceless household servant. Having served her usefulness, she dies, with no word from the text about the joys and frustrations of marriage and motherhood or the grief she must have felt when her sons had died.

There are instances, however, when the text cannot keep a determined woman down. Such is the case with Tamar, Judah's daughter-in-law. Despite the impulse to pass over her existence in silence• in order to get on with the adventures of Jacob's favorite son Joseph, the story pauses, seduced by scandal. Tamar refuses to stay hidden between the lines. She creates a breach, pushing herself into the light (as her son is to do at the end of the story), guaranteeing for herself a place, however marginal, in the family of Judah and in the memory of Israel.

Tamar, a young Canaanite woman, is Judah's hand-picked choice for his firstborn son Er. Unfortunately, Er, who is "evil in YHWH's sight," is not long for this world. Enter YHWH, a god of swift justice. YHWH, the widow-maker. We do not know the nature of Er's evil. We do not know if Tamar was a victim (or survivor) of his "evil." We only know that upon his death, she is left childless, and thus without status in society.

Judah enjoins his next son, Onan, to act as *levir*, that is, to impregnate Tamar in order to "raise seed" for his dead brother. Onan, however, not eager to share his inheritance with another son, whether his in fact or his brother's in fiction, spills his semen on the ground. YHWH does not look favorably on this show of greed and kills Onan as well.

Fearing Tamar to be the cause of these deaths and unwilling to risk his third and only remaining son, Judah sends his daughter-in-law back to her father's house, deceptively promising her that he will send for her as soon as his third son is grown. In Judah we see the patriarchy flourish: unable to acknowledge any fault in his own male offspring, he shifts the blame onto the woman. He wants to keep her at a distance, to keep her Other, completely marginal (a widow in her father's house), and yet he wants to control her sexuality. He does not want her to remain part of his family, but he won't release her to become part of someone else's. He plays games while her future hangs in the balance.

Time goes by, Judah's third son grows up, and still Tamar is not summoned back to Judah's house. One day Tamar is told that her father-in-law, now a widower, is planning to attend a sheep-shearing festival. She makes plans to intercept him. She takes off her widow's garments, dons a veil, and waits for him at the gate to Enaim—literally, "the opening of the eyes"—on the road to Timnah, or more playfully, "on the way to a reckoning" (38:14).

Why does she change her clothes? Because Judah mistakes her for a prostitute, interpreters usually assume that she has dressed as such intending to solicit (!) from him that very assumption.[9] Another reading is possible, however. The veil she puts on is the same kind of veil that Rebekah wears when she first encounters Isaac. Is it the veil of a bride? Is it the veil of a woman betrothed? Is it the veil of a young woman available for marriage? Only mentioned here and in Genesis 24, it is clearly not an article of clothing associated with prostitution. (Most likely prostitutes would have left their faces brazenly uncovered.)

She puts on clothes that signify a status other than that of a widow. By redefining herself symbolically, perhaps she hopes to confront Judah with his responsibility toward her. Perhaps she hopes that, when he sees her, he will be reminded that she is still betrothed to his family, that she should be married. If these are her intentions, it is all the more ironic that Judah mistakes her for a prostitute.

His failure to differentiate between a bride and a prostitute sparks for us another pang of sympathy for his late wife. His failure to recognize his own daughter-in-law points to just how far she is from his mind. He sees what he wants to see, defining this woman in a way that is convenient to him.

Once he propositions her, we might imagine her ire rising and, with it, her determination to beat him at his own game. He wants a prostitute, so she gives him a prostitute, a hard-bargaining business woman who shows him to be the fool. She meets his needs and, unwittingly, he meets hers by not only giving her his seed but also giving her all the necessary articles by which to identify him as the father.

When her pregnancy becomes community knowledge, Judah is set to have her burned. Not only would he be rid of his problematic obligation to her, but he could practice a little "righteousness" in public view. Like YHWH, he could be a swift bringer of justice. Of course, Judah's justice proves to be arbitrary and obviously self-serving. A suspicious reader might say: So, too, YHWH's. After all, where is YHWH in the middle of the story, when the woman must deal with the serpent? YHWH is quick to punish the evil of Er and Onan but is slow to correct the injustice against Tamar. Instead, Tamar must work out her own salvation.

In the face of Judah's self-righteousness, in front of the whole community, Tamar produces Judah's things: his staff, his cord, and his signet. Judah has no choice but to acquit her and bring her back into his family. He had sought to control her sexuality; in the final analysis, she controls his.

Tamar bears not one son but two. It is through these sons that Judah's line continues, and it is particularly through Tamar's first-born Perez that Judah's line comes to renown.

That's the problem with these veiled women. They can make the patriarchy mighty uncomfortable. Sometimes they refuse to be ignored. They have been known to be subversive. They can make a man lose confidence in himself (if only briefly!). They can even turn him into a laughingstock. They can occasionally force him to recognize his responsibility. And sometimes they can save his tribe and his/story.

They are bound to appear on occasion. Indeed some of them must appear if the others are to remain safely hidden. After all, no one would believe a story in which no women appeared. Better to reveal a few, lest others grow suspicious that this story might not be representing the truth. Nevertheless, all things considered, it is far better to keep as many of these women as possible under "wraps." So says the patriarchy. So says the text.

The promise as it is enacted in the ancestral stories of Genesis is de-limited by a familial focus. The issue of descendants (to use a pun) is an ever present concern and an opportunity for God to show his power to bring forth children in unlikely circumstances. Upon the fertility of the present is propped the future vision of land and nationhood.

In Genesis the immediate problem is the getting of many descendants. It is hardly surprising, then, that women are allowed a prominent role. The pressure is on them, so to speak, to make God's promise come to life. In the beginning God involves women directly: he insists that Sarah bear the child of promise; he assures Hagar that she too will become a great nation; he explains to Rebekah that she will mother not one nation but two.

Taking her revealed knowledge to heart, Rebekah becomes the first voluntary guardian of the promise, ensuring, through whatever

dubious means, that Jacob (Israel) inherits the choice land and prosperity rather than Esau (Edom).

After Rebekah, however, God deigns not to speak to the other
women of Genesis. Women, as mothers, are necessary, but the crisis
is over. Israel (Jacob) has been born. From this point on women (as
mothers) become unwitting caretakers of the promise. Leah and
Rachel (Genesis 29–30), together, "build up the house of Israel" (see
Ruth 4:11) despite jealousy's attempt to tear it apart. Tamar (Genesis
38), in an effort to secure her own economic well-being, keeps
Judah's line intact, holding in trust the future monarch David.

By the beginning of Exodus the twelve sons of Israel with their
families (seventy in all) are living in Egypt, becoming so numerous
that the Pharaoh is threatened by their increasing population. God's
promise of many descendants has been fulfilled. Israel is well on its
way to becoming a "great nation." Even the Pharaoh recognizes that
Israel has become a "people" (Exod 1:9). Only the promise of the
land has yet to be realized. It is here that the ominous shadow of
servitude, foretold by God to Abraham (Gen 15:13-14), creeps across
the page.

God's precise prediction ("Know for sure that your seed will be
aliens in a land that does not belong to them. They shall be enslaved
and oppressed for four hundred years, but I will judge the nation
whom they serve and afterward they shall come out with great
possessions" [Gen 15:13-14].) casts the exodus story in something of
a cardboard construction. Collective characters ("your seed" and "the
nation whom they serve") play their prescripted roles with little variation or internal differentiation. Large groups are lumped together—
the Egyptians, the Israelites, the Hebrew women, the male babies to be
thrown into the Nile—with no sense of the individuals that comprise
those groups. The collectivity is exacerbated as the story continues.
The Israelites become "the people" or "the congregation" speaking,
acting, complaining as one. The firstborn of Egypt are condemned
and die in one fell swoop. Pharaoh's army, serving as an extension
of Pharaoh and symbolic of oppressive Egypt, pursue the Israelites
and meet their destruction all in unison.

There is a kind of simplicity to this kind of characterization that
keeps the reader from becoming too emotionally involved in the
events taking place. The Hebrew boys being thrown into the Nile are
quickly decentered by the one male baby who is rescued. The firstborn of Egypt, presented *en masse*, render invisible the deaths of
individual children, the grief of mothers and fathers. By collectivizing
the firstborn, they simply stand for the oppressive enemy, the

rhetorical opposite to Israel, God's firstborn son. Simplicity translates into polarity, coaxing the reader to read over the ethical and theological ambiguities and problems that arise when one tries to imagine real people in these roles.

Set against these vague cardboard collections, the women in the early chapters of Exodus emerge as some of the few independent personalities in the story of the exodus and wandering. As characters, they are perhaps no match for Moses. They are hardly singled out by God personally for confrontation and leadership. For them there is no burning bush, there are no signs and wonders. They are not called upon to leave their mundane lives and do something extraordinary. God gives them no instructions, offers them no assurances. Yet they, like their predecessors in Genesis, are unknowing but indispensable caretakers of God's promise.

Through their "mothering," the role so firmly assigned to women in Genesis 3, they continue to salvage the promise long after the seed has been multiplied, numerous descendants secured. It is their "mothering" that distinguishes these women as characters and makes way for the nation's leadership. Without them, there would have been no Moses.

The midwives, Shiphrah and Puah, are introduced first (Exod 1:15), summoned into the story by the Pharaoh, whose social and physical abuse of the Israelites has failed to reduce their numbers. The two women stand, named, before an unnamed and paranoid king. "When you assist in delivering babies for the Hebrew women," he instructs them, "look for the two stones [i.e., testicles]. If it is a son, kill him; but if it is a daughter, let her live" (1:16).

> The shadow of Pharaoh squatted in the dark corners of every birthing place in Goshen. Hebrew women shuddered with terror at the indifference of their wombs to the Egyptian law. (Zorah Neale Hurston, *Moses, Man of the Mountain*, 11)

The midwives say nothing in response. They simply go about their business of bringing life into the world. Fearing "the gods" (*ha-elohim*) more than the Pharaoh, they allow the baby boys to live. Who are these women and why do they behave in this manner? Their nationality is left obscure in the text. They may be Hebrew midwives or they may be Egyptian midwives to the Hebrews. An ambiguous word choice leaves their piety vague. Do they fear God, that is, the god of the Hebrews, or do they fear "the gods," that is, divinity in general? Are they protecting their own people or are they taking up the cause of a community alien to them? Whoever they are, whatever their motives, they refuse to turn birth into death no matter how intimidating the political powers that be.

When called upon the royal carpet for their seeming ineffective-ness, the midwives merely shrug, "The Hebrew women are not like Egyptian women for they are *ḥayot*. They deliver before the midwife comes to them" (1:19). Their response to Pharaoh, like Rachel's to Laban in his search for the household gods, is wonderfully resource-ful. In the first place they speak of women's experience. The topic of women in labor, like Rachel's appeal to menstruation, is not some-thing this male monarch is likely to know much about. Any further interrogation of the matter would only publicize his ignorance about such matters. In the second place they appeal to the Pharaoh's "us/them" mentality. These Hebrew women are not like Egyptian women, they claim. With this sentiment the Pharaoh is sure to agree. Hebrew women are *ḥayot*, "animals." ("They multiply like rabbits" might be an analogous sentiment.) Like animals, they are really in no need of midwives. The implication is that these women are born to breed. That is what—perhaps all—they are good for. Consequently, they deliver before the midwife can arrive. How can Pharaoh argue with information that confirms his suspicions of the Hebrews' differ-ence?

In the third place they affirm what the Pharaoh cannot hear. The Hebrew women are, they urge, *ḥayot*, "full of life." They stand in the tradition of Eve, the mother of all living (*ḥay*). These mothers are so full of life that even a death-dealing Pharaoh cannot quench its force. And indeed Pharaoh is no match for maternal power.

These women hear no instructions from a burning bush. Some other sense of responsibility guides their actions—explicitly, their fear of the gods, implicitly their respect for life, their love of children. They have no authority to confront Pharaoh directly, no strength to make demands of him, no power to call down plagues upon him. They simply side-step him. They out-maneuver him, appealing to his ignorance and his prejudice. Their quiet rebellion buys time for Hebrew children. More children are born and thrive (1:20). God rewards the midwives with households of their own (1:21).

Eventually, however, the Pharaoh renews his assault, this time assigning all Egyptians the task of Hebrew infanticide. Into this vicious context the baby Moses is born.

Since he is a healthy child, Moses's mother does her best to protect him. First she hides him in her house for as long as she can. Then she ironically obeys the Pharaoh's command: she puts the child in the river! The Nile, however, is for Moses his salvation rather than his grave. Secured in a water-tight basket and watched over by his sister, the baby is placed among the reeds on the bank of the river.

What did the mother expect to happen? Obviously something of significance, since the sister is stationed so that she can observe "what would be done to him" (2:4). The rapid sequence of events may give us a clue. The child is hardly there in its basket any time before *Pharaoh's daughter* and her entourage come down to the river to bathe. It is highly doubtful, considering the young woman's elevated station, the presence of crocodiles in the water, and the contours of any river bank, that the daughter of Pharaoh would bathe at just any place in the river. More likely the young woman had a favorite bathing spot which was no secret to Moses's mother. Moses's mother, in a sense, places the fate of her baby at the feet of Pharaoh's daughter, somehow trusting that this young woman could never carry through the brutal policy of her father.

Her gamble pays off. Pharaoh's daughter sees the child, hears his cry, and is moved to compassion for him, knowing full well "this is one of the Hebrews' children" (2:6). When it becomes clear that, whatever the nature of her sentiment, she seems ready to take responsibility for the infant, the sister steps forward with a proposal. A crying baby, no doubt hungry, needs to be fed. "Shall I go summon for you from among the Hebrew women a woman able to nurse that she may nurse the child for you?" (2:7) Pharaoh's daughter dispatches her immediately on this errand.

Commentators have been quick to see the text ridiculing the naiveté of Pharaoh's daughter, that she is conned into paying a Hebrew mother to nurse her own child. But we might well wonder, is she so unaware of what is transpiring? Is she so simple to think that this young Hebrew girl's appearance is coincidental? Is she so slow to be unable to connect the woman who instantly materializes, her breasts filled with milk, with the child's mother? Rather, one can easily imagine this daughter of the court ascertaining in silence all the dimensions of this desperate attempt to save a baby's life. One might hear in the interchange carefully avoided questions and painstakingly controlled understatement. One might visualize the exchange of knowing looks even as infant and money changes hands.

Where would Moses be, where would the people Israel be, where the divine promise, if not for the mothering of this foreign woman? As Terence Fretheim points out (1991:38), the actions of this non-Israelite are presented in direct parallel to those of the God of Israel: "She 'comes down,' 'sees' the child, 'hears' its cry, takes pity on him, draws him out of the water, and provides for his daily needs" (cf. 3:7-8). What she does for Moses, God is soon to do for Israel.

Chapter Five

THE SUBJECT OF THE LAW

Now these are the rules which you shall set before them. (Exod 21:1)

God's deliverance of Israel results in the birth of a new nation. Narratively speaking, God is something of a midwife, pulling Israel out of Egypt, through the Red Sea, into a new life and a new world. Israel's growth depends upon guidance which is provided at Sinai in the form of God's instruction. With the giving of the Law, God's relation to Israel assumes a different metaphor, with distinct elements of patriarchal authority and contractual arrangement. The people, identified as God's firstborn son (Exod 4:22) and a special possession (Exod 19:5, Deut 7:6; 14:2; Deut 26:18), are characterized as a collective that moves and speaks as one. The Law reveals, however, that, within this seemingly unified body of Israel, there are differences and hierarchies.

Is a wife (a man's woman) included in the prohibition against working on the sabbath day or is she not? The fact that the question can be asked at all is a measure of women's marginality to the Law. "Six days you shall work and engage in any business," says the Decalogue (the "Ten Commandments"), "but the seventh day is a sabbath to YHWH your God, you shall not engage in any business—you, or your son, or your daughter, your male worker, or your female servant, or your cattle, or your resident alien who is within your gates" (Exod 20:9-10). The person addressed ("you") is masculine singular. This person is an adult male, with children, servants, and cattle; in some way, too, the resident alien comes under his control. He is also the person addressed a few verses later: "You shall not covet your neighbor's house; that is, you shall not covet your neighbor's wife (woman), or his male worker, or his female servant, or his ox, or his ass, or anything that belongs to your neighbor." He and his neighbor are the same. They are well-to-do male heads of households. They are the Subject the Law is constructing. Everyone else is presented as Other.

The conventional explanation for the missing wife is that the second singular masculine pronoun ("you" or "your") is gender inclusive. Tikva Frymer-Kensky even makes a virtue of the absent item, claiming that it *shows* "that the 'you' that the Law addresses includes both women and men, each treated as a separate moral agent" (1992:54). How it shows so much is far from obvious. What *is* clear is that if there is any inclusiveness to be asserted it is not a matter of women and men but specifically wives and husbands. What is missing is the term "your *wife*" as distinct from "your *daughter*" or "your *female servant.*"

More to the point, however, the inclusiveness claim in this particular case both ignores the plain contrary witness of the immediate context (vs. 17: "you shall not desire your neighbor's wife") and defies the extensive evidence regarding the Subject of the legal discourse in general. As the injunctions just quoted indicate, this Subject is the male head of household (a "father's house"). Nowhere does the Law entertain another subject. Though women, children, servants, slaves or sojourners may sometimes be the grammatical subjects of legal sentences, they are always grammatically or contextually placed in relation, as object or Other, to the Subject of the discourse.[1] Jewish and Christian interpretive traditions have formulated strategies to relate to women and children even a text like the law against desiring your neighbor's wife. But these strategies, while on the face of it "inclusive," can too easily tinker with the surface while leaving the structural exclusion intact. The subliminal message remains: women are primarily of interest to the Law when they affect men's interests.

The interests, however, are usually more specific than those of all men. As just observed, the subject is frequently specified as the male head of household. The Decalogue itself begins (Exod 20:1-6) by depicting a jealous god who forbids any relationship with any other god. The root metaphor, as has sometimes been observed (cf. Fretheim 1991:227), is drawn from the marriage sphere.[2] Its perspective is the husband's. The deity is the model of the jealous husband. Any infraction of the exclusive loyalty due to him (spoken of as "iniquity"—see Fretheim) will be met with punishment that has lasting consequences upon the children (sons).

The consequence clause ("for I YHWH your God am a jealous god, punishing your children for the iniquity of the parents, to the third and the fourth generation of those who hate me") at least partially sustains the metaphor:[3] after all, if a wife is put to death for having a relationship outside her marriage, or if a husband sends away his wife (as he may do virtually at will according to the Law), the judgment will inevitably affect any children of the marriage. The underlying value system is revealing: clearly here the husband's right to dispose of his wife—itself a mechanism of male control over women's sexuality—is assumed to be paramount and to override the interests of the children.

Finally, even the crude binary language of love and hate that ends the paragraph ("those who hate me" [20:5] and "those who love me" [20:6]) has a deepseated connection with the root metaphor. There are no middle terms for the jealous husband. The woman either loves him or hates him. That polarizing is a regular characteristic of divorce and one of the primary iniquities that are visited upon the children of divorce. It is a hallmark of patriarchal husbands who perceive their ownership and authority to be undermined.

The Decalogue ends by marking out even more extensively the husband's (head of household's) exclusive domain: one such man shall not desire, or take pleasure in (ḥamad), another such man's woman, or male worker, or female servant, or ox, or ass, or anything at all belonging to that man. The commandment seeks to ensure harmonious relationships between heads of households. It also implicitly validates the status quo between these men, including inequities of wealth. The "politics of envy"—a favorite phrase of the wealthy—have no place here.

Thus, framing the Decalogue are powerful images—not of the gods of Egypt or Canaan but of the family or household, where the husband/father/master/owner is focal. The message is clear: God speaks to those who matter; God is depicted in the image of those who matter. Those who matter are well-to-do patriarchs who rule their households with authority and who respect each other's property. All other people have significance in relation to them.

Almost the first commandment in the Book of the Covenant, the collection of laws which follows the Decalogue in Exodus, concerns the family. Like the laws of the Decalogue it is addressed to a property-owning adult male. Its object of concern in the first instance is a Hebrew male slave. Hard on the heels of the story of YHWH's freeing the Hebrews from slavery to Pharaoh comes the unblinking preamble, "When you [Hebrew property owning man] buy a Hebrew slave . . ." (21:2). So the problem in Egypt was not slavery, only the conditions of slavery. The social order is to remain strictly stratified. For some Hebrews deliverance from Egypt will mean transfer from one slave owner to another. On the other hand, whatever the conditions of slavery among the Israelites are to be (and the Law will have more to say about them) here they are at least made finite: the Hebrew slave must be allowed to go free after six years. That seems to be some improvement, even if it is only an incremental one. But that is hardly the last word to be said. After all, the term *Hebrew* slave can only mean that any other slave will not enjoy sabbatical release. Hebrew is set over non-Hebrew and privileged by law.

Social stratification includes discrimination against the foreigner. Having delivered Israel from oppression as aliens, YHWH now encodes inequity toward aliens into its primary value system.

Now comes the construction of family. If the slave "comes in" single he shall "go out" single. If he comes in "possessor of a woman" (ba'al ishshah; cf. Rashkow 1992:63) he shall go out with his woman with him. The patriarchal hierarchy reaches into the bottom ranks of society. The male slave can possess a female just like his master, and her fate hangs on his. But what if he is enslaved as a single man, and his master gives him a woman, and she bears him sons or daughters (21:4-6)? Then the woman and children belong to the master, and the man must leave alone. By determining this outcome, the law constructs the master's motive in giving a woman: it is to produce more slaves, not to offer the man or the woman the comfort of a spouse or sexual partner, or the both of them the joy of children. The master's property interest comes before any interest in the slave's family (man, woman and children) as a basic social unit. (As the lawgiver puts it succinctly later in the same chapter, verse 21, "the slave is [the master's] money.") This finding confirms our earlier conclusion from the Decalogue that the primary construction of family in this textual world is determined by class as well as gender. Without the property-owning adult Israelite male there is no family.

The fact that the slave law now goes on apparently to rescue the family does not alter our observation. "If indeed the slave says, 'I love my master, my wife and my sons (children)—I will not go out free,' then his master shall bring him close to God and bring him close to the door or to the doorpost [m^{e}zuzah); and his master shall bore through his ear with an awl. And he shall be his slave for the future." If the male slave is unwilling to see the relationship between him, his woman, and his children broken up—if, that is, he covets his own family—then with divine sanction the master can obtain not only more child slaves but the adult male permanently and his woman as well. Clothed as it is in rectitude, a more insidiously pernicious incentive to prostitute women and enslave men, women, and children is hard to imagine.

The code continues its construction of family values. Again there is a deep irony in the juxtaposition of this next law (21:7-11) with the Exodus story. YHWH redeems his children (sons?) from slavery. The law concerns a man selling his daughter into slavery (l^e'amah). The man and his daughter are Hebrews, as the context makes clear—the law is dealing further with the question of sabbatical release. The female slave "shall not go out as the male slaves." What follows is not entirely clear, but the gist is that her sexuality is at the master's disposal. On the other hand, he must provide for her economic security in some fashion. If he designates her for himself, and then decides that she is "evil in his sight," he must allow her to be redeemed and may not sell her to foreigners, for he has "dealt unfaithfully" with her. That is to say, while it is his right to use her sexually, he then has to accord her a place in his household as a woman belonging to him, or allow her to be released to an Israelite (her father?) for the redemption price; he may not sell her out of the country, which could mean permanent slavery.

If he designates her for his son, he must treat her according to the "rules for daughters." That is unlikely to mean that he must treat her as his own daughter, as some translations suggest. Rather it defines her sexuality and her place in the generational hierarchy of the household, without naming her as his son's wife. If he takes another, presumably similar (i.e., slave) woman for himself, he is obliged to keep on feeding and clothing the first woman (21:10).[4]

If he fails to fulfill these provisions she is entitled to go free, without payment. But, we might ask, go where? What if she has no redeemer, no one willing to take her in? Does she end up a slave again, or a prostitute?

In terms of family we see a father's absolute right to sell his daughter into slavery. We see another father's right to use his female slaves sexually, one or more at a time, or to give them sexually to his son, together with an obligation to provide subsistence for only as long as it suits him. Though the text does not indicate precisely what standing any children of this kind of relationship might have—that is, whether or not they would have inheritance rights—the earlier provision makes clear that the children would belong to him, not her. For their part, they would grow up in a set of relationships wholly dependent for any continuity upon the father/master's say so. The woman's position is simple: her body, her livelihood, her roles as mate and mother, all are hostage to male power.

In the parallel provisions in Deuteronomy, we see a somewhat "kinder and gentler" legal code at work on the topic of household slaves. The sabbath day commandment is a case in point. Moses's version of the sabbath commandment stays close to the previous account until it comes to the list of those in the addressee's household who are expected to desist from work. As in Exodus, the wife is missing. Unlike Exodus, however, where YHWH's rest on the seventh day of creation, back at the beginning of time, justifies the sabbath law, Moses in Deuteronomy appeals to Israel's deliverance from Egypt for rationale (Deut 5:12-15):

> [You shall not work] . . . so that your male slave and your female slave may rest like you. Remember that you were a male slave in the land of Egypt, and YHWH your God caused you to go out from there with a mighty hand and an outstretched arm. Therefore YHWH your God commanded you to observe the sabbath day.

Here we have a text that works in a similar double-edged way to the slave law in Exod 21:2-11. The memory of deliverance from slavery in Egypt leads on the one hand to the mitigation of some of slavery's oppressive conditions. On the other hand, it leads to slavery's legitimation. In this case the sabbath law is turned into a salve for the conscience of a slave turned slave owner.

Despite this basic contradiction that compromises all the slavery laws, in whatever code, Moses's new version of the law of sabbatical release in Deut 15:12-18 is a strenuous attempt to confront the iniquities of slavery. For a start, the commandment is preceded by another law concerning the sabbatical year (Deut 15:1-11; cf. Leviticus 25), stipulating that creditors should grant their debtors release from their debts, and urging, in cases of need prior to the sabbatical year, that the law not be made any excuse for mean-spirited action toward the poor and needy neighbor. Though not cited as special objects, wives and children of poor men are obvious potential beneficiaries of the law, while the reiterated concern for the poor and needy—a characteristic of Deuteronomy—has a cumulative countervailing effect to the laws that so patently have the interests of the rich and powerful at heart.

The law then adds a significant provision that would enable a released slave to have some chance of economic survival (15:12-15):

> And when you send him [i.e., a male Hebrew slave] out from you a free person you shall not send him out empty-handed. Truly provide for him from your flock, your threshing floor, and your wine press, which YHWH your God has blessed you with and given you. Remember that you were a slave in the land of Egypt, and YHWH your God redeemed you; therefore I am commanding you this thing today.

The provision for the slave to remain in the household is still there but the objectionable stipulations about the man's family are gone, their place taken by the command to provide decently for the man. In its new form the text leaves open the possibility of taking "you shall not send him out empty" to include his family and proper provision for them. Such an injunction would then begin to make a slave owner seriously accountable for the persons he owns. The clause concerning the man who wishes to stay with the household remains, but again it is significantly recast. His motivation no longer need pivot, if he has a wife and children, on the legal blackmail which in Exodus threatens him with their loss. Rather the text simply recognizes that he might indeed decide that, all things considered, he could not hope to make a better life on his own.

> But it shall be that if he says to you, "I will not go out from you," because he loves you and your house, because he has well-being with you, then you shall take the awl and put it through his ear into the door, and he shall belong to you as a slave for the future. (15:16-17)

Finally comes another movement toward some kind of equity within inequity. The clauses concerning the Hebrew daughter sold into slavery by her father are also gone. In their place we find the simple stipulation: "And you shall do the same with your female slave."

In Exod 21:15 and 17 we move to the topic of mothers and fathers. We meet two injunctions that could be said to afford equal status to men and women as fathers and mothers: whoever strikes (21:15) or curses (21:17) his father or his mother shall be put to death. This apparent equivalence may remind us of the words of the Decalogue that enjoin honoring (treating seriously and taking care of) your father and your mother (in their later years).

Given what we have already seen of the inequity of power between men and women in general and in "family" relationships in particular, it is highly likely that any equivalence between father and mother in these laws is more apparent than real. In the case of the draconian laws against striking or cursing the mother as well as the father, the patriarchal interest lies in the first instance probably in maintaining the generational hierarchy.

As we shall see shortly in discussing the list of women proscribed for a man's sexual intercourse (Leviticus 18), patriarchy is a system of discrimination based on age (or generation) as well as gender. Women can derive position within the hierarchy from their husbands. Though systemic power resides in the men, the fathers, the man's woman to some extent symbolizes his power. Thus Absalom in 2 Samuel 16:20-22 symbolically as well as practically demonstrates his usurpation of his father's place by publicly "going into" his father's women. To strike the woman, therefore, is to strike the man. Only the man himself may strike his woman.[5] More specifically, to strike or curse the mother is to strike or curse the father. And to strike or curse the father is symbolically to bring into disrepute the patriarchy itself, the rule of the fathers.

Moreover, generational power confronted with the exigencies of old age or incapacity through war or accident means that the system must adapt to the possibility of compromise: the father may be forced at some time to yield power to the son even while still living.

(See Devora Steinmetz 1991 on the struggle between father and son in the Genesis narratives.) For both these reasons it is in the interest of the adult male in his prime to insist that the son accords the father the most profound respect. That will include respecting likewise the father's woman, the son's mother.

In the Decalogue the principle of profound respect (honoring) is enjoined explicitly, with an explanatory clause added: "in order that you may lengthen your [own] days upon the ground which YHWH your God is giving you" (20:12). The motivation suggests that respect entails more than refraining from physical or verbal assault. It also has a positive practical dimension. As others have observed, the commandment is probably best understood as encouraging decent provision for elderly parents (Fretheim 1990:231-32), though the pertinent condition of the parent is better thought of as dependency rather than age. One day the adult male addressee may find himself dependent upon his son(s) for his livelihood. The law therefore expresses his interest in seeing that not only he but also any of his women with whom he wants to go on living are properly supported. In other words, it is in the interest of the active male head of household to establish with his parents the model for his children.[6]

The law of seduction in 22:16-17 (vss. 15-16 in Hebrew) is a stipulation about a daughter's monetary value to a father. If a man talks (*pittah*) an unbetrothed young woman of marriageable age (*b^etulah*) into having sex, he must give the father the bride-price and make her his wife. If, however, the father refuses to give the woman to him, he must pay money equivalent to the bride-price for *b^etulot*. While there are problems in understanding the details here—depending upon whether *b^etulah* means a woman who has not had sexual intercourse or more broadly, a nubile young woman, of marriageable age—for our purposes it is enough to note that the text constructs this kind of young woman essentially as a chattel of her father. The subjects of the stipulation are the seducing man and the owning father. The young woman has no say in her disposition. While we may imagine that the father may have privately various reasons for refusing to give his daughter to the seducer, including his daughter's wishes, these reasons are accorded no focus here. Rather the issue appears to be that the unmarried daughter loses a significant measure of marketable value once she has had sexual intercourse, so that the father must be compensated appropriately. Like the slave, the daughter as family member is conceived strictly in economic terms.

One other provision in the Book of the Covenant touches directly on our topic. Following a general injunction against maltreating or oppressing a resident alien, "for you were resident aliens in the land of Egypt," comes a further charge (Exod 22:21-24 [20-23]):

> You shall not abuse any widow or orphan. If you do indeed abuse any of them, if they indeed cry for help to me, I shall indeed hear their cry. And my anger will burn and I shall kill you by the sword, and your wives will become widows and your children orphans.

What appears on the face of it an admirable sentiment—the protection of the most vulnerable family members, widows and orphans—becomes on closer inspection an ambiguous message. Of course, the reason widows and orphans are so highly vulnerable is just because they are systemically denied economic security in their own right. Though it is a truism to say so, it bears repeating: widows and orphans are such because they no longer belong to an adult male. The charge not to abuse them in their powerlessness is then patriarchy's attempt to salve its conscience, painlessly, without any redistribution of capital or income that would infringe on the male monopoly of political and economic power. The charge is backed by YHWH's anger, impressive enough to deter any god-fearing Israelite man, though expressed in a way that subverts the very values it purports to be defending. Apparently in the defense of widows and orphans it is acceptable to create more widows and orphans! Once again the Subject is revealed as exclusively adult male. The speaking voice can only conceive of the punishment as deprivation of the male. Reconceive the Subject, and women and children are seen to be the ones required by YHWH to pay the price of the sins of their husbands and fathers.

We have touched upon the issue of sexuality at various points in the preceding discussion. The most concentrated legal pronouncement on the matter is, however, found in Leviticus 18.[7]

The code opens with a broadly couched prohibition against sexual intercourse with blood relations—"No man shall go near any flesh of his flesh [*sh^e'er b^{e}saro*; cf. Gen 2:23, *basar mibb^{e}sari*] to uncover nakedness" (Lev 18:6). It then elaborates to an adult male audience a list of specific forbidden relationships (Lev 18:7-18).

> You [masc. sing., here and subsequently] shall not uncover the nakedness of your father, that is, the nakedness of your mother . . . You shall not uncover the nakedness of your father's wife; that is your father's nakedness. You shall not uncover the nakedness of your sister, the daughter of your father or the daughter of your mother . . . You shall not uncover the nakedness of your son's daughter or of your daughter's daughter, for that is your nakedness. You shall not uncover the nakedness of the daughter of your father's wife, begotten by your father; she

> is your sister . . . You shall not uncover the nakedness of your father's
> sister; she is flesh [sh$^{e'}$er, "close blood relation"?] of your father. You
> shall not uncover the nakedness of your mother's sister, for she is flesh
> [sh$^{e'}$er] of your mother. You shall not uncover the nakedness of your
> father's brother, [that is,] you shall not approach his woman; she is your
> aunt. You shall not uncover the nakedness of your daughter-in-law; she
> is your son's woman . . . You shall not uncover the nakedness of your
> brother's woman; she is your brother's nakedness. You shall not uncov-
> er the nakedness of a woman and of her daughter, and you shall not
> take her son's daughter or her daughter's daughter to uncover her na-
> kedness; they are flesh [sha^{ia}rah]; it is wickedness. And you shall not
> take a woman to distress/harass [litsror 'el, "be a rival to"?—cf. 1 Sam
> 1:6] her sister, uncovering her [i.e., the woman's] nakedness on account
> of [or "against"] her [i.e., the sister] while she [the sister] is still alive.

Recent readers have observed that biological/genetic advantages do
not alone account for this list. Genetics has no problem with a
woman and her daughter, or two living sisters, both conceiving children by the same man. The list is a complex social construction. Its
subject, as often noted, is exclusively male, so that our reading might
well seek male interests at work. And such interests are not hard to
see. There are at least three principles encoded here which are of
particular relevance to our inquiry.

First, nakedness (that is, exterior genitals implying sexuality—a
typically male construction) belongs to men. Men own the "nakedness" of women, that is, men control women's sexuality. (This is
graphically spelled out in the ordeal of the woman suspected of adultery in Numbers 5 which will be discussed in further detail below.)

Second, society is built on an intricate hierarchy defined (at least
in significant part) by the generational sequence of its males relative
to a "father." Women find their place in the hierarchy in relation to
the males, whether by birth or marriage, and so indirectly can
sometimes become reference points in the system. (By extension, age
is a correlative definer of the hierarchy.)

This second principle at work here is expressed via an implication
of the phrase "uncovering nakedness," namely, that sexual relations
between men and women are a matter of men depositing their seed
in women, which may lead to the birth of children.[8] The children of
the proscribed relations would create havoc with the hierarchy.

This brings us to the third principle. By owning women's nakedness in the context of a well-defined male-dominated hierarchy,
men can control the means of production (for example, through
inheritance) and the propagation of a man's line/name/identity (as is
made clear by the levirate proposal, a striking exception to the
proscribed sexual relations [Deut 25:5-10; cf. Genesis 38]).

In short, this list in this form is a classic construction of patriarchal control. This point is underscored by what the passage does
not say. There is missing one sexual relationship which a present-
day reader would expect in a consanguinity list. There is no specific
prohibition against the father having sex with his daughter. Such an
omission is not a commendation of such a practice (the broad opening prohibition in verse 6 clearly covers this case); rather it is the
patriarchal subject's subliminal refusal to acknowledge, to name, any
compromise over the relationship which most obviously epitomizes
the patriarchal hierarchy. The father exclusively owns his daughter
and her sexuality; the relationship expresses the domination of
male over female, generation over generation, and age over youth—
with no complications.

Despite this highly regulated construction, there are yet a few
texts (and silences) that indicate more positive aspects of human
(hetero)sexuality. Though they take us outside the Law, they are
relevant to the discussion. For one thing, because of the premium
put on offspring (e.g., Gen 1:28; 15:5), sexuality is consistently
viewed as something good, intended by God. It is not portrayed as
something "dirty." The only times when it is described as "defiling"
have to do with the transgression against the male ownership of a
woman's sexuality (e.g., Gen 34:13; Num 5:13). Though there are
numerous restrictions placed upon (hetero)sexual activity, all of
which can be linked to the patriarchal system of control, there are no
prohibitions against sexual activity in general. Women, particularly
virgins, widows, and divorced women, may be obliged to be chaste
because of the male system of lineage and inheritance, but no one is
required or even encouraged to be celibate because sexual activity is
evil in and of itself.

Undercutting the patriarchal Subject in Leviticus 18 is a minor
thread, rarely visible, that voices the subject of women's pleasure.
We have two instances of Sarah's laughter, both concerning her
physical pleasure. First, she chuckles at the thought of intercourse
with her aging husband (Gen 18:2): "Shall I have pleasure—with my
lord so old?" Later, we listen to her contented laugh as she discovers
physical and emotional satisfaction while nursing Isaac (Gen 21:6-7).
Leah's "hiring" of Jacob with her son's mandrakes is a humorous
ridicule of the notion of the patriarch's control of either his wife's or
his own sexuality. Here it is the wife, not the husband, who insists
on intimacy, and she "buys" his "services" with a bunch of turnips!
We see a similar turning of tables in Tamar's trickery of Judah
(Genesis 38) and Ruth's overtures to Boaz (Ruth 3). Whatever their

ultimate desires, these two women manipulate male sexuality to pleasure themselves. Deut 24:5 recognizes that one way of controlling a woman's sexuality is to keep her sexually satisfied, thus the onus of fidelity is put back on the husband: "When a man has taken a new wife, he shall not go forth to war and he shall not be charged with any duty. He shall be free at home for one year to pleasure his wife whom he has taken." In other words, he cannot expect her to wait faithfully for him if he has not given her something to wait faithfully for! (But contrast NRSV: "to be happy with [his] wife.") Of course, the text that deconstructs Leviticus 18 most powerfully is the Song of Songs, an astonishingly unreserved celebration of love and (hetero)sexuality. And its Subject, for the most part, is a woman.

A few verses beyond the list of proscribed heterosexual relations in Lev 18:7-18 we come across the often-cited condemnation of homosexual relations:

> You shall not lie with a male as with a woman; it is objectionable [to'ebah, "an abomination"]. (18:22)

> A man who lies with a male as with a woman—the two of them have done an objectionable thing [to'ebah]; they shall be put to death, their blood is upon them. (20:13)

The immediate context of the injunction in Lev 18:19-23 is rarely brought to bear on any understanding of the prohibition. However, a consideration of this law in relation to both its immediate context (vss. 19-23) and the earlier list (vss. 7-18) proves illuminating:

> And to a woman in the impurity of her uncleanness [that is, who is menstruating] you shall not go near, to uncover her nakedness. And to your neighbor's wife you shall not give your lying down for seed, to make yourself unclean by her. And of your seed you shall not give, to cause it to pass over to Molech, so you do not pollute the name of your God: I am YHWH. And with a male you shall not lie down, as lying down with a woman; that is a to'ebah ["rejected," "unacceptable," "objectionable": in a ritual sense]. And with no animal shall you give your lying down, to make yourself unclean by it; nor shall a woman present herself before an animal to lie with it; it is a tebel ["confusion" (from bll, "mingle," "mix," "confuse") or "waste" (from blh, "wear out," "waste away")]. (18:19-23)

Commentators have often wondered what the Molech prohibition has to do with the others here. Whatever precisely the sentence means, whether it implies child sacrifice or some other form of dedication, it clearly has a connection with the passage through the term "seed."[9] Moreover, if, as George Heider (1985:256) suggests, the term "cause to pass over to" in cultic contexts such as this means "to transfer ownership or control," then we have a stipulation designed to prevent a loss to YHWH of seed that rightfully belongs to him. Indeed, such loss would pollute his very "name." Chapter 20 elaborates the point: such behavior is described as whoring after Molech (20:5) as if Molech were a prostitute on whom the seed of the men of Israel, YHWH's seed, is wantonly wasted. Read thus, the prohibition regarding Molech in 18:21 is far from being alien to its context, as many modern critics have thought. On the contrary, it can be interpreted as encapsulating major themes of the passage as a whole.

First, it situates men's seed as a central subject. The inappropriate disposition of seed is a misuse of what in the first instance belongs to men but ultimately to YHWH. By ascribing the seed to the divinity the male subject obliquely divinizes the seed.

Second, the prohibition against passing seed to Molech establishes the issue of ownership and control (the control and ownership of issue!) as another central subject. The hierarchy is clear: control devolves from YHWH through men. Or put another way, the patriarchy of Israel finds its justification in the divine.

Third, the prohibition centers our attention on the importance of name. Name is identity, reputation, and lineage. Name is also inheritance and property. And name can be polluted, corrupted, and negated.

Let us reread verses 19-23 in light of these themes. The passage begins by prohibiting for men sex with a menstruating woman: that is a waste of seed, in that the ancients believed that a menstruating woman could not possibly be fertile. (It is likely that they thought the seed would simply be washed away by the menstrual flow.) A man is not to lie with his neighbor's wife: that is unacceptable because it conflicts with the neighbor's ownership of the woman, and the birth of a boy-child would confuse the hierarchy of inheritance. The Molech prohibition, already discussed, is next. It is followed by the prohibition against a man lying with another man as with a woman. That, like sex with the menstruating woman, is a waste of seed and potentially a loss of name.

So, too, if a man lies with an animal. For a woman to have sex with an animal (domestic, as usually with *bᵉhemah*; a male is assumed) is a waste (*tebel*) of seed just because it is a confusion (*tebel*): the seed wasted is in the first instance the animal's but ultimately it belongs to a man, the animal's owner. Men have better use for their male animal's seed than to waste it on women.

The passage prohibiting homosexual relations is of a piece with the earlier strictures regarding (hetero)sexual relations with "relatives": it is a document of patriarchy which constructs rules of behavior in the interests of a male dominated social system. And like the earlier section it has, for many a present-day reader, a missing stipulation.

What is missing is any prohibition against women having sex with women. For readers bent on culling from the Bible a blanket condemnation of "homosexuality" this omission is an embarrassment. It is, however, eminently understandable. The text does not construct an essential category of "homosexuality"[10] but rather it defines sexual boundaries which are part of the construction of patriarchy through the privileging of male control of seed.[11]

Women lying with women have nothing to do with the disposition of male seed (whether human or animal), and although such actions could be construed as a challenge to male ownership of women's genitals, that issue is plainly secondary in the immediate context (vss. 19-23), even if it is present in verses 6-18. (Of course, the patriarchal Subject might have difficulty even conceiving that a woman might desire any other than a male like himself, as seems to have been the case with some Christian patristic commentators [Boswell 1980:158].)

There is, however, a further dimension to the stricture against a man lying with another man as with a woman, as well as to the lack of any comment about women with women. This dimension derives from the fundamental principle of patriarchy, namely, that it comprises a hierarchy in which males have dominion over women. For this hierarchy to maintain itself, males must be socially constructed to be "men," which is to say they must play dominant roles in their relationships with women. It is bad enough when women become "uppity" and attempt to usurp men's dominant functions. They must be suppressed and the system has elaborate and often brutal mechanisms for that suppression (see the discussion of Numbers 12 below). But perhaps the most fearful prospect for patriarchy is the possibility that males might not be "men." As Chrysostom, one of the great church "fathers," expresses it eloquently when remarking on men having sex with men:[12]

> What shall we say of this insanity, which is worse than fornication? For I maintain that not only are you made by it into a woman, but you also cease to be a man!

For such persons to exist, even potentially, is for patriarchy to harbor its worst enemy in its midst. Such persons then, must be sought out and destroyed.

The problem, then, is not so much the man who lies as a man with another man (the inserter—this, of course, is the not the only way to envision such sexual relations, as plenty of evidence from the

ancient world bears out, but it is, commonly, the patriarchy's stereotypical envisioning). The problem is essentially the man who lies as
a woman with another man (the insertee, catamite, *malakos*). The ultimate confusion is for a man, equipped with phallus and the divine
seed, to equate himself with a woman, phallus-less and (from the
male point of view) seed-less. For patriarchy, that confusion is intolerable, unacceptable, an abomination. Indeed the legal history of the
persecution of homosexuals in patriarchal societies has been often, in
the first instance, a history of the persecution of men by men, probably for this very reason.[13] The active legal persecution of women for
female-with-female sex has often followed pogroms against men
almost as a rider, a logical extension of what is proclaimed and
probably perceived to be the universal perversity of same sex relations, when the deeper logic of patriarchal fearfulness against men
who appear to aspire to be women is suppressed.

Of course, those who have expressed their sexuality through
homosexual relations have probably always been a minority presence
in human society. Their suppression, like most suppression of minori-
ties, has therefore inevitably been a fluctuating thing. (It is very hard
to maintain oppression at the same level of intensity at all times and
at all places—even oppressors can tire of their oppression!). At times,
of course, male-with-male sex has been accommodated, as in classical
Athens for a period.

Consistent with patriarchy, however, have generally been the
social codes that have governed the compromise. Almost always,
accommodation has dictated that important aspects of the patriarchal
hierarchy and stereotypical male/female (active/passive) roles be
maintained, at least symbolically, once adulthood is reached. Thus a
relationship between an older man and a youth could be tolerated—as long as the youth was perceived to play the "woman's" role.
Likewise, difference in class could allow an upper class man to take
a lower class man as a lover on condition that they affected (at least
in public) active and passive roles respectively.

Thus patriarchy has attempted to sustain its construction of men
and women even while acknowledging its failure to control fully the
men on whom the system rests. More often, though, it has fearfully
resorted to outright oppression of those who, whether knowingly or
not, would subvert its dominion. Hence the prohibitions of Leviticus.[14]

The Law as a whole is formulated in terms of a covenant. We
suggest that, despite the attempt to see in the Law a reflection of
ancient Near Eastern treaties, there are basically two root metaphors

at work here. One employs the image of parent and child: YHWH is the father and Israel the child, usually the son. The more predominant metaphor, however, is that of a marriage contract: YHWH is the husband, Israel is the wife. Each metaphor implies a strict code of conduct between YHWH and Israel. YHWH, as husband and father, is provider and authority figure. He, in essence, possesses the wife/child Israel. For the wife/child Israel the stipulated mode of behavior is that of grateful obedience, the specifics of which are outlined in the Law. Israel is to be willing to obey YHWH's instruction, thus submitting to YHWH's control.

YHWH is a jealous husband. He is obsessed with the issue of fidelity, insisting over and over again that his wife Israel is not to commit adultery against him, that is, to go whoring after other gods. There should be no infidelity and no resistance to divine authority. So how does a jealous husband deal with his suspicions in ancient Israel? In a manner not unlike many husbands today: the threat of violence is the mechanism by which women are kept in line with a jealous husband's will. At least in ancient Israel, there is some pretense of communal constraint, though physical violence is invoked nonetheless. A good example is found in Num 5:11-31:

> And YHWH spoke to Moses: "Speak to the men of Israel thus: 'When any man's wife turns aside [from him], and is unfaithful to him [or "behaves treacherously against him"]; and a man lies with her, lying with semen, and it has been concealed from her husband's eyes, and it is kept hidden that she has been defiled and there is no witness against her and she has not been caught, and a spirit of jealousy passes over him and he is jealous of his wife when she has been defiled or a spirit of jealousy passes over him and he is jealous of his wife when she has not been defiled, then the man shall bring his wife to the priest . . .
> And the priest shall bring her near and stand her before YHWH. The priest shall take holy water in an earthen vessel and put into it some of the dust which is on the floor of the tabernacle and the priest shall stand the woman before YHWH and loosen the hair of her head . . . and in the priest's hand shall be the bitter waters which cause the curse.
> The priest shall make her swear and he shall say to the woman, "If no man has lain with you and if you have not turned aside to defilement under your husband, be free from these bitter waters which cause the curse. But if you have turned aside under your husband and if you have been defiled and a man besides your husband has given to you his 'lying down'"—then the priest shall make the woman swear with the oath of the curse. The priest shall say to the woman, "May YHWH make you a curse and an oath among your people, when YHWH makes your sexual parts drop [something from within] and your womb discharge. May these waters causing curse enter your bowels and cause your womb to discharge and your sexual parts to drop [something]!" And the

woman shall say, "Amen, amen."

And the priest shall write these curses in a book and blot with the bitter waters and he shall make the woman drink the bitter waters which cause the curse. The waters which cause the curse shall enter her, causing bitter pain . . .

And when he makes her drink the water, it then shall be the case that if she has been defiled and has been unfaithful to ["behaved treacherously against"] her husband, the waters which cause the curse shall enter her causing bitter pain and her womb will discharge and her sexual parts drop [something] and the woman will become a curse in the midst of her people. If the woman has not been defiled and she is pure, then she shall be clean and conceive children ["she shall be seeded seed"].'"

This is the law of jealousies when a wife turns aside under her husband and has been defiled or when a man over whom the spirit of jealousy passes, is jealous of his wife: he shall stand the woman before YHWH and the priest shall do to her all this instruction. The man shall be cleared from sin, but that woman shall bear her sin.

What we notice here is that only the husband has the prerogative to bring charges of infidelity. The woman has no recourse when she suspects her husband of "behaving treacherously" against her. Implicit in this is the notion that the wife has no right to question the husband's sexual behavior at all. He owns her sexuality, not vice versa. She is "under her husband" in such things (if not all things). He has exclusive right to her body; any other man's seed "defiles" her.

We notice further that the woman is assumed guilty until proven innocent, and that the ritual itself is tilted toward the guilty verdict. The woman is forced to undergo the ordeal whether or not there is any evidence against her. She is physically portrayed, by the loosening of her hair, as a woman who has been promiscuous. She is compelled to drink the bitter waters, the contents of which could be anything that might produce violent internal contractions. The potion is obviously designed to induce abortion should the woman be pregnant as a result of her "turning aside from under her husband." But any ingredient that could cause a miscarriage in a pregnant woman could also bring on an early menstrual period. All the concoction need do is produce a little blood, tissue, or mucus and the woman is as good as "a curse in the midst of her people."

Whether the woman is guilty or not, her privacy has been invaded and she has been publicly humiliated. The nature of her sexual activity has been decided by a tribunal of males: YHWH, the one who commissions and sanctions this ordeal; the priest, who controls the amount of "bitterness" in the water; and the husband, susceptible to fits of jealousy. Some man besides her husband has been allowed to loosen her hair and gaze on her with it down. And who checks for this "discharge," and how is the checking done? Is the priest indeed immune to all these sexually charged actions? If she survives the pain and the humiliation seemingly innocent, how can she return to her husband's house to be "seeded with seed," as if nothing has happened? Not to mention the fact that a man overcome with jealousy once is just as likely to be so again.

The divine-human marriage metaphor shares much with this scenario. God, the jealous husband is the one worried about infidelity. Indeed, in Deuteronomy, where this obsession with fidelity reaches its height, we find YHWH imposing the same kind of conditions on Israel that are described in Numbers 5. The mere potential of disobedience warrants the recitation of self-curse (Deut 27:11-26; 28:15-19), just as was the case with the woman under suspicion of adultery. And as in the case of the suspected woman, the ultimate threat is a threat to their bodies and their offspring:

> YHWH shall make the plague cling to you until he has consumed you . . . YHWH shall strike you with consumption and with fever and with inflammation . . . Your body shall be food to all the birds of the heavens and to beasts of the land and there shall be no one to frighten them away. YHWH shall strike you with the ulcer of Egypt and with tumors and with the scab and with itch of which you cannot be healed . . .
>
> You shall eat the fruit of your womb, the flesh of your sons and your daughters whom YHWH your God has given to you—thus shall your enemies so distress you . . . The man who is most tender and delicate among you shall begrudge his brother and the wife of his bosom and the remnant of his sons so that he will not give them any of the flesh of his sons that he may eat because he has nothing left to him . . . She who is most tender and delicate among you, who would not have ventured to put the sole of her foot on ground, so delicate and tender is she, she will begrudge the husband of her bosom and her son and her daughter, begrudging even the after-birth that comes out between her legs and even her sons that she bears for she shall eat them in secret of lack of anything else . . .
>
> If you are not careful to do all the words of this Law which are written in this book, to fear this glorious and fearful name, YHWH your God, then YHWH will bring extraordinary plagues on you and your seed, great and persistent plagues with evil and endless sicknesses. He shall bring on you all the diseases of Egypt of which you were afraid and they shall cling to you, also every sickness and every plague which is not written in the book of this Law, YHWH will bring them upon you until you are destroyed. (28:21-27, 53-61)

YHWH tries to control Israel by threatening the body. Only YHWH has the power to bring such a threat to pass; only YHWH has the prerog-

ative to accuse Israel of infidelity. In later expressions of this metaphor, Israel may voice the notion that she has been abandoned by
her husband (e.g., Isa 49:14; 50:1; 54:4-8), but what can she, in
actuality, do? Israel has no power over YHWH. Israel cannot threaten
God, because God, unlike Israel, has no body.

The theological metaphor of father and child works in much the
same way, only in this metaphor, any sign of ingratitude or any
questioning of God's judgment leads to bodily punishment. Our
paradigm for this metaphor is Numbers 11 and 12.

In Numbers 11 the people of Israel are trekking through the wilderness, uncertain of their future in Canaan and idealizing their past
in Egypt.

> O that we had meat to eat [or, "flesh to consume"]! We remember the
> fish we ate in Egypt—for nothing!—and the cucumbers, and the melons,
> and the leeks, and the onions, and the garlic! But now our strength is
> dried up, and there is nothing at all but this manna to look at! (11:4-6)

God, a father unaccustomed to ingratitude, responds to the complaint with anger; and Moses, caught in the middle, is frustrated
with the entire situation. Moses, like Pharaoh's daughter, finds
himself in need of someone who can nurse this crying baby.

> Why [he demands of YHWH] have you dealt ill with your servant? And
> why have I not found favour in your sight, that you lay upon me the
> burden of all this people? Did I conceive all this people? Did I give them
> birth, that you should say to me, "Carry them in your bosom, as a nurse
> carries the sucking child, to the land which you swore to give their
> ancestors?" Where am I to get meat to give all this people? For they
> weep before me and say, "Give us meat, that we may eat." I am not able
> to carry all this people alone, the burden is too heavy for me, kill me at
> once, if I find favour in your sight, that I may not see my wretchedness
> [evil]." (11:11-15)

Moses is not the one who has borne this child. Moses is not
physically capable of providing them nourishment. As Moses sees it,
God is in fact the mother, and she is not doing her job. But despite
Moses's effort to shift the metaphor, to redefine God's role in terms
of mother and nurse, God, it seems, is nevertheless heavily identified with patriarchy at this point.

The previous chapter has been full of the hierarchical ordering of
the people/army. Under Moses stand officers and chosen men—a the
son of b, and c the son of d—men who stand over the hosts of the
tribes. Even as chapter 11 continues, God's response to Moses is one
of ambivalence. His answer is to alleviate Moses's burden by estab-
lishing further hierarchy: he instructs Moses to gather the seventy

elders at the tent of meeting, so that "they shall bear the burden of the people with you . . ." (11:17). God withholds some of the spirit that is upon Moses and lays it on the elders instead; at which point they begin to prophesy. "And when the spirit rested upon them, they prophesied. But they did not do so further" (11.25).[15]

Something is wrong with this spirit of prophecy. Not only does it seem to be temporary, but its value is also in question. There is a wicked wordplay in the term used here for prophesying, *hitnabeh*, which can also mean "raving." Prophets and lunatics, as we all know, are often hard to distinguish. (Perhaps, then, the cessation of the prophesying might be viewed as a blessing in disguise.) God makes a gesture to disperse responsibility, but he does so by organizing a more intricate hierarchy. Then it seems that the new structure is not terribly effective after all. God seems to be saying to Moses that life would be simpler with autocratic rule. Seventy ruling elders raving might be an even greater challenge than Pharaoh, king of Egypt!

In addition, God instructs Moses to tell the people that they will get meat to eat, more than enough, more indeed than they will care to think about, until it comes out their nostrils and is loathsome to them. Soon we see a wind (spirit) from God bringing huge numbers of quails. Yet the promised overeating of quails never comes about—rather God's anger intervenes: "With the meat still between their teeth, before it was eaten, YHWH's anger was kindled against the people and YHWH struck the people with a great plague" (11:33).

God shows himself to be desperate. As God sees it, the people stand at a crossroads, having lost their sense of priority. Their yearning for the imagined comforts of Egypt will destroy their relationship with God, undo their liberation: "You have rejected YHWH who is in your midst, and have wept before him, saying, 'Why did we come forth out of Egypt?'" Their questioning of God's judgment is a personal affront. All he can do is take out his frustration on their bodies, the all-too-common response of a distressed parent.

But what about the people's perspective? They stand at the doors of their tents, weeping. They are indeed on the threshold, in a liminal space, between Egypt and the promised land. The language of mothering, nursing, bearing, and coming forth suggests for the reader a way of perceiving the situation. Moses sees God as the mother who gave the people birth. The people see Egypt as their womb and they want its comfort. God, they sense, is less concerned with nurturing than with rule and order. God, in a nutshell, is removed, distant, and unwilling to tolerate rebellion.

The next episode in Numbers 12 concerns Miriam and Aaron, sister and brother of Moses.

> Miriam spoke, and Aaron, against Moses because of the Cushite woman
> whom he had taken (for he had taken a Cushite woman). They said,
> "Has YHWH indeed spoken only through Moses? Has he not spoken
> through us also?" And YHWH heard it. Now the man Moses was very
> humble, more than all humankind upon the face of the earth. (12:1-3)

The story starts with the complaint by Miriam and Aaron against
Moses, because of the Cushite woman he had taken. So what had
happened to Zipporah, the wife who had mediated between Moses
and God way back at the beginning of Moses' commission? Earlier in
Exodus (18:2) we are told that Moses had "sent her away." Has he
divorced her? For such is a possible rendering. Or is Zipporah alive
and well, returned and married to Moses? If that is the case, are the
sister and brother protesting "for her sake" (*'al-'odot*)? That would be
characteristic of Miriam, at least; for it was Miriam whose timely
intervention had reunited the infant Moses and his mother, at his
mother's breast. Could this protest be a protest against the rupture
of a relationship and their demand a demand that God's chosen
leader not be above reproach?

Phrased as they are, their rhetorical questions are difficult for
Moses to answer: "Has YHWH indeed spoken only by Moses? Has he
not spoken by us as well?" Not only does this claim come from
Aaron the mouthpiece of Moses, and Miriam the prophetess (Exod
15:20), but also it embodies the beginnings of what earlier Moses had
so earnestly wished for: "Would that all YHWH's people were prophets" (Num 11:29)! God's response, however, shows a reluctance to
diffuse power.

God summons the three siblings to the tent of meeting, comes
down in pillar of cloud and reproves Miriam and Aaron, telling them
that whereas visions and dreams may be the way communication
usually takes place between God and prophet, with Moses there is
something special (12:8-9):

> "With him I speak mouth to mouth, clearly ['in a vision'!] and not in
> riddles . . . Why then were you not afraid to speak out against my
> servant Moses?" And the anger of YHWH was kindled against them, and
> he departed.

Implicitly, God defends his vassal ruler against the weakening of his
authority; explicitly he claims a special revelation through Moses.
One commentator approvingly puts it this way: normally communication between God and prophet takes place by way of visions and
dreams—"riddles" which require further interpretation. However,
"between the Lord and Moses there is, so to speak, direct communication. And, like all direct verbal communication, it is clear and
unambiguous, unlike dreams and visions."

But alas, while a touching sentiment, we must insist that language *does* more than it *says*. God's speech, spoken directly to Miriam and Aaron, subverts his very point. He comes, not in a dream or vision or riddle, but as the author of direct discourse. And Miriam and Aaron have no need to rely on Moses to make sense of what God has said. Just as we must, God takes great risks with words. For words are powerful, surpassing their speaker's intentions.

As the cloud lifts, Miriam is seen to be leprous. Aaron beseeches Moses (12:11-15),

> "My lord, do not lay sin upon us, because we have acted foolishly, because we have sinned; let her not be as one dead, whose flesh is half consumed on coming out of its mother's womb." And Moses cried to YHWH, "Heal her, O God, I beg you." But YHWH said to Moses, "If her father spat on her face [because of some offense] would she not be shamed seven days? Let her be shut outside the camp for seven days, and after that she may be brought back in." So Miriam was shut outside the camp for seven days. The people did not set out on the march until Miriam was brought back in; after that the people set out . . .

Why is Miriam alone stricken with the leprosy? That question has teased countless commentators. Among other possibilities, two ways of answering this question strike us as worth considering.

The first has to do with gender. It is possible that she is struck just because she is a woman. Perhaps she embodies feminine concerns ("feminine," that is, as expressed in this particular construction of gender) for contiguity over against separation, for equality over against hierarchy, values that God is in no mood to adopt. She speaks against a patriarchal Moses who takes the Cushite woman despite his prior commitment to another. She aligns with the motherly Moses who desires that the intimacy of God's spirit be given to all. Her punishment, to be struck "leprous, as snow" is then a harsh kind of poetic justice: it is her flesh, that correlate of comfort yearned for by the children of Israel, that is attacked and, in rhetorical terms, turned cold. Even in its mitigation her punishment follows these lines: she is as a daughter rebuked by the patriarch, and she is sentenced to separation from her people.

The second explanation has to do with the social hierarchy and cannot be divorced from the issue of gender. Aaron is not punished with leprosy because he is the high priest. Such an affliction would render him unclean, unable to perform priestly duties (so Sakenfeld 1992:48). God has need of Aaron. On the other hand, Miriam, as a woman, spends much of her life unclean anyway (from menstruation, sexual intercourse, childbirth, caring for the sick and the dead). As a woman and a non-priest, and therefore as a "lower class" citizen, Miriam is "unnecessary" and becomes the scapegoat of YHWH's indignation.

The language of Aaron's petition to Moses and of God's response brings together the issues of gender, relationship, and uncleanness and pushes the nature of divine-human relationship to a head. "Do not let her be like a dead [baby] coming out of its mother's womb with its flesh half consumed!" pleads Aaron. An anomaly—something dead that should be alive. Something unclean because it is both a newborn and a corpse. Miriam, alive but covered with death. Aaron depicts her as a stillborn baby, a loss to her mother. But God rejoins with a deliberate shift of metaphor. She is not a baby lost to her mother, but a daughter whose father has spit in her face. Miriam, implies God, is not innocent, but willful. This was no natural misfortune, but culturally constructed defiance and curse. And God is no grieving mother; he is an angered father who will not tolerate insubordination—not from a "daughter." Even here God desperately maintains hierarchy (the father is the head of the house while a daughter is the least valued member), refusing to have his role and his relationship to his people reinterpreted.

The fact remains that if God is (erroneously, we think) to fault Miriam and Aaron for their complaint against Moses, the blame should fall equally on both. But here again we see, as in the garden, an unscrupulous shifting of the blame. The woman's body suffers the brunt of divine anger, whether that anger is legitimate or not.

What we shall find, in the chapters that follow, is that in the social construction of men and women and in the theological mirror of divine-human relationship, women's bodies, far more often than men's, bear the punishment for insubordination. Whether they "turn aside from under their husbands," or whether they assert a will independent of their father, or whether they just happen to be a convenient scapegoat for the male Subject of the story, women pay with their bodies. Sometimes with their lives.

Chapter Six

POSSESSED AND DISPOSSESSED

From the law code of Deuteronomy, with its injunctions to wipe out the population of Canaan and to worship YHWH alone, and its prohibition against involvement with foreign women, the narrative ventures into the land of promise with a tentative testing of the waters. Two young men (*n^e'arim*; 6:23) are sent to spy out the land and the city of Jericho. Once across the river their first stop is a prostitute's house where, we are told, they "lay" (*shakab*). The notice that they have arrived in Jericho is completely omitted—we deduce their arrival from the next verse—suggesting that, despite Joshua's orders, their primary mission is to visit a prostitute and only secondarily are they interested in spying out the land.

The spies' behavior has been commonly defended by the argument that a brothel would be the best place for them to secure information about the city. The text, however, gives no indication that their place of lodging is in fact a brothel. It says merely that "they went and entered the house of a woman, a prostitute, whose name was Rahab" (Josh 2:1). The place is not clearly identified as any sort of "establishment." There do not seem to be any other "working women" or their clientele there. The two men ask no questions. They eavesdrop on no conversations. Rahab's house does not appear, after all, to be an ideal place to glean a great deal of information. While we might imagine that, in explaining to Joshua upon their return how they had come to make a pact with a prostitute, the two young men may have tried to convince Joshua that consorting with prostitutes was a slick trick of the spy trade, we have every right to suspect that, at the time, these young men had something besides spying on their minds!

A scenario is not difficult to reconstruct. The men are young. Their identification as such suggests that they are quite likely unmarried. They are part of a community with a strict code of sexual conduct that (technically) allows them no access to women before marriage. Once outside Israel's purview the two young men decide to make the most of their temporary independence. They visit a prostitute. It would not be as if they were defiling an Israelite woman or doing anything that would corrupt their own community. This woman was Other. A foreigner. Besides, they were, under the directive of

YHWH, eventually supposed to wipe out all these foreigners anyway. Who would ever know? The only witness, the woman herself, would be dead along with all the rest of the citizens of Jericho.

But something happens. In their haste to find a woman to meet their needs, they commit some sort of indiscretion. Perhaps they have to ask someone where such a woman might be found. (How else would one find a prostitute in a strange city? Was there a "red lamp" district? Or graffiti on the city wall?) That would be a dead give-away to any man in Jericho that they were strangers in the city. Perhaps they simply looked and spoke differently. Perhaps someone had seen them leave the Israelite camp, cross the Jordan, and enter the city.

Whatever the case, the king of Jericho is informed that very night that two Israelites have come to survey the land. Immediately, he sends men to Rahab's house to take the spies into custody. How Rahab detains the king's guard at the door long enough to hide the spies, we are not told, but clearly she does a better job of resisting threatening intruders than either Lot (Genesis 19) or the old man in Gibeah (Judges 19). She takes the two Israelites up onto her roof and camouflages them among some stalks of flax that she had laid out there. She returns to the door to screen them further with her words to the king's men. We might imagine her feigning surprise at the news that the two were spies. Spying was not the business that they had done with her, she assures the men. "Oh yes, the men came to me, but I did not know where they had come from. The men left at dark, about the time the gate was to close. I do not know where the men have gone. Hurry after them—you may catch them!" (2:4-5) Persuaded by her tone of urgency, the king's men quickly depart to pursue their quarry.

Her ruse successful, Rahab rejoins the two Israelites on the roof, uttering to them a speech (Josh 2:9-11) that sounds as though she has just been reading the book of Deuteronomy!

> I know that YHWH has given the land to you and that terror of you has fallen upon us and that all the inhabitants of the land have melted before you. For we have heard how YHWH dried up the water of the Red Sea in front of you when you came forth out of Egypt and what you have done to the two kings of the Amorites who were beyond the Jordan, to Sihon and to Og, how you totally destroyed them. We have heard and our hearts have melted and everyone is dispirited because of you. YHWH your god is indeed god in the heavens above and on the earth below. (Josh 2:9-11)

What is the import of this speech? Is it confession? Is it concession? Is it a con? Are the words even Rahab's at all?

Let us start with the last question. It is commonly observed that the speech sits awkwardly on the lips of this foreign prostitute. The Deuteronomistic flavor of the discourse suggests, as many commentators have observed, that the words express the theological message of the editor (or we might say narrator), rather than viewpoint of the woman.

Is Rahab set up by the narrator to communicate the Deuteronomistic thesis? If so, why was a more credible character not chosen? Why not a person with more authority, a person with more integrity? Who is likely to accept the perspective of a foreign prostitute?

But perhaps the problem is not where to put the speech, but what this particular woman is allowed to say. She is a "hero" in ancient Israelite tradition, but she has three strikes against her: she is a woman; she is a foreigner; and she is a prostitute. She is the quintessential Other. She is, as her name suggests, a chaotic force[1] that threatens a clearly delineated community where "male" and "Israelite" are defining norms, and where prostitution undermines male control of female sexuality. In order for Rahab to be acceptable, she must be tamed. She is tamed by this speech. Her Yahwistic confession saves her. She may have three strikes to her detriment, but her piety renders her tolerable, "safe," for the Israelite community. This is necessary because, once she is delivered from the destruction, she becomes part of Israel's community, part of Israel's tradition, and part of Israel's society: "She lives in the midst of Israel to this day because she hid the messengers Joshua sent to spy out Jericho" (6:25).

There are, of course, less subtle dimensions to her characterization. Whatever the ideological agendas embedded in the choice of her speech, the fact remains that, as far as this version of the story goes, the speech is attributed to her. She is characterized as a woman with uncanny insight, capable of crossing theological and national boundaries. Based upon what she has heard about the power of YHWH and the violence of the Israelites, she confesses, or concedes, that YHWH, Israel's god, is god of heaven and earth. The hearsay (as well as the massive troop of Israelites poised just across the Jordan) may have indeed convinced her that this deity must be more powerful than any other and that she would be wise to acknowledge that to be the case.

A sincere confession on the lips of Rahab casts her in direct contrast to the spies, who have forfeited Mosaic law by consorting with her in the first place and who have for the most part ignored Joshua's instructions in their haste to pleasure themselves. Her steadfast deliverance of the men, when they themselves try to maneuver out of their agreement to deliver her and her family from the destruction (2:17-20), further contrasts her faith(fulness) with theirs. Once she has deposited them safely outside the city wall and outlined for them a plan of escape, the spies place all kinds of contingencies upon their arrangement, leaving the impression that they hope she will fail to adhere their conditions. Although she has risked her life for them, their fear of having their indiscretion disclosed ("do not tell this business [or 'affair'] of ours" [2:14, 20]) seems to inspire their hope that Rahab will not survive.

The overall effect of this picture is to question the clear-cut notion of insiders and outsiders. In other words, it seriously disturbs the patriarchal notion of the world as a set of binary opposites. When foreigners can quote Deuteronomy with more facility than Israelites can, what does that say about the grand theological ideas of chosenness and exclusivity? When foreigners show themselves to be more courageous and dependable than Israelites, what does that say about the integrity of Israel? In the context of imminent "holy" war, where everything and everyone foreign is to be utterly destroyed, the story leads us to ask, how many Rahabs, how many prophets, how many protectors, indeed, how many innocents, are out there in Canaan, doomed to die on account of their Otherness. The bellicose and exclusive rhetoric of Moses and Joshua—and YHWH, too, for that matter—is irreparably undercut.

On the other hand, we might wonder if Rahab's speech is completely ingenuous. She may be hedging her bets. She is, after all, a prostitute, a woman who knows more than a little about sheer survival. With the Israelites obviously about to invade the land, with rumors floating everywhere about the havoc they have wreaked, she may see here an opportunity to have her cake and eat it too. She can bargain with the Israelites for her life and for the lives of her family. Should Israel destroy Jericho (and if they keep their word), then she is in good stead. If they fail in their attack on the city, no one in Jericho is any the wiser. She still continues to live, her secret pact with the Israelites known to her alone.

In support of this reading, we note that she tells the spies what they want to hear. When she returns to the roof to talk to them, she seems to play their game. She speaks their language in order to secure from them the promise of her deliverance. "Do you want to know what I know?" she seems to be asking. "Well, I'll tell you what I know. I know that your god is making a gift of our land to you. I know that everyone is terrified, melting in fear before you. I know the stories about you and your god. I know that we will not be able to resist you."

Indeed, this information is all that the spies learn about the land. When they return to Joshua to make their report, they can only quote Rahab: "YHWH has surely given all the land into our hands.

Moreover, all the inhabitants of the land have melted before us" (2:24). This, too, is what Joshua wants to hear, though he might have appreciated some specifics about the strength of the military forces and the city's fortifications.

On this reading, Rahab is a trickster or, more appropriately, a survivor. Religious confession, in the face of a violent god and his violent people, is a means of survival. This, too, raises grave theological questions about the either-or mentality of Deuteronomy's concern with correct worship. The reward for religious fidelity, the punishment for infidelity, is barren ground upon which to base a relationship. Freedom ("choose life" [Deut 30:19]) becomes the freedom to submit to divine control or bear the consequences. Rahab can play YHWH's game. In the end, survival is what is important. Where is her heart and mind and soul? Who can say? But her story suggests that there needs to be more to relationships (divine-human or otherwise) than possession and control.

From the perspective of Israel, Rahab is both dispossessed and re-possessed. She loses her home and community in Jericho to find new ones in the midst of Israel. She is an outsider who becomes an insider, a person inhabiting the margin (a prostitute living in the city wall) who moves to the center of Israel, confusing Israel's self-identification.

If the depiction of Rahab problematizes the notions of Israel as norm and foreigner as threatening Other, the stories in Judges further complicate the image of a united Israel. Over against Rahab the nation in Joshua had, for the most part, been homogeneous, a cardboard collective with few individual groups or people emerging. The book ends with national, univocal acclamation: "YHWH our God we will serve and we will listen to his voice" (24:24). The people stand united, ready to march against the promised land.

Upon entering the world of Judges, however, the image of the uniform nation fractures. The unified advance upon the promised land splinters into scattered glimpses of particular tribes in crisis, specific people and their contributions to the survival of the nation.

The focus often falls on families but the angle of that focus is somehow different from that witnessed in the stories of Genesis and the instructional literature of Exodus–Deuteronomy. Interest in lineage and male descendants has dissipated. The acquisition of land and property gradually ceases to be of chief concern. The role of mother takes on varied dimensions. The integrity of fathers is often undermined. Yet some things do not seem to change. We find that every success, and sometimes even survival itself, is riddled with sacrifice, the scapegoating of women and children, usually daughters.

The first daughter is Achsah (Judg 1:11-15; cf. Josh 15:13-19). Her sacrifice is a "minor" one. Her father Caleb simply uses her to inspire military zeal for the conquest of the promised land. Whoever takes Kiriath-sepher ("city of writing") can take Achsah for his wife. The city is taken and the young woman is taken by her first cousin Othniel, a man with good lineage and courage to commend him (cf. Judg 3:7-11).

Achsah, however, is no silent instrument as was her ancestress Sarah. She makes the best of her new bond (undoubtedly her father could have made a worse match for her), immediately procuring the conditions of a desirable family life. When she joins her new husband, she persuades him (some translations emend to read "he persuaded her") to ask her father for land. Having secured a field, Achsah arrives on her donkey to confront her father with an additional request. "Give me a blessing," she insists. "Since you have given me desert land, you should give me springs of water." Caleb, moved by her initiative, complies by giving her not one set of springs, but two. The upper and lower springs become hers to bring life to her land.

In a sense Achsah is like Tamar seducing Judah, Rachel buying mandrakes, Rebekah rerouting the patriarchal blessing. She is like Jacob wrestling by the Jabbok, stubborn, tenacious, and bent on a blessing. She is doing what must be done to insure a good life for her and her family. A woman determined to participate in the divine promise, Achsah insists on possessing the land, all the while recognizing that it comes to her as a gift.

Other daughters in Judges do not fare as well as Achsah. The daughters we hear of next (Judg 3:5) are not given to heroes within the family. Neither are they given land or blessing. Rather, they are Israelite daughters given to foreigners, traded to other nations to insure Israel's peaceful coexistence in the land. These daughters are allowed no part in the promise, for they are, in essence, dispossessed. Their fate foreshadows not only the plight of other women in Judges but the future of all Israel in exile.

From daughters possessed and dispossessed by men, we move to a woman of self-autonomy and power (Judges 4–5). Deborah is introduced by the epithet 'eshet lappidot. On first reading we might assume that this is a familial identification: Deborah, wife of Lappidoth. We might expect her importance to the story to lie in her role as wife. Yet we soon discover that wifehood reveals little about Deborah. It is not her relationship to her husband that will prove significant, but her relationship to Israel and to her appointed commander. The "wife of Lappidoth" is more aptly a "woman of fire" or "spirited woman." As we shall soon see in this story, familial categories are constructed only to be imbued with radically different meaning.

Deborah is a prophet and a judge who settles disputes for Israel beneath a palm in the hills of Ephraim. She relates to Israel as both religious and judiciary leader, but her leadership is portrayed also in terms of family. Later she will be called a "mother in Israel" (5:7) because, as Cheryl Exum (1985:74) notes, her accomplishments are like those of other mothers in Israel: she is a woman of "counsel, inspiration, and leadership." Her motherhood has other dimensions, however. We might well envision a Spartan mother who goads her children to fight. Allusion, too, may say something of Deborah's relationship to Israel. The only other Deborah in the Hebrew scriptures, Rebekah's nurse, is also associated with a tree in this same territory (Gen 35:8). Hence one is invited to see Deborah the judge as nursemaid to a politically incapacitated Israel. Like Moses's mother, she is both mother and nurse to a fledgling and, like Moses's mother, she is willing to risk her child in order to save it.

Battle is imminent as in the days of Achsah and Caleb, but the situation differs greatly. The war now is defensive rather than offensive. The Israelites, having done evil in YHWH's sight, have been oppressed by the Canaanites for twenty years.

Deborah summons Barak son of Abinoam and instructs him, on the word of YHWH, to raise a large army from the tribes of Naphtali and Zebulun and to fight the Canaanite army of Sisera at the Wadi Kishon. Barak responds cautiously "If you will go with me, I will go; but if you will not go with me, I will not go" (4:8). It is unclear whether Barak's response indicates cowardice, lack of self-confidence (the Greek text adds here "for I do not know the day that the messenger of YHWH will grant me success"), or distrust of Deborah's authority. The response is, however, in keeping with the changed times. In Caleb's day all the people heard God's command to conquer the land and Israel was assured of victory (1:2). One can imagine, on the other hand, that Deborah's authority, though well recognized, is hardly a match for the commanding voices of Moses, Joshua, and Caleb. Neither Barak nor any of the people has heard YHWH speak. He has only this woman's word for it, a word that has come out of the blue after twenty years of persecution, a word backed by no military experience, a word that is strategically naive, that hardly takes into account the Canaanites' nine hundred iron chariots. Barak may well be testing Deborah. If she will stake her own life on this message from God, then so will he.

Deborah mocks his hesitance: "I will indeed go with you, but the path you take will not lead to your glory, for YHWH will sell Sisera into the hand of a woman" (4:9). How far this is from the story of Caleb, Achsah, and Othniel! A woman rather than a man raises the rallying cry, a hesitant hero replaces an eager one, and a woman, not a man, will win the glory.

'We might also hear here echoes of Rebekah and Jacob, Rebekah sending Jacob to fight for his blessing, Jacob hesitant because he fears a curse. It is only after Rebekah takes the curse upon herself that Jacob agrees to do as he is told. Only after Deborah agrees to go with him does Barak do as he is instructed.

In the meantime, Sisera, the commander of the Canaanite army, hears of Barak's forces gathering at Mount Tabor. We might well visualize Sisera, in his haste and arrogance, leading his chariots down the dry river bed to his destination. Barak's troops swarm down the steep banks, trapping the chariots where they cannot maneuver. Sisera's only means of escape is to abandon his chariot and flee on foot (4:12-16).

While his army is being slaughtered, Sisera flees to the tent of Jael, wife of Heber the Kenite ("Joiner the Smith"). In an earlier aside (4:11), the narrator noted that Heber had moved away from the other Kenites and had camped near the Canaanites. The latter, with their iron chariotry, no doubt provided the smith ample trade. An alliance with the smith ("peace between King Jabin of Hazor and the clan of Heber the Kenite"; 4:17) assures Sisera that he can find asylum with Heber's wife, Jael.

Wives, however, are not always so easily pegged (though as we shall see, male attitudes sometimes are!). Jael has more pressing matters to consider than an obsolete political and economic alliance between her husband and this defeated commander. Though her thoughts are never revealed, she is clearly a woman caught in the middle. The Israelites have obviously won. They cannot be far behind Sisera, and they are unlikely to take kindly to a family that has allied itself with the enemy—especially if found to be hiding the Canaanite commander. Jael does what she has to do. She offers Sisera a seductive welcome, treats him with maternal care (giving him milk and tucking him in) and, when he falls asleep assured of his safety, she drives a tent peg through his mouth (*rqq*="parted lips," often mistranslated as "temple"), severing his spinal column, leaving him to die a convulsive death.

Like Leah intercepting Jacob, summoning him to her tent after having purchased his "services" with her son's mandrakes, Jael intercepts the approaching Israelite forces, leading them to her tent and to their quarry. The dead general purchases her safety from the men of Israel. Jael wins not only her security, but in the song of Deborah and Barak, she wins Israel's praise as well (5:24-27). In their description of her feat, her violent act becomes larger than life. No seduction and deceit here. No ambush of a sleeping giant. In the song Jael does combat with a standing Sisera. The killing and the dying take place in slow motion with Sisera falling between her legs, ravaged.

As the song continues, the graphically violent and rapacious imagery colors Sisera's downfall with poetic justice. Deborah and Barak move from Jael and Sisera to imagine Sisera's mother standing at her window awaiting her son. As soon as the listener is captured by the poignancy of the scene, the singers wrench sympathy away by attributing to the mother words that make the blood run cold: "Are they not finding and splitting the spoil?—A womb, two wombs, per head, per hero . . . ?" (5:30)

On the one hand, the speech makes explicit what has been implicit in the story, that is, the threat to women during war. Women on the losing side can expect to be captured and raped if not killed. Hence the poetic justice with which the Israelite singers depict Sisera's death: the one who would threaten their women, and perhaps has threatened them in the past, is himself ravaged by a woman. On the other hand, by attributing to Sisera's mother such a casual approval of rape, they show her to be deserving of violation herself. The hoofbeats for which she listens will not be those of her son but those of the Israelite army. Whatever violence the Israelites use, it is justified in the rhetoric of the song. They will do to the Canaanites what Canaanites would have done to them.

As Deborah and Barak contend that Sisera and his mother get what they deserve, the reader might surmise that, in the end, the difference between Israel and Canaan is not so vast after all. Israel, though now identified as YHWH's friend (5:31), has been and will be again YHWH's enemy. In forty years time they will again do evil in the sight of YHWH and the cycle will begin again. And though she stands outside the window, Deborah, Israelite mother, envisions a Canaanite mother not unlike herself. Deborah is a bellicose mother who pushes her "children" to victory; hence, she easily invents the callous Canaanite mother eagerly awaiting the spoils of war. One mother reduces her enemy to a "womb," while the other reduces hers to a caricature of moral insensitivity. Each mother has justified the violence of her "children" by dehumanizing their victims.

And what of Jael, the woman who "mothers" Sisera to death? Some might call her a hero. Others have labeled her sinister, a *femme fatale*. More likely, she is simply a survivor, a victim of her husband's politics who acts as she must in order to save herself and the remnant of her family.

There are some surprising images of motherhood in this story, fixed somewhere between good and evil. Mothers who are leaders, protectors, counsellors, and portraits of courage, are also mothers who condone violence, deceit, and the possession of other women. The same mothers who resolutely guard their own families savagely, set out to destroy the families of others not (un)like them. Their motivations vary: survival, liberation, conquest, revenge. But however ambiguous and mixed their motives, Deborah and Jael, witting and unwitting, are caretakers of Israel, "mothers" lauded for accomplishments quite other than the bearing of sons.

Judges 11 is the story of two abused children, a boy and a girl. The boy is Jephthah whose story begins with the hypocrisy of patriarchy. Jephthah is a child of the margin, the son of a prostitute. His father is a subject who slides from an individual named Gilead to the entire town called by that name. In other words, Jephthah's father might be any man in the town of Gilead. The town maintains the prostitute, sires a son by her, but then in righteous indignation kicks the child out because he is a prostitute's son. The child grows up to become an outlaw, a magnet for other "empty men" (11:3) like himself, who are given no place in settled society.

When the town of Gilead is threatened by the Ammonites, the elders scout for a military leader. Jephthah, the "street-smart" unscrupulous fighter, emerges as the candidate of convenience. He and his rough riders would be a formidable mercenary force and, should he fall in battle, the community would suffer no loss.

The elders set about luring the outcast home. They offer him the rank of general, but Jephthah is no easy mark. He will not let them forget their earlier spite. "Are you not the very ones who hated me, driving me from my home? Why turn to me now when you are in trouble?" The elders have no answer. They merely shrug and up the ante: "Nevertheless, we have now turned back to you, that you may go with us and fight the Ammonites. You could become head over us and over all the inhabitants of Gilead." Jephthah concedes to the offer of this more permanent and prestigious political position (11:9-11).

When Jephthah returns to his hometown of Mizpah to rally his troops, YHWH's spirit, a sure sign of divine favor, comes upon him. Nevertheless, Jephthah proceeds to bargain with God. For assured victory he trades the life of whoever (or whatever) comes first to meet him when he returns home (11:29-31). Does he not recognize the spirit's presence? Is he not satisfied with its power? Is his bravado driven by the spirit and its mighty rush? Does he make the vow (as Saul does later) in order to fire up his troops for battle? There are no clear answers, only the picture of a man desperate to succeed, desperate to belong to a community that only wishes to exploit him.

The battle won, we meet the second mistreated child. Jephthah's daughter, his only child, comes out to greet him. Jephthah, a prisoner of his childhood, is destined to repeat and to inflict the sorrow of his youth. He sees his family lost again before his very eyes as he realizes he has vowed to destroy his own daughter.

In his surprise and sorrow he blames her for the predicament he has brought upon them. "Alas, my daughter, *you* have brought me down. *You* are among my troublers. I have opened my mouth to YHWH and I cannot recant" (11:35).

Is the daughter an unwitting victim, as so many commentators have assumed? She does not ask her father for clarification. Though he has referred only obliquely to his vow, she seems to know what his vow entails (11:36):

> My father, you have opened your mouth to YHWH. Do to me that which has gone forth from your mouth. After all, YHWH has given you vengeance over your enemies, the Ammonites.

This is hardly the response of someone who has unknowingly ensnared herself in a secret. Jephthah's vow was most likely made in public at Mizpah in order to rouse zeal for the war effort. Others knew of the vow—why else would they have stayed indoors as their troops returned victorious? Hence, Jephthah's pained exasperation with his daughter: Did she not know better? Had he not made it plain? Has she done this on purpose to wound him, her father? On this reading she *is* one of Jephthah's troublers. She has stepped forth aware of her fate. Her voluntary action passes judgment on her father's willingness to bargain for glory with the life of another. His priorities (and perhaps those of all Israel) stand condemned. In this sense, she is not unlike Achsah confronting her father with the short-sightedness of his promise of dry land.

If we can concede such initiative in this young woman, we can see her taking control of the vow, turning it from a weapon of victory accidentally causing unavoidable collateral damage to a chilling lesson about recklessness, thoughtlessness, and human worth. As she redirects the vow, she dictates its conditions. She and her female companions retreat to the mountains for two months to mourn her young womanhood. She chooses to take upon herself her father's vow, but she does not choose his company. She spends her remaining days with other young women who know her, who know what it is like to be a young woman in the midst of a violent society, and

who, in the end, will not forget what she has done and what has
been done to her. After she returns to her father to be burned, the
women of Israel, young and old, continue each year to gather and
recount her story.

Do they continue, inspired by her self-sacrifice? Some readers
would like to think so. As one turn-of-the century interpreter wrote,

> [They] came back to be far better daughters than they went out. They
> came back softened, and purified, and sobered at heart. They came back
> ready to die for their fathers, and for their brothers, and for their hus-
> bands, and for their God. (Alexander Whyte, cited in Beal and Gunn 1994)

No doubt they come back sobered, but hardly softened. More likely
they come back angry, frightened, defiant, and determined that such
a story would never be enacted again. They recount her story as Deborah had "recounted," in song, the triumphs of YHWH (5:11, the only
other occurrence of this verb). But the songs of these women recount
no triumph, only the grim reality of a family and a society gone
awry.

As for Jephthah, he knows no way or seeks no way to redeem
his vow. He seems destined to continue the cycle of abuse. While he
awaits his daughter's return, he continues to be a man of violence,
victory, and verbal manipulation. But, only six years after he kills his
daughter, he dies and is buried in the same obscurity in which he
was born. Just as (all of) Gilead is his father (11:1), he is buried
(somewhere) in the towns of Gilead (12:7). He paid a high price for
such short-lived glory.

A reader who recalls God's last-minute deliverance of Isaac in
Genesis 22 might legitimately ask, Where is God in this story? Or
one who remembers Saul's willingness to keep his vow and execute
his son Jonathan (1 Samuel 14) might question, Where are the people
who, as in Saul's case, might stay a violent father's hand? The sons
are saved; the daughter is not. Are the values of God and society
now exposed? Or does the story urge an ironic look at a world in
which this is allowed to happen? Are the death of the daughter, the
silence of God, and the absence of the people signs of something
amiss with the promise?

What was implicit in Judges 4 becomes explicit in Judges 13: God
communicates again in the world of women. An angel (or "messenger") appears to the wife of Manoah the Danite and announces that
though she is barren, she shall in fact bear a son. Moreover she is to
observe certain rules, both she and her child, like those enjoined
upon a "Nazirite" (Num 6:1-21). This is to be no ordinary child, but
one born out of barrenness to be dedicated, separated to God.

The wife or woman (she is given no name of her own) senses from the outset that she is in the presence of the divine (13:6). "A man of God came to me," the woman tells her man, "and his appearance was like the appearance of a divine messenger, very awesome [or 'fearful']" (13:6). For her that appears to be sufficient. She recognizes the divine message. She does not need more. "I did not ask him where he came from, and he did not tell me his name, but he said to me . . . ."

Manoah, by contrast, is far from content. His wife tells him that she has had a man visit her and, in the same breath, that she is going to have a baby! We can only imagine what is going through Manoah's mind. Who exactly was this "man of God"? Was he really a messenger from God? What business did he have going directly to Manoah's wife with this "communication" instead of introducing himself first to the man of the house as only right and proper? And what if, *if*, the visitor were a messenger of YHWH? Was he, Manoah, sure that he knew precisely what being a Nazirite entailed? Should they not have plans for the boy, a pedagogical program, some clear instructions? Manoah is in need of answers (13:8-9):

> So Manoah entreated YHWH and said, "YHWH, please, let the man of God whom you sent come again to us, and teach us what we are to do with the boy who is to be born." And God listened to the voice of Manoah—and the messenger of God came again to the woman as she sat in the field, and Manoah her man was not with her.

Irony is piled on gentle irony. Despite Manoah's subtle inclusion of himself into the audience ("come again to *us*, and teach *us* what *we* are to do"), God "listens to" Manoah but deliberately sends his messenger back to the woman when Manoah is not with her, just as before. This time the wife fetches Manoah (13:10-11):

> And the woman hurried and ran and told her man and said to him, "Look, he has appeared to me, the man who came that day to me." And Manoah got up and went after his woman, and came to the man and said to him, "Are you the man who spoke to this woman?"

The wife's words are interestingly divided between her trust in the epiphany ("he has appeared to me," not "he has come to me") and her sense of her husband's doubt ("the man," not "the messenger" or even "the man of God"). Manoah's words may be read as bluntly skeptical. Eliminating all talk of divine possibilities he rather insinuates impropriety by setting "the man" in relation to "this woman." Compounding the insinuation, moreover, is his impersonal objectification of her as "this woman" as though that were the visitor's point of view. By not using "my woman" as we might have expected, he distances himself from her further. His suspicion is showing.

The visitor's frankness (and perhaps his refusal to be rankled), however, pushes Manoah into playing his next card: "When [or "If"!] your words come to pass, what guidelines exist for the boy, and what is he to do?" (Judg 13:12) Notice that he does not, to the man, include himself in this attempt to clarify responsibility—no "us" or "we." And perhaps in the same spirit, he gets in reply even less than the original message to his wife on the previous occasion! Pointedly, *nothing* is said of Samson or Manoah. And though the instructions to the woman about herself are repeated, they are now framed, for Manoah's benefit, by an audacious claim to authority over her: "All that I have told the woman, let her observe . . . All that I have commanded her, she shall observe" (13:13-14). Or, as the REB puts it, "She must do whatever I say"! The visitor even impishly adopts Manoah's language, referring not to "your wife" but to "the woman." We can almost hear divine laughter.

Manoah, however, is not through (13:15) and he is not yet willing to let the visitor go: "May we urge you to stay? Let us prepare a young goat for you" (REB). Perhaps he is testing the visitor. Is this stranger indeed a divine messenger, that is, an angel, or is he merely a human who will eat meat? Or perhaps this is a test of hospitality. A man who has had sex with his wife would surely be unwilling to accept his hospitality, because to do so would massively compound the injury.

Without completely giving away the guessing game, the messenger of YHWH tries valiantly to make it easy for Manoah. "Though you urge me to stay, I shall not eat your food; but prepare a whole-offering if you will, and offer that to the LORD" (REB).

But the visitor's refusal to eat and his suggestion that his portion instead be offered to God are still not enough for Manoah who *still* "did not know that he was the messenger of YHWH." (By this stage a reader may be strongly reminded of Gideon's interminable tests in Judges 6–7—Gideon who also had difficulty recognizing a divine visitor and also tried the food test [6:11-24].) Manoah presses to know the man's name, wrapping the request, as he had done earlier, in an ambiguous expression of expectation. "What is your name? So when [if!] your words come to pass we may honor you" (13:17).

The visitor declines to answer but offers one last verbal clue: "How come you ask my name, when it is too extraordinary?" But Manoah is too stubbornly in search of the tangible.

The messenger resorts to a final strategy. He vanishes up into the heavens in the sacrificial flame. At last, his skepticism assuaged, Manoah recognizes the visitor's identity. Manoah's wife knows the divine when it appears; Manoah knows it only when it disappears.

But what he now knows, he fears—"We shall surely die, for we have seen God" (13:22). Manoah knows the rules of holiness. He panics, as indeed those "rules" suggest he should. Again we are reminded of Gideon, who cries, when recognition finally dawns, "Alas, O YHWH God! For now I have seen the messenger of YHWH face to face." On that occasion, YHWH reassures Gideon, "Peace to you; do not fear, you shall not die" (Judg 6:22-23). On this occasion, Manoah's wife plays God's role. Her attitude is clear: What matter the rules? Manoah has seen God but learned little. If killing were intended, why accept the offering, quite apart from taking so much trouble to announce these things?

> And the woman bore a son, and called his name Samson; and the
> boy grew, and YHWH blessed him. (13:24)

We see in this woman shadows of Rebekah, a woman with special knowledge, some of which she shares, some of which she keeps to herself. As Robert Alter has noticed (1981:101), when reporting to her husband the first time what the angel has said to her, she withholds something. "For the boy shall be a Nazirite to God from the womb," the messenger announces, "and he shall begin to deliver Israel from the hand of the Philistines" (13:5). "For the boy shall be a Nazirite to God from the womb," reports the woman, "to the day of his death" (13:7). Intuitively substituting death for deliverance, she becomes prophetic. Samson's eventual suicide will effect the beginning of deliverance, as he brings low Dagon, the oppressing god of the Philistines, and implicitly manifests the power of YHWH, the delivering god of Israel (16:28-30). Thus when she substitutes the one phrase for the other, she reveals what she knows, that deliverance has its price.

She does not, however, talk to her husband about deliverance. She keeps the point of the pronouncement, with all its intimations of violent danger and death, to herself. Like Mary in Luke's Gospel, she keeps this thing, pondering it in her heart (Luke 2:19). She has a life independent of her husband, and she has the power to keep powerful knowledge from him. Does she fear to put the idea of a child destined for warfare in her husband's head? Does she hope to thwart the divine purpose? Or does she wish to see divine purpose work out its own way, unencumbered by her husband's control? Of course, more simply, she may be simply blocking her fear, as she trembles for the future of her unborn child. Whatever her reasons, we find that her actions and her knowledge of good and evil (and the slippery divide between them) set her apart from the man who ostensibly defines her.

Another mother and son introduce this final portion of the book of Judges. As the story of Micah and his mother begins (Judges 17–18), we learn that the son has betrayed his mother. The reader is not allowed to witness the betrayal itself but is permitted to overhear the son's confession. Micah, fearing his mother's curse, admits that he has stolen from her eleven hundred pieces of silver (cf. 16:5). The mother replies not with a curse but with a blessing upon her son. When he returns the money, the mother announces that she is consecrating the silver to Yhwh for her son and (according to the Hebrew text) promises to return the silver to her son. She has a smith cast two hundred pieces of the silver into an idol which finds its home in the house of Micah. What becomes of the remainder of the money is not disclosed, but, in the end, one might assume that she keeps it for herself.

Micah builds a shrine for the idol. He contributes other sacred objects and installs one of his sons as priest. In this religious family, however, there is no reliance upon Yhwh. The divine name gets bandied around, but the deity is never addressed. Yhwh's identity is lost upon tangible objects. Somewhere along the way the expectation of Abraham, that he would "charge his sons and his household after him to keep the way of Yhwh by doing righteousness and justice" (Gen 18:19) has been lost. Private shrines, idols, and unordained priests have little to do with righteousness and justice. Abraham's household-become-nation has now splintered into individuals making up their own rules and seeking religious security in the privacy of their homes.

The disintegration of Yahwism, like the loss of Eden, is conveniently blamed on a woman. Micah's father is absent. What remains is a twisted picture of mothers and sons. What kind of son steals from his own mother? And what kind of mother leads her son into idolatry? She is not like the mother of Samson, carefully keeping religious tradition for the sake of her son, nor a "mother in Israel," making judicious decisions and leading her people in liberation. Micah and his mother are looking for the secret to security—a little silver, a family chapel, a private priest. Security finally comes, so they think (17:13), in the form of a Levite whom Micah hires to officiate in his shrine. Security, however, is short-lived as his possession soon becomes the possession of an entire tribe (18:1-31). The security of priesthood goes to the highest bidder.

The final story in Judges also involves a Levite (chs. 19–21). The Levite in question, a resident of the hill country of Ephraim, takes for himself a woman from Bethlehem in Judah.[2]

Things do not go well in the Levite's household. The young woman, for some reason, leaves him and returns to her father's house in Bethlehem. The nature of the domestic problem is not disclosed. The Hebrew text states that the young woman "whored against him," though what that means is not as obvious as it might at first appear. Would a woman who has actually committed adultery return to her father's house, given the social shame that this would bring upon him? By the same token, would the Levite, in such a case, be likely to go to the father to woo her ("speak to her heart") and bring her back? And why is there no mention of legal consequences (cf. Genesis 38)? It is possible, as Koala Jones-Warsaw (1992) argues, that upon marriage, the young woman was accused of not being a virgin. On this reading, she might return to her father's house as an appeal to her honor. Or, one might surmise that, as in our culture, women could be accused of being "whores" for any number of reasons besides sexual ones. Indeed her very leaving could make her, in a patriarchal worldview, a "whore." Her very independence earns her this epithet from both husband and narrator. (The narrator, in this case, is feeding the reader the husband's point of view and seemingly adopting it himself.) Why might she leave her husband? Judging from the Levite's later behavior, one might easily imagine that she has been subjected to abuse.

Four months pass before the Levite decides to go after his wife in order to bring about a reconciliation. Why does he wait so long? Is it because, as Jones-Warsaw suggests, the woman's status as secondary wife would not, as in the case of Abraham and the fleeing of Hagar, occasion immediate response? Is it perhaps a matter of pride? His honor has already been wounded by her leaving. His going after her would only compound the injury. And so he waits for her to return to him. But return she does not. With each passing day, we might imagine his resentment growing.

Although the narrator says the Levite went to "speak to her heart," we never hear him speak to her at all. Instead, we witness the Levite and his father-in-law engaged in a tactful tug-of-war. The young woman's father, seemingly pleased to see his son-in-law, makes an elaborate show of hospitality, encouraging the Levite to stay three, then four, then five days. We might wonder if the father, reluctant to send his daughter back into a situation of possible mistreatment, intentionally delays his guest. The Levite, bound by customary obligation to his host, is trapped. Though he wants to leave, he cannot. His culture dictates that he succumb to the wishes of his host. The days pass, his plans to depart repeatedly thwarted, his rancor steadily rising.

When, on the evening of the fifth day, the Levite insists on leaving with his wife, still nothing has been said as to the wishes of the young woman. Neither her husband nor her father consult her about returning. We do not know if she wanted to return with her husband or if the two men had simply reached some understanding regarding her future. Whatever the case, she is transported away from her father's house in silence.

Neither is the young woman consulted when the travelling party faces the decision about where to spend the night. Their late start forces them to travel late to Gibeah, a settlement the Levite believes will be a friendly town. The inconvenience of late travel and the difficulty of finding shelter for the night are piled upon the Levite's other grievances.

Finally, an old man, himself a native of Ephraim, takes the tired troop in. While they are relaxing in the old man's house, the men of the city, a worthless lot, surround the house insisting that the Levite be brought out that they might "know" him. Hardly a welcoming committee, their intent is torture and humiliation, "sport" at the expense of the Levite. The old man protests, offering them his daughter and the Levite's wife instead. The men, however, are adamant and the Levite, in desperation and no doubt blaming his wife for the situation he is in, seizes her and throws her out to the mob.

It is not difficult to reconstruct his rationale. If she had not left him, if she had not refused to return on her own so that he was forced to fetch her, and if her father had not detained him, they would not be in this predicament. This is clearly her fault. She must pay the price.

While he spends a safe night, seemingly replete with sleep (19:27), the woman is gang raped by the mob until the wee hours of the morning. In the dawn the men let her go, and she stumbles back to the old man's house and collapses at the door. Abandoned by her father, betrayed by her husband, raped and tortured by a mob, the woman is trapped in a world of men. She has nowhere to go but back to the husband who threw her out, only to find that the door of hospitality and safety is still closed against her.

The Levite arises to go on his way as if nothing has happened. Opening the door, he finds his wife lying with her hands on the threshold. "Get up, let's go," he says. But there is no answer.

Putting her battered body upon his donkey, he takes her home. When he enters the house he takes his knife, seizes his wife (just as he had seized her and thrown her to the mob in 19:25), and cuts her body into twelve pieces, as if she were some sort of sacrificial animal. At what point the woman dies we are not told. He sends her piece by piece throughout the tribes of Israel in an effort to summon an assembly.

Throughout the story the woman has been allowed no speech. Now it is her broken body that speaks to all Israel. What her body says, what the Levite intends for it to say, and what Israel hears, however, are hardly congruent. Just as her body became every man's that night in Gibeah, now her body is given to all Israel. Her message is that she has been abandoned and betrayed by all the men with whom she has come in contact. The Levite's message is that his honor has been insulted, his life threatened, and his property damaged. Even his version of the story (20:4-7) removes him from culpability. Like Dinah's brothers, what Israel hears is a message of outrage and an excuse for war.

As Israel rallies against Benjamin, they are careful to inquire of YHWH. They are not careful, however, to ask the right question, which is whether or not they should fight at all. Having already decided to fight, they arrogantly ask, "Who shall go up first?" YHWH, allowing them to do as they please, responds, just as he had at the beginning of the settlement of the land (1:1-2), but this time with what might be interpreted as ironic indifference: "Judah shall go up first" (20:18).

The ending of the book is filled with echoes of its beginning— Judah leading the fight (1:1-2), a story of dismemberment (1:5-7), a woman on a donkey (1:11-15)—all images that have been skewed in the course of time. Judah goes up first, not against a foreign enemy, but against fellow Israelites. The dismemberment is not that of an enemy king, but that of an innocent and unprotected woman of Bethlehem. The woman on a donkey rides not erect and determined to secure life for herself and her family, but limp and immobile, a victim of violence, the embodiment of betrayal and death.

The war against Benjamin is bloody, the tribe left all but extinct. Six hundred men remain, but all the women and children have been slaughtered. The Israelites, stained with the blood of other Israelites, men, women, and children, cry again to YHWH with ironic gall: "O YHWH, God of Israel, why has it come to pass that today there should be one tribe missing from Israel?" (21:3) Like the Levite, they accept no responsibility and use violence to beget violence. They slaughter yet another town, Jabesh-Gilead, to secure virgins for the remaining Benjaminite men. These women not being enough, the Israelites, further relieving themselves of blame, seek to repair the damage that YHWH has done: "The people had compassion on Benjamin because YHWH had made a breach in the tribes of Israel" (21:15). They conspire against the young women of Shiloh, permitting the men of Benjamin to abduct them while engaged in their festal dances. Two hundred young women are seized to satisfy the needs of Benjamin.

Neither the Levite's wife nor the women who are subsequently murdered or abducted and raped are allowed speech. The world of Israel has become a place where women have neither voice nor choice. Their future is decided for them, and they have no place in the land. The woman, in the end, is caught between her father's house and her husband's. No other house offers refuge to her. Trapped on the threshold, unable to move, she is torn apart and displaced by the men of Israel.

Despite the people's eagerness to blame YHWH for the utter devastation at the end of Judges, the narrator is quick to remind us that "in those days there was no king in Israel"—not even YHWH was sovereign—"and all the people did what was right in their own eyes." It is into this world of rationalized violence and silenced women, of fragmented nation and fractured promise, that the figure of Hannah comes (1 Samuel 1), ominously traveling with a husband from the hill country of Ephraim to a yearly festival in Shiloh (cf. Judg 19:1; 21:19-23).

Hannah travels not only with her husband, Elkanah, but with her husband's other wife, Peninnah. Elkanah ("God acquires"), it seems, is a man of means, financially capable of acquiring and supporting two wives and standing, on account of this, diametrically opposed to the men of Benjamin who are desperately scrambling to abduct even one woman per man. Hannah's marriage to Elkanah is described against the brutal background of women being taken against their will. For Elkanah the marriage to two women is most likely a sign of great prestige, but for the two women, it is a source of great bitterness.

How and in what order Elkanah acquired these two women is not disclosed. We are only told that Peninnah has children while Hannah has none (1 Sam 1:2), and that Elkanah loved Hannah (1:5). We are immediately led to think of Jacob's love for Rachel, of Rachel's barrenness, and of Leah's fertility. Jacob had been tricked into his double marriage. What about Elkanah? Had Elkanah married Hannah first and, upon discovering her infertility (like Abraham), taken a second woman to bear his children? Had Elkanah married Peninnah first but, considering her less desirable after having borne his children, found a more pleasing woman in Hannah? Did he, like David, take the two women at the same time (cf. 1 Sam 25:42-43), so that it was clear to both of them from the beginning that they were partial and replaceable?

Any one of these possibilities marks this a marriage of male convenience. For the women involved it is a different matter. Whatever the order of matrimony, whatever the reasons for the taking and possessing of two women, Hannah and Peninnah are pitted against one another in a desperate effort to claim their self-worth.

Annually Elkanah would take his family to Shiloh to offer sacrifices to YHWH. On such occasions he would make sure Peninnah and her children all received portions, but to Hannah he would give a double portion,[3] "for it was Hannah that he loved [even though] YHWH had closed her womb" (1:5). With such blatant favoritism in constant view, it is hardly any wonder that Peninnah responds with jealous provocation. Hannah lacks children and yet she takes preeminence at the table and in her husband's heart. It is a bitter pill to swallow and, in self-defense, Peninnah magnifies Hannah's shortcoming. Considering Elkanah's devotion to Hannah, Peninnah probably says nothing overtly to her, especially not in the company of their husband. More likely she torments her with incessant, oblique commentary, indirect reminders of her barrenness and thus her lack of value. She provokes Hannah "so that she would storm [literally, 'thunder'] that YHWH had closed her womb" (1:6; see McCarter 1980:49).

Peninnah's strategy, however callous, cleverly creates tension between Hannah and Elkanah. She targets the family gathering at Shiloh, gouges Hannah on the topic of children, and lets Hannah's reaction ruin the family meal. Hannah weeps and refuses to eat. Elkanah is first bewildered, but gradually loses his patience, taking her behavior personally. "Hannah, why are you weeping? Why don't you eat? Why are you so resentful?[4] Am I not good enough for you— better than ten sons?" (1:8).

On the one hand Elkanah says what every woman needs to hear at least once in her life, namely, that she does not have to be a mother to be a person of worth. On the other hand Elkanah firmly ensconces himself as the center of Hannah's world. How ironic is this speech coming from a man who thinks he is good enough for two wives, who would probably never (indeed he would never have to) consider valuing a wife over ten sons. Not only is this man so short-sighted as to think that he, shared with another, is all this woman needs to be fulfilled in life, but he is also oblivious to what is going on in his household. He cannot see how this system of marriage is afflicting his wife. He cannot hear his wife's pain. He turns her sorrow into something about himself. Her desire, her need for value is refocused on him and his worth. As he twists her experience, he portrays her to be ungrateful and obnoxious.

Aware that she cannot possibly make her husband understand the depths of her desire and despair, she arises after the meal to present her case before YHWH. YHWH is, as far as she is concerned, to blame for her condition.

She prays, weeping, bitter of spirit. She pleads with God to look upon her affliction and to remember her and to give her a boy-child. She is willing to bargain: if God will give her a son, she will give him back to God "all the days of his life" (1:11). How strange to want a child so badly and yet be willing to give up that child! What is the point of having the child in the first place? Is this vow but a symbol of her utter desperation? Is even a baby for a short length of time better than no baby at all? Is the status of motherhood, rather than the child himself, really what is at stake? Does she believe that if God will "open her womb" for the first child, others are sure to follow? Is she giving up the first one in order to ensure that there will be others? What drives Hannah to make this vow?

Commentators are ever eager to speak of Hannah's faith and faithfulness and God's graciousness. But we might take a more critical look at this story. What view of God controls Hannah's prayer? What sort of god does Hannah have faith in? A god who only gives when he gets something in return? A god who requires a mother to give up her child in order to live up to society's conditions of value? And what about Hannah's view of herself? What compels her to negotiate with this "god of armies" (1:11; more often translated "hosts")?

This arrangement, despite common talk about faith and grace, is indeed a sad one: a woman so desperate as to bargain with her child; a god so willing to be complicit in such sacrifice. The son is born to Hannah. She dedicates him to God from the very beginning with his very name: Samuel, "His name is God." As she delays releasing the child until he is weaned, we see her pain in letting him go. Yet when the time comes, she takes him to the house of God in Shiloh that he should grow up in the service of YHWH.

The story is not unlike that of Jephthah and his daughter. Jephthah, so desperate to win his victory, gives up his daughter. Hannah, in desperation, gives up her child-to-be. Is Hannah, too, motivated by "victory"? The psalm attributed to her might so indicate that. Jephthah kills his daughter; Hannah merely sends her son into the care of the old priest Eli (yet another man who could not hear her pain or understand her distress) who, the narrator suggests, has had enough trouble raising his own sons. Is she faithful or is she foolish? The same question has been asked of Jephthah.

However we assess her sacrifice and the cultural and religious conditions that require it, we do recognize that she keeps her word to YHWH. She delivers her son, acknowledging that he is a gift, asked from and given by YHWH, and proclaiming that he is now being given back (1:28).

The song Hannah then sings is curiously appropriate yet inappropriate (see also Polzin 1989:30-36). On the one hand it captures with alacrity Hannah's personal and domestic triumph. It acknowledges God as the source of her success, praising his power and sense of justice (2:2-10). The song celebrates the fact that she has prevailed over her "enemies" (2:1), in this context pointing not only to her rival but any others (Elkanah and Eli, for example) who may have refused to take her plight seriously. The song indicates that she has been one of the poor made rich, the low made high, the weak who are now strong (2:4, 7-8). She is the barren woman who is soon to be the mother of many (2:21); her rival is the mother of many who is now forlorn (2:5). The song commemorates her vindication, firmly identifying her among the faithful (2:9), even subtly suggesting that her "thundering" (1:6) has sparked the "thundering" of YHWH (2:10).

In the end, however, we keep hearing the song as not hers—as a common song, composed by someone else, and sung by others in situations not unlike Hannah's. Although it may suit her voice in places, we hear its incongruity in others. Her experience is not best described in images of warfare and economic poverty. Her success is not best visualized in the phallic image of a "raised horn," the symbol of male dominance and virility in the animal kingdom. And why should her experience of suffering and triumph—that is, her story—be subordinated to a concern for the monarchy (2:10)?

Perhaps Hannah's voice has been "dubbed over" by a narrator bent on exploiting her story for political ends, making it into an exposition to the story of *real* importance in the books of Samuel and Kings, namely, that of the monarchy. Just as the dying words of Eli's daughter-in-law (1 Sam 4:19-22) are reinscribed to express concern for Israel and the ark of YHWH, so Hannah's words are here scripted as a foreshadowing of and support for the coming monarchy, a precursor to David's own psalm in 2 Samuel 22 (see Polzin 1989:33-35). If Robert Polzin's argument is correct (1989:18-36), Hannah's entire story is then but a parable about kingship. Her asking for and receiving a son is a metaphor for Israel's asking for and receiving a king. The mention of kingship in 2:10 is simply one more instance in which the true Subject of the story clearly surfaces.

Or perhaps Hannah song is both her own and not her own. She lives and sings under the sign of patriarchy, and her subjectivity, like the subjectivities of all who live under the same sign, men as well as women, is not free of patriarchy's claim on her. On this reading, perhaps the incongruity of her song reflects her own poignant ambivalence, as she struggles to live with the incongruities of a world in which women's experiences are always subject to men's concerns, because a woman must not herself be Subject.

Unlike the women at the end of Judges, Hannah is a woman of speech and action. Dismembered and dispossessed women had signaled the anarchy of Israel. Hannah hails a new day. She is not a victim. Like Achsah she is willing to speak up for what she wants. She is, however, another unwitting caretaker of the promise as it takes a new turn into the next phase of Israel's relation to YHWH. Her desire for a child becomes strategic for the ongoing story of Israel's political heroes. A mother sacrificing for the sake of the monarchy, sacrificing her son, sacrificing her own story, in the service of those men who, literarily speaking, have more power and promise.

Chapter Seven

IN THE SHADOW OF THE KING

> You may indeed set up over you a king whom YHWH your God
> shall choose . . . But let him not multiply for himself women, so that
> his heart turns away . . . . (Deut 17:15, 17)

> And David came to his house in Jerusalem. And the king took the
> ten women, concubines, whom he had left to guard the house and
> he put them in a house under guard, and he provided for them but
> did not come to them. So they became shut up until the day of their
> death, living widows. (2 Sam 20:3)

Ten women, whom the great king multiplied for himself, attract
little attention from the host of commentators on the career of
David. Abandoned to guard (or watch over, or keep) the palace from
which David flees with all the rest of his house(hold) at the outset of
his son Absalom's rebellion, they are themselves left wholly defense-
less (2 Sam 15:13-16). Thus when Absalom arrives in Jerusalem with
his army they are his to treat as he pleases. The usurping son seeks
advice from Ahithophel, David's erstwhile counselor. Now this
man's advice, the narrator tells us, was regarded by both David and
Absalom as if they consulted the divine oracle. "Go into your father's concubines," says this paragon of wisdom, "those whom he
left behind to watch over the house, so that all Israel will hear that
you have made yourself odious to your father and the hands of all
who are with you will be strengthened" (2 Sam 16:20-21). His possession of the concubines, so conveniently delivered into his hands by
his father, will enable Absalom to make a public statement of his
irrevocable break with his father. This is the logic of patriarchal
power. That the son has entered his father's city is not enough; he
must enter his father's women. This is the act that will signal the
ultimate dispossession of the king his father. Thus politics are written on women's bodies—not for the first time, nor the last—in this
story of kingship and nationhood.

So a tent is pitched on the roof of the palace—the roof from
which David gazed at Bathsheba—and there Absalom enters his
father's concubines "in the sight of all Israel" (16:22). We can infer
that any hands that were thereby strengthened were male hands,[1]
just as the gazing eyes of "all Israel" were in practice male eyes, at

least those that mattered to the fledgling king. The place of women in this episode is to be abandoned and raped in the interests of male power. Whether Absalom was able to mark all ten of their bodies in the time that remained to him before being called out to battle the narrator does not specify. The generality of the statement that Absalom went in to (into?) them is sufficient. They are, after all, in the larger scheme of things, only a generality themselves—a tent of ten concubines waiting to lend significance to affairs of state.

From the temporary tent on the rooftop, where they waited to be sexually entered by the new man Absalom, the narrator transposes these ten women to a permanent house of detention, where the old man David never entered, and where they wait for the day of their death. Between tent and prison house the narrator relates the action that determines their fate—a battle lost and won and the new man himself caught between heaven and earth and pierced to death by Joab and his ten armor-bearers (18:9-13). But if we glimpse here an ironic connection between the impaling of Absalom and the rape of the concubines, and we are moved to consider again their situation, the unfolding story leads not to the subject or the subjectivity of the concubines but rather to that of their (re)possessor, King David.

Absalom's death is told in terms of David's political enmeshment with his general, Joab, and of the tension generated between his public and private roles, as king and father. David's yearning for his son is famous (18:38 [19:1]):

> The king became agitated, and he went up to the gate chamber and wept; and as he went he said: "O my son Absalom, my son, my son Absalom! O that I had died instead of you, Absalom, my son, my son!"

Has he heard, like all Israel, that his son has violated his concubines? If so, it makes no difference. His grief for his son is everything. It takes that other power player, Joab, to drive home another viewpoint (19:5-6):

> You have covered with shame today the faces of all your servants who have saved your life today—and the lives of your sons and your daughters, and the lives of your wives, and the lives of your concubines—by loving those who hate you and hating those who love you.

Since Joab's purpose is to shore up the military victory by retaining the allegiance of the army, we may doubt that he has much concern for David's many sons, daughters and wives, let alone his concubines. Yet his very act of naming, for whatever other purpose, brings them back into the reader's view. We may choose to pass over them rapidly, as Joab would probably prefer, or we may pause. If we pause it will be because we have a concern that is not Joab's but that can come to expression through Joab's speech.

What of these concubines? Did they—do they—love David? Did he—does he—hate them? What had he been thinking of when he abandoned these women to Absalom? Had it never crossed his mind that this was what he was doing? Had he thought that Absalom would never take that final step, that the concubines might represent to Absalom his father's paternal authority (cf. Lev 18:8) and prove an insuperable barrier to complete and irrevocable usurpation? Whatever the case, what the concubines might have wanted (or feared) appears to have been of no concern to David. He sheds no tears for them, either as left behind by him, violated by his son, or as lifelong prisoners in a "widowhood" of his making.

Neither, it would appear, are the women's concerns a pressing concern of the narrator, given the cursory account of the women's final imprisonment. We may, of course, speculate. Perhaps some of the women were glad never to see the king again, glad that he was dead to them. Perhaps some found satisfaction in each other's company. Perhaps some mourned their confined sexuality. Perhaps some found sexual freedom. Perhaps some longed for their children. Perhaps their children were imprisoned with them. Perhaps some longed for the children they would never have. Ten women confined in a verse. But although David can seem to shrug them off—a political embarrassment, a slight to his paternal authority, to his man-hood—a reader can choose to do otherwise. As we contemplate the brief story of these women we may wonder what kind of man caught up in what kind of social values could so brazenly shift responsibility for the consequences of his own actions.

We may also ponder Joab's invocation of the term "love." David, he spat out, had loved those who hated him and hated those who loved him. Such a confusion of love and hate may remind us of an earlier episode in David's family history. Amnon, son of David and Ahinoam, loved Tamar, daughter of David and Maacah, and sister of Absalom. In this story, as in the story of the concubines, the personal is enmeshed in the political.

> And it came to pass after this that Absalom son of David had a beautiful sister whose name was Tamar, and Amnon son of David loved her. And it was distressing to Amnon, to the point of making himself sick, on account of Tamar his sister, for she was a virgin and it was impossible in Amnon's view to do anything to her. (13:1-2)

This harrowing story of incest, rape and fratricide introduces its characters in terms of familial relationships—son, sister, and, by implication, brother. As the tale unfolds, the narrator loads it with these reminders of family connection: "And Amnon had a friend, whose name was Jonadab, the son of Shimeah, David's brother . . .

and he said to him, 'Why are you so low, king's son? . . .' And Amnon said to him, 'I love Tamar, my brother Absalom's sister.'" After Amnon has set in motion Jonadab's plan to gain access to Tamar, "David sent word to Tamar at home, saying 'Go to your brother Amnon's house, and prepare food for him.' So Tamar went to her brother Amnon's house . . ." Amnon himself perversely exploits the ambivalence of the term "sister," both calling upon it to invoke the authority of brother over sister and pressing it into service as language of courtship and affection: "Come lie with me, my sister." ("Open to me, my sister, my love," one lover entreats the other in the Song of Songs 5:2.)[2] Tamar, however, names the act: "No, my brother, do not rape me . . . ."

Having done what he wanted to do, however, "then Amnon hated her with a very great hatred; indeed the hatred with which he hated her was greater than the love with which he had loved her" (13:15). His "love" exposed and expended as lust, he cannot be rid of her fast enough: "Get up and get out!" She is no longer "my sister," but nameless. And though Tamar desperately seeks to hold him to a responsible relationship ("No, my brother . . ." [vs. 16, reading a widely accepted emended text]), Amnon cannot abide to be reminded. His language now matches his behavior, treating her as a disposable object. "Put this [woman? thing?] out of my presence, and bolt the door after her." So thrust out, the door bolted behind her, she finds her way, weeping, to her brother Absalom's house.

If Amnon has tried to obliterate his brotherly connection with her, so Absalom seems just as quick to marginalize the matter, though we may notice that he carefully avoids claiming Amnon as his own brother: "And her brother Absalom said to her, 'Has Amnon your brother been with you? Well then, my sister, keep quiet about it; he is your brother; do not take this thing to heart.' So Tamar dwelt, desolate, in the house of Absalom, her brother"(13:20).

This ending of Tamar's life is not, however, the narrative's ending, for the narrator adds, "But Absalom spoke to Amnon neither good nor evil; for Absalom hated Amnon, for he had raped his sister Tamar." In due course, when hating Amnon turns into killing him (vss. 23-29), we may understand why Absalom is reluctant to own his fraternal connection.

Tamar is trapped in a story of male possession and competition. "Absalom son of David," the story begins, "had a beautiful sister whose name was Tamar, and Amnon son of David loved her." Tamar starts her narrative life as a possession, competed for. Absalom son of David has something that Amnon son of David wants—namely, Tamar. The narrator identifies the men not as brothers but as

sons of David. As David is pulled into the story we see him as father but especially as king. "And when the king came to see him,
Amnon said to the king, 'Let my sister come, please . . .'" (vs. 6);
"So now [says Tamar to Amnon], please speak to the king; for he
will not withhold me from you" (vs. 13); "And as for King David, he
heard of all these things and was very angry, but he would not
punish him, for he loved him for he was his firstborn [son]" (vs. 21,
following LXX and Qumran; cf. NRSV). The genealogically attentive
reader may remember that Amnon was David's first son and Absalom was David's third (3:2-3). That Absalom moves closer to
succession to the throne is a factor we cannot overlook in contem-
plating his motivation for murder. Where is Tamar in her story's
aftermath? Is she uppermost in her brother's mind, or is she displaced by the prospect of royal power?

Amnon's love of Tamar turned out to be hate. What of David's
love for his daughter? Joab speaks of sons, daughters, wives and
concubines. Tamar is the only daughter of David to be named in the
books of Samuel. Does she love her father? We are not told, though
we see her dutifully following out his instructions to the point of
being raped. Does he love her? We are not told and we hear no
word of lament from him. We see no tears. "O my daughter Tamar,
my daughter, my daughter Tamar! O that I had not sent you to my
son's house, O Tamar, my daughter, my daughter." When we read
David's lament for Absalom we may mark the absence of such an
outcry for Tamar. When he learns of the rape he is angry, but it is
less clear that his anger is on behalf of Tamar more than it is frustration at the behavior of Amnon, "for he loved him, for he was his
firstborn [son]."

Having observed David's grief over Absalom and glimpsed the
possibility that he loved Amnon, even if only because he was his
firstborn son and heir, we might ask, What further part does love
play in David's life? Of course, that question subverts our program
and once more places a man in the Subject position. Yet not entirely
so, since if we explore that question at all we shall find ourselves
investigating, among others, the women whose subjectivity we seek
to restore. (In many ways that was what we saw happening in our
reading of what has for so long been called the "Abraham" story.)

Seeking a beginning, we could seek David's mother—and not
find her, not even her name. Actually, finding any females in the
story of the kingship's origins is not easy. Between the birth of
Ichabod ("the glory has departed") to the wife of Phineas (1 Samuel
4) and the young David's triumphal reception by the women of Israel

(ch. 18), there are but a handful of references to women. Samuel, in
his tirade against the kingship that YHWH has promised (not necessarily with enthusiasm) the elders of Israel, promises them in turn
that the king "will take your daughters to be perfumers and cooks
and bakers . . . and he will take your male and female slaves . . ."
(8:13, 16). Later, urging king Saul to wipe out the Amalekites, he
instructs him to "utterly destroy all that they have; do not spare
them, but kill both man and woman, child and infant, ox and sheep,
camel and donkey" (15:3). Impatient at Saul's sparing of Agag, he
hews the captive Amalekite to pieces before YHWH at Gilgal while
intoning the law of retaliation, "As your sword has made women
childless, / So shall your mother be childless among women" (15:33),
a point perhaps lost on a victim whose mother has already perished,
we assume, at the edge of an Israelite sword.

The women of King Saul's family emerge into the story of kingship within this patriarchal context of military and political power.
Saul, like David, has no textual mother, but in addition to three sons
he does have a wife, Ahinoam daughter of Ahimaaz, and two daughters, "and the names of his two daughters were these: the name of the
firstborn was Merab, and the name of the younger was Michal" (1
Sam 14:49, 50). Daughters and David meet, in a manner of speaking,
as a transaction of war. Visiting his brothers at the front, David over-
hears something that interests him greatly. "The king will make the
man who kills [Goliath] wealthy, and will give him his daughter and
make his family free in Israel" (17:25). Feigning ignorance of the
promise—and with a suitable display of piety—he seeks and gains its
verification (17:16-7). Thus when he is celebrated by the women of
Israel (who have come out to meet King Saul!) we know that, despite
his public claims to have acted solely to the glory of God (17:41-7),
this young man privately harbors powerful ambitions.

Unable to shake himself free of the intruder whose military and
political power accumulates relentlessly, expedition by successful
expedition, Saul, jealous and fearful, finally makes good his promise.
He offers David his elder daughter, Merab, on condition David
would continue, as he put it, "to be valiant for me and to fight
YHWH's battles" (18:17). His unexpressed intention, however, is to
have the Philistines kill David and spare him the political embarrassment of doing it himself. (David himself is to become the unsur-
passed master of this technique of murder by proxy.) But at David's
extravagant flourish of (false) servility on being made this offer—
"Who am I and who are my living [kin], my father's clan in Israel,
that I should be son-in-law to the king?"—Saul either cannot resist
demonstrating his superior status or loses his nerve. Either way he

rubs David's nose in his servility by taking him at his word—indeed, who *is* he?—and giving Merab to Adriel the Meholathite as wife! Promised by her father to one man, given by him to another, Merab is truly a pawn on the royal chess board. And David makes no move.

Then the plot takes an unexpected turn. "Now Saul's daughter Michal loved David. When it was told to Saul, the thing seemed just right to him" (18:20). At first it seems as though we shall see a repetition of the fate of Merab, for Saul immediately revives his earlier plan. "Let me give her to him," he decides, "that she may be a snare for him and the hand of the Philistines may be against him." But this time the plan is different. The operative word is "snare." His daughter offers him the perfect snare: her love as bait. The negotiations this time take place by proxy, suggestive of the hostility and estrangement that have divided the men, and David's reply via Saul's servants is this time humility laced with sarcasm: "Is it trifling in your eyes, being the king's son-in-law, seeing that I myself am but a poor, trifling man." Saul refuses to be ruffled. He makes his play. He sends word that the price of his daughter is a hundred Philistine foreskins. When it is told to him, "the thing seemed just right to David, to become the king's son-in-law" (vs. 24). And so, in his inimitable fashion, the prospective son-in-law kills *two* hundred Philistines and presents their phallic tokens to the king, "that he might be the king's son-in-law." Which is to say, the man who has been trifled with ("lightly esteemed") presents himself with not one but two hundred and one phalluses before the king, his father-in-law. Saul has lost, and doubly so. He gives David his daughter Michal as a wife, a wife who loves the man. And knowing that YHWH is in David's camp as well, Saul can only be still more afraid of him than ever.

In due course, Saul can hold his hand no more. He plans to kill David, "in the morning" (19:11-17). His fears about his daughter materialize. The narrator at last gives her a voice: "But she told David, Michal his wife did, saying, 'Unless you escape with your life tonight, tomorrow you will be put to death.' Like Rahab rescuing the spies at Jericho (Josh 2:15), she lets him down from the window and he escapes. Like Rachel foiling her father Laban's pursuit of her husband Jacob (Gen 31:19-55), she skillfully dissembles, enabling her husband's escape and saving herself in the process. Both know how to take charge of the household gods (*teraphim*), and both are more than a match for their father when it comes to words. Each grounds the power of her words in an aspect of women's experience that, for differing reasons, renders male reply impossible. Each leaves her father speechless. Rachel turns the taboo of menstruation—the taboo which secludes a woman as "unclean"—into an impassable wall around her body, and the stolen *teraphim*. Michal delays her father first by asserting "he is sick" as the reason David cannot leave. When, however, her deception is uncovered and she is challenged to explain her apparent betrayal of her father, she invokes another gender construction typical in an androcentric world, namely the understanding that women are physically vulnerable to men: "He said to me, 'Let me go; why should I kill you?'"

So Michal has the last word. But it proves only episodic. She is a woman and daughter and princess, her husband a fugitive. Her story thus remains under the control of King Saul, her father. Before long, in the aftermath of the account of David's marriage to Abigail, the widow of Nabal, we learn that "David also married Ahinoam of Jezreel; both of them became his wives" (1 Sam 25:43). And almost as an afterthought the narrator adds, "Saul had given his daughter Michal, David's wife, to Palti[el] son of Laish, who was from Gallim." From pawn to queen to pawn.

What might she have thought when the news came of David's marriages? Did she feel deserted? She had betrayed her father for him. What commitment to her had he ever shown? Did she wonder whether he had ever loved her, or only used her? Did she love him still? She must have heard enough in the house of the king to suspect that her father had used her. Had she felt like Leah? Laban, Leah, and Rachel. Saul, Merab, and Michal. But at least Jacob had loved Rachel. Had David ever loved Michal?

Had David ever really loved anyone?

Well, Jonathan had loved David, that much can be said. Michal must have known this about her brother—must have known, too, that her father had both loved and hated David. A whole family in the emotional grip of a man whose commitments elude us as they eluded Michal, Saul, and even Jonathan. We need to contemplate Jonathan further, accord him some subjectivity in our story, for he complicates our construction of women and men in this story world.

Though the suggestion has long been voiced, few commentators afford serious consideration to reading a homosexual dimension in the story of David and Jonathan. That is hardly surprising, given that until recently, most have been writing out of a strongly homophobic tradition. Artists, however, have been less fearful, as the bronze David of Donatello supremely attests. In this century, André Gide wrote a play he considered perhaps his best work, on just this subject. Indeed he complicates the plot further by seeing Saul, too, as enamored of David from first seeing him as a young lyre player. As Gide reads it, the father and son find themselves trapped in a lover's rivalry over the young man who is to usurp them both.[3]

We venture our own reading by starting with the verb "to love" (*'ahab*), remarking on its shifting translations in a standard commentary (Anchor Bible). When used of Michal, we read "Now Saul's daughter, Michal, fell in love with David" (*'ahab*, 1 Sam 18:20). But with Jonathan it is different. Jonathan, like all Israel and Judah (18:16), simply "loved" him (*'ahab*; 18:1, etc.). This is the Jonathan whose "life" (or "soul" or "being" [*nephesh*]), we are told, "was bound to the life of David" (18:1). This is the Jonathan who "took great delight in David" (19:1), the Jonathan whose love for David, reiterated several times, was like "loving his own life" (18:1, 3; 20:17), the Jonathan whose love towards him, says David, was "more than the love of women" (2 Sam 1:26). Michal "fell in love with" David. Jonathan "loved" him. The difference in translation of the same verb is transparently a transcription of conventional heterosexist interpretation of the text in question (and something we have done ourselves without giving the matter a second thought). Where commentators do raise the question of different kinds of love, they usually (and quickly) conclude that reading a homosexual relationship is "reading in" what is not there, stretching the bounds of interpretive moderation, or is simply "perverse." Yet no few modern interpreters are willing to devote discussion and extend credibility to reading "love" here as a cipher for political commitment—borrowing from ancient treaty language. What counts as stretching the bounds turns out to be a highly prejudicial decision.

On the contrary, far from stretching probability, a homosexual reading, as the passages mentioned above indicate, finds many anchor points in the text. To be sure, everyone loves David. But as we have already seen in this story of David, powerful words have a way of turning up in very different senses. There is love and love (as Amnon's story reminds us). Saul may have loved David's music. All Israel and Judah may have loved his military panache. Jonathan and Michal may have loved him as lovers. But, if we take any notice of the text at all, it is Jonathan who shows an abiding passion.

At the very beginning Jonathan strips himself for David, offering him his clothes and weapons. As the story progresses he risks his father's huge displeasure in order to try to keep David at court and so to keep him close to him. He even abdicates his own royal position. As David Jobling once neatly put it, Jonathan "empties his heirdom into David" (1978:18). Saul himself can be read as becoming aware of the nature of his son's feelings. Unable finally to contain his

anger, he bursts out at Jonathan: "You son of perversity and rebellion! Do I not know that you are choosing the son of Jesse, to your
own shame and to the shame of your mother's nakedness?" (20:30)
He identifies Jonathan with perversity and women. The idiom "son
of" signifies essence: Jonathan is quintessentially perverse and
rebellious. But as the outburst goes on to make clear, Saul is also
talking about Jonathan's mother: in the misogynist mythology of
patriarchy, woman as Other is always potentially the perverse and
rebellious. Jonathan, perverse and rebellious, is truly the offspring of
a woman. Jonathan *is* a woman. Indeed, the son who is a woman
shames the very (female) genitals from which he has come forth.
Saul, on this reading, speaks from a heterosexist, patriarchal position. Jonathan, too, is trapped in the same social system, so that he
falls back in anger but also, says the narrator, in shame (vs. 34),
"because he hurt ['*atsab*] for David and because his father had humiliated him."

But, it will doubtless be objected, Jonathan is said to have fa-
thered a child (2 Sam 21:7; 9:3); and David is constantly connected
with women from early in his career, so that finally his failure to be
aroused by Abishag (1 Kgs 1:1-4) is worthy of the narrator's attention. Of Jonathan we would observe that, quite apart from the possibility that he was bisexual, it is common in patriarchal societies for
men whose primary sexual orientation is homosexual to live out a
heterosexual role for at least some part of their lives, and in doing so
to father children. Of David something a little different may be said.

We come back to the question with which we began this discussion. Did David love anyone? As already observed, while several
characters in the story are said to love David, nowhere unambiguously is David ever said to love anyone.[4] Moreover, in the recounting of the relationship between David and Jonathan, there is a
remarkable asymmetry in the use of affective terms generally. What
emerges from this imbalance is a reading that either has Jonathan's
passion unrequited or at least unconsummated, or perhaps David
playing out a lover's role only so far as it suits him to keep Jonathan's affections strongly alive.

Consistent with the latter interpretation are David's famous final
lines in his lament for the dead king and his son (2 Sam 1:19-27).
The lament as a whole is richly layered and typically, for David,
double-edged. When we hear him proclaim that the father and son
were not divided, whether in life or death, we ought to take pause.
Saul had come close to killing Jonathan—over David (1 Sam 20:33).
So too we might wonder at the picture of Jonathan slain upon "your
high places," a phrase that hints at apostasy. And as David laments

Jonathan's love for him, we may hear another message. Very precisely he speaks of how extremely lovely Jonathan was to him—the first time we have been given such a view. So David perceived Jonathan as lovely? But it is David who has been the object of everyone's gaze up to this point. For a convenient moment David turns this loveliness around—and lays it on Jonathan. Then he continues: "Wonderful your love to me, more than love of women." He carefully casts the relationship in a particular light. The point of comparison is women. Jonathan belongs in the relationship in the position of a woman, even if only to surpass her. We are reminded of Saul's invective. Jonathan is such a "son of perversity and rebellion" that he puts (even) a woman to shame. The explicit tone is different in each case, but the construction of Jonathan's sexuality by Saul and David is the same: Jonathan is a woman, more woman than women are.

David's move here is characteristically astute. Having enjoyed every advantage of Jonathan's attachment, he now finally capitalizes on it. He publicly acknowledges what was no doubt rumored, if not commonly known, but he seizes the opportunity to define the relationship in a way that is highly favorable to himself. He proclaims himself an object of affection. Moreover, Jonathan's loveliness and love do indeed become political endorsements. On the other hand, Jonathan's love comes to rest in the comparison with women; and, in the kind of patriarchal stereotyping we have already spoken about, that makes David the "man." Doubly so, since David's experience of women must have been a matter of notoriety. Who else better to judge what kind of love might be valued more than the love of women! Thus the words that praise Jonathan at the same time subtly devalue him. And even more so, for as royal prince he should have played the "man" to the commoner's "woman." David has reversed the sexual roles just as he has reversed the political roles. By claiming the sexual relationship, but strictly on his terms, he turns it into a proclamation of his own ascendancy, his inevitable dominion, and of the inevitable end of the house of Saul. Saul's is wasted seed.

Saul had begged David to swear that he would not cut off Saul's seed after him, and that he would not wipe out Saul's name from his father's house (24:20). David's lament implies that Saul might as well have saved his breath: Saul's seed was already cut off—Jonathan had seen to that. And there is David, dominant, a "man," and waiting to be king.

Waiting to be king. Is that what shapes David's life from that fateful moment when Samuel anoints him, the youngest of all those

brothers? Saul tried to hide from kingship. David sought it out. Is
that what Michal learned, finally, that David's whole *raison d'etre*
was to accumulate and mediate royal power? Was she jealous of her
brother as she watched him give himself to David? Was she aware that
he continued to meet David after she herself had seen the last of
him? Did she see Saul's crown slipping away from Jonathan into
David's hands? With satisfaction, perhaps, but later regret? Did she
feel any kinship of loss with her brother as the time went by and
word came of David's growing army and entourage, and of his
marriages, and they waited, but no word from him for them? Did
they grieve together, sister and brother, or live out separate lives in
this family that David had disrupted? And then she found herself
sent off to Paltiel, as though she were David's widow, or as though
her marriage had never been.

Word did come, but not auspiciously, and by then, anyway, the
years had passed and things had changed in Michal's life. By this
time things had changed for David, too.

Following the death of Saul and Jonathan (and his two brothers)
in battle against the Philistines, David becomes king of Judah in
Hebron. War breaks out between south and north, between David
and Saul's son, Ishbosheth, a long war, during which "the house of
David grew stronger and stronger, while the house of Saul grew
weaker and weaker" (2 Sam 3:1). Key to Ishbosheth's survival is Abner, his father's general.

Prefacing the final episode in this story of struggle is a list of
David's sons—along with their mothers, David's wives, now swollen
in number to six.

A quarrel breaks out between Abner and Ishbosheth over Rizpah,
a concubine who had belonged to Saul (3:6-11). The king's accusing
question—"Why have you gone into my father's concubine?"—is met
with an angry rebuff by Abner: "Am I a dog's head belonging to
Judah? Today I keep showing loyalty to the house of your father
Saul . . . and yet you charge me now with a crime concerning this
woman!" He threatens to shift allegiance to David and "to transfer
the kingdom from the house of Saul, and set up the throne of David
over Israel and over Judah, from Dan to Beersheba."

Immediately Abner begins negotiations with David, who agrees
to make a covenant with him on the condition that Abner demonstrate that he is negotiating in good faith (3:12-16): "But one thing I
require of you, namely, you shall not come into my presence unless
you bring before me Michal, Saul's daughter, when you come into
my presence." At the same time David demands of Ishbosheth,
"Give me my wife Michal, whom I betrothed at the price of one

hundred Philistine foreskins." David's manner of naming Michal is transparent: she is "Saul's daughter" to Abner, for she is to betoken Abner's betrayal of the house of Saul and will confer dynastic legitimacy upon David; she is "my wife Michal, whom I betrothed at a price" to Ishbosheth, to whom he represents his claim as no more than a request to have his legitimate wife returned.

Ishbosheth, without further ado, we are told, sends to have her taken from her husband, Paltiel the son of Laish. The reader, surprised at Ishbosheth's immediate capitulation, may suspect Abner's threatening presence. And indeed the strong man shows up within a sentence or two, with Michal firmly in his charge. But there is for Abner a minor inconvenience, a husband 3:16). "But her husband went with her, weeping as he went behind her to Bahurim. So Abner said to him, 'Go on back!' And he went on back." Like a dog sent home with its tail between its legs, this weeping husband.

Something had changed for Michal. Seized from her home, from a husband who cares enough to weep for her, she is shuttled between her father's general, who is selling his loyalty for being grudged possession of a concubine, and a husband king, whose regard for her has been marked by his multiplication of wives. None of the power players addresses a word to her. The only voice raised on her behalf is that of the weeping, cowed Paltiel. Something had changed for Michal. Someone cared enough for her to weep.

Our judgment that she matters not one whit as a person to David or to the narrator is reinforced by her disappearance from the narrative at this point. Her arrival in Hebron is unmarked. It is the maneuvering of the male players that draws the narrator's attention: David, Abner, and his mortal rival, David's general Joab. If Michal found the experience replete with not only loss but also humiliation, we would not be surprised. This event could hardly have left her feelings for David (quite apart from her brother and Abner) unscathed.

Michal's story finds its conclusion in 2 Samuel 6. David, now king of all Israel, victor over the Philistines, established in Jerusalem, and living in a splendid palace, decides to bring into his new capital the prime symbol of the cult, the ark of God, "which is called by the name of YHWH of hosts who is enthroned on the cherubim." As the ark entered the royal city to the sound of shouts and trumpets, Saul's daughter saw the king, girded with some special priestly garment, "dancing before YHWH." Years before, she had stood at her window in defiance of her father as she lowered her young hero husband through it to safety. Now she gazed through her window watching her father's supplanter leaping and dancing, "and she

despised him in her heart." The narrator shifts perspective back to
David for several sentences, recounting the culmination of the
celebrations, but then returns us to Michal.

David blessed the people, and gave gifts of food to all, men and
women, and then they returned, "[each] man to his house." David
himself returned to bless his own house.

> But Michal the daughter of Saul came out to meet David, and said,
> "How the king of Israel has distinguished himself [or 'gained power' in
> an oppressive sense; kbd] today! Exposing himself today in front of his
> servants' maidservants, like the posing and exposing of one of the riff-
> raff!" (6:20)

Michal's words are scathing. They are also her last in the story.
The king behaves no better than riff-raff, says a king's daughter. She
accuses him of "uncovering himself"—exposing himself, showing off,
flaunting himself—and as his response strongly suggests, there is a
sexual dimension to her scorn. This is not the first time he has
exposed himself before his subordinate's women, nor, she knows,
will it be the last. David, smarting at the attack, flings back his own
barbed taunt. He rubs her nose in the eclipse of her father's house,
typically wrapping his self-righteousness in piety and flaunting his
(apparently well justified) confidence that YHWH is on his side (6:21):

> [It was] before YHWH, who chose me instead of your father and all his
> house, appointing me prince over the people of YHWH, over Israel; so I
> will make sport [tsahaq] before YHWH.

He also goes on the offensive with regard to the matter of exposure,
though his offensiveness sounds more than a touch defensive. (Doth
he protest too much?) He will uncover himself even more degrading-
ly, he boasts, and will do so in the confidence that he has something
"weighty" (kbd) to show (6:22):

> I will be even more trifling than this and I will become low in my own
> eyes, and yet with the maidservants of whom you have spoken, with
> them I shall be held in esteem [kbd].

The implication is clear. (Unquestionably, this is the man with the
two hundred foreskins.) He is YHWH's gift to women and if Michal
does not appreciate that, he can do without her admiration. And he
can certainly do without her criticism. He no longer has any use for
her. That, at least, is what she may have heard in his words.

What did she know of his need for her? He wanted her back
when his throne was still not secured. She could buttress his claim
to the throne and, hopefully, produce a son who would then conveniently inherit both royal houses. But now he had the throne, the
power of north and south was centralized in Jerusalem, his personal

fiefdom, the tide was turned against the Philistines, and the populace was there on his side again, as he danced before YHWH and distributed largesse to the crowds. So why should he need Michal, daughter of Saul, any more? Her body had outlived its usefulness to him.

And Michal daughter of Saul had no child to the day of her death. (6:23)

Readers have responded variously to this sentence that punctuates Michal's story. The due divine reward, many have supposed, for opposing YHWH's chosen. Or, on the understanding that David still sees advantage in having an heir by Michal, does this proud woman, a king's daughter, refuse to lend her body to any further political (ab)use? Alive to another reality than the one for whom she betrayed her father's house—she had belonged, after all, to another house and husband—does she now refuse to be further complicit in the uniting of the houses of Saul and David? Or, assuming that such an heir is no longer of interest to David, is it that he makes good his implied threat, and disdains intercourse with her, to the day of her death? Michal and the ten concubines, living widows to the day of their death. And is his sexual absence then a weighty thing or a trifle, a threat to her, or a blessing?

So Michal's subjectivity is swallowed up in the ongoing drama of David the great king, the man whom YHWH chose to rule over all Israel. The daughter of Saul disappears into the king's house. (Yet though she disappears, her presence will be felt, if only in the son she never had. For without her son, the obvious heir, the way would lie open for a plague of bitter struggle between brothers in the house of David.) So Michal disappears into the king's house, along with other women, wives and concubines, named and nameless. Did they live separately or in each other's company, those many women?

Among the named: Ahinoam of Jezreel, whose son Amnon, David's firstborn, would rape Tamar, daughter of Maacah; Maacah, mother of the raped daughter, whose son Absalom would murder Amnon and for a brief time seize his father's throne; Abigail the widow of Nabal of Carmel whose son Chileab, strategically second born, vanishes from the narrative without trace; Haggith, whose son Adonijah, expected to succeed his father after the deaths of Amnon and Absalom, instead is murdered by Solomon, son of Bathsheba, wife of Uriah the Hittite whom David had murdered; Abital, mother of Shephatiah; and Eglah, mother of Ithream.

Most of these women find no voice in the story. Of the two who do speak, Abigail (1 Samuel 25) belongs to the formative stages of David's power as, pursued by Saul, he builds an effective fighting force. Bathsheba (2 Samuel 11–12; 1 Kings 1–2), on the other hand, belongs to its fulcrum and decline, first as David's empire is being consolidated, and then as the crown passes from him to Solomon.

Abigail seizes the initiative from her husband, Nabal, and intercepts David as he moves angrily with overwhelming armed force to wipe out Nabal and his household. Abigail's eloquence is voluble, meandering, and brilliantly persuasive. She knows the man's vanity and ambition and targets it to perfection (1 Sam 25:28-29):

> Please forgive your maidservant's trespass; for YHWH will assuredly make my lord a secure house, because my lord is fighting YHWH's battles; and evil shall not be found in you so long as you live. If anyone should arise to pursue you and to seek your life, my lord's life shall be bound in the bundle of the living in the care of YHWH your God; but the lives of your enemies he shall fling away as from the hollow of a sling.

And understanding that her husband's days of wealth and independence are numbered, she seeks to insinuate herself into David's future: "And when YHWH has dealt well with my lord," she concludes, "remember your maidservant" (25:31).

Like Rahab, Abigail has a keen eye for the future and the wit and tongue to place herself in it to her advantage. And sure enough, when David hears of Nabal's death he sends for her. The message is blunt and to the point. Clearly he had heard her message. "And David's servants came to Abigail at Carmel and spoke to her, saying, 'David has sent us to you to take you to be his wife'" (1 Sam 25:40). Immediately she resumes her obsequious role and plays it to the hilt (25:41):

> She rose and bowed down, her face to the ground, and said, "Behold, your maidservant is a serving girl to wash the feet of the servants of my lord."

She signals, ingratiatingly, her recognition of male power, the messengers' as well as that of their (and her) overlord. Perhaps she also signals, intriguingly, a hint of sexual promise as she speaks of washing their feet—later David, having made Bathsheba pregnant and needing to pass off paternity, will urge her husband Uriah to go down to his house and, as David puts it euphemistically, "wash your feet" (2 Sam 11:8; cf. vs. 11).[5] But if Abigail's words hold out such a hint, she then carefully fences promise with propriety—the feet are the feet of the servants of "my lord." In short, Abigail is already building her place in the hierarchy of royal power.

The narrator adds a touch of irony to move the episode towards its close. The maidservant who is but a "serving girl" rides off in haste, "and her five women servants going along in attendance [literally, 'at her foot'!]." Her rhetoric belies the truth: this is a woman of wealth and ambition. But a shadow falls across her even as she reaches eagerly for her place of power (25:42-43):

> So she followed the messengers of David and became his wife. And then there was Ahinoam; David took her from Jezreel—and the two of them became his wives.

David's policy is to dissipate all power but his own. He will have not one wife but several. And no wife will be first in his house. He will keep his political options open and Abigail, whose options now are closing, will have to learn to live in their shadow.

Bathsheba's story (2 Samuel 11-12) intersects with David's right at the pinnacle of empire. As the king's army ravages the Ammonites and besieges Rabbah, the final prize, Bathsheba, is spied by David from the rooftop of the king's house as she is washing herself. She is seen to be very beautiful. Like Abigail before her, she is sent for by David and she comes to him. "And he lay with her." Unlike Abigail, she returns to her house, for she is married—to a man away fighting the king's wars. She conceives. Now she finds her voice for the only time in this story, and it is powerfully laconic. She sends word to David: "I am pregnant!"

Is she taken, as Rabbah is taken, as the fruit of royal power? After all, what could a woman do, confronted by the king's demand, and her absent husband himself the king's vassal? Maacah's daughter Tamar might have said, "No, my lord, do not force me; for such a thing is not done in Israel!," though she could not then have appealed to the king to make things right ("So now, please speak to the king, for he will not withhold me from you" [2 Sam 12-13]). But we hear no other words from Bathsheba, either because the narrator would have us think that she speaks none or because the narrator denies us access to them—or perhaps has no interest in what they might have been. Without those words, Bathsheba's subjectivity remains veiled, ambiguous.

Androcentric interpretive tradition, anxious to lessen the blame that falls so unavoidably in this episode upon the great man, have not been slow to point their finger at the woman. The woman made him do it! Why was she bathing where she could be seen, flaunting her body, tempting him? Patriarchy quickly invokes its controlling stereotypes, its Others. Bathsheba joins Eve, along with countless other Sirens of male mythology, in embodying woman as temptress.

Recent feminist critics (cf. Bal 1987) have returned the question of responsibility back to the king, by insisting on raising the question of power. Who in this story has the power to act upon their desires? Unquestionably the man. Whatever precisely the circumstances of

Bathsheba's washing, whether or not her being seen could have been preventable (and the narrator cloaks the matter by specifying David's vantage point on the roof of the palace and withholding any details of Bathsheba's location), is not the point. For a man to see a woman's body is no license for him to possess it. Some such precept would likely have received a degree of formal accord in patriarchal ancient Israel, as it would today in north America. But the reality has been and is, even in some courts in this country today, otherwise. Seeing remains for many men a license for possessing, via unequal power, whether physical or political, or both. The question of blame in this story then is also a contemporary one, of gender and power. Feminist critics have seen Bathsheba as a classic victim (or perhaps better, survivor) of male abuse of power.

From another perspective, however, Randall Bailey reads a different story, of a conspiracy to effect a political marriage (1990:83-90). Here David, in typical fashion with an eye to property and political connection (Bathsheba is the powerful Ahithophel's granddaughter; cf. 23:34), deals with an equally ambitious woman (like Abigail?), a woman of initiative and cool nerve who is also interested in power and will use whatever means she has as a woman to gain it. Bailey reads with an eye to the character of the woman who is later involved in the coup which places her son on the throne. The critic carefully builds his reading out of the text. He notes, for example, that David already knows the woman he is dealing with ("David sent and made inquiries about the woman, and said, 'Is this not Bathsheba the daughter of Eliam, wife of Uriah the Hittite?'" [11:3]). Among other observations about word choice, he notes that each character is reciprocally the subject of the much repeated verb, "he/she sent" (*shalah*), which seems to signal both the transactional nature of the event—this is a deal being worked out—and a degree of autonomy in Bathsheba's action. The woman, moreover, is not "brought," she "comes." Bailey, an African-American liberationist critic, is reluctant to assume that the woman, because disadvantaged, has no power to effect change to her own benefit.

Whatever Bathsheba's role, one thing is clear: Nathan's enunciation of YHWH's displeasure with his chosen king transposes the king's punishment onto the bodies of women and a newborn baby.

"Let not this thing be evil in your sight," David said to Joab in the aftermath of Uriah's death (murder), "for sometimes the sword devours one, sometimes another" (11:25). "So now," says Nathan on YHWH's behalf, "a sword will not turn aside from your house, a lasting sword . . . Thus says YHWH, 'Behold, I am raising up evil against you from your house'" (12:10-11). Rapist son Amnon, and fratricide usurper son Absalom come into our view.

"I gave you," says YHWH, "your master's house . . . I gave you the house of Israel and Judah" (12:8). "House" is ambiguous. It is kingdom, dynasty, extended family. Just so, the king's private and political lives merge, mirror each other. "I gave you," continues YHWH, "your lord's women into your breast." Politics are written on the bodies of women. But YHWH's gift of another man's women has been met by David's grasping of another man's woman. Therefore, "I will take your women in your sight, and give them to your neighbor, and he shall sleep with your women in the sight of this sun [i.e., with everyone's knowledge]" (12:11). The rape of daughter Tamar and the rape of the king's concubines come into our view.

"I have sinned against YHWH," says David (12:13). "The child born to you shall surely die," replies the prophet (12:15).

So David gets on with his life. The story ends with him taking the city of Rabbah. Or does he? Is it not Joab who really takes the city?

> And Joab fought against Rabbah of the Ammonites, and took the queenly city. And Joab sent messengers to David, and said, "I have fought against Rabbah; further, I have taken the city of waters. So now gather the rest of the army together, and encamp against the city, and take her, lest I be the one who takes the city and my name be proclaimed over her." So David gathered all the army and went to Rabbah, and fought against her, and took her. (12:26-29)

The siege of Rabbah frames the story of Bathsheba. Cities are feminine. The taking of Rabbah frames the taking of Bathsheba. How could the king who takes another man's woman not be the one who takes another king's city? Joab makes way for the king so that the symmetry is clear. David takes both woman and city. War is written on women's bodies.[6]

The confrontation between king and prophet, a turning point in the larger story of David, is sparked by Nathan's parable of the rich man with his many flocks and herds and the poor man with only his ewe lamb (12:3-4):

> And he nurtured her and she grew up together with him and his children [sons]. Of his morsel she ate and from his cup she drank and at his breast she lay. And she became to him like a daughter. Now there came a traveler to the rich man, who spared himself taking from his own flocks or his own herds to prepare a meal for the wayfarer who had come to him by taking instead the poor man's ewe lamb and preparing her for the man who had come to him. (12:3-4)

The lamb is pictured as a girl child, a daughter (Heb. *bath* as in Bathsheba bath-Eliam!). But she is also the one who "ate his morsel and drank his cup"—language often used in sexual imagery (cf. Proverbs

1–9)—and "slept at his breast." The daughter who is at the same time a woman is taken from her father/husband and given to another man. The parable makes very clear the analogy between eating/drinking and sex. The female body is a meal for the man. It is not only the sword that devours (literally "eats") in this story.

And what is YHWH's response to the rich man, David? As Tod Linafelt (1992:107) pungently observes, it is to behave as the rich man! "I will take your women in your sight," says YHWH, "and give them to your neighbor, and he shall sleep with your women in the sight of this sun."

YHWH takes David's concubines and makes them into a meal for Absalom. He takes David's daughter (his "ewe lamb") and makes her into a meal for Amnon. Her body is seized and devoured by her rapist precisely in the course of her preparing and offering him a meal—at her father's urging. The fruit of Tamar the date palm—which is what her name means—is plucked and eaten. A promise fulfilled. So are we to imagine YHWH enjoying its ironic flavor?

Yet if YHWH and the men of Israel are intent on devouring women's bodies as their expression of power, a silent woman struggles to uphold another view of politics and the body. Rizpah's story flares up red on a cold blue canvas. It is a loose thread, one among a cluster the narrator has left waiting to be pulled in the closing chapters of the book (2 Samuel 21–24). These are threads that can quickly unravel YHWH's chosen king, perhaps YHWH himself.[7]

The story starts with food, or rather the lack of it. A long famine leads David to "seek the face of YHWH." The oracle responds: there is "bloodguilt" on the house of Saul "because he put to death the Gibeonites" (21:1-2). Ironically, it would appear that, in seeking to implement what the Israelites had originally been commanded, namely to destroy the original inhabitants of the land (Deuteronomy 7), Saul now stands condemned for violating the Israelites' subsequent oath to spare the Gibeonites, made through deception (Joshua 9). The issues of "guilt" and justice here turn out to be complex. When does one covenant—or promise, or commandment—override another? For how long must "bloodguilt" haunt a house? If Saul's house has blood on its hands, what of David's?

David's response is to allow the Gibeonites to name their compensation. Their request, obliquely, is for blood (21:4). The king, anxious to deal with his current political problem, the plague, takes them up with alacrity, though prudently making sure to except Jonathan's son Mephibosheth "because of the oath of YHWH which was between them, between David and Jonathan son of Saul" (21:77). So seven sons of Saul are given over for execution. Once again, conveniently for David, the house of Saul is reduced, and the blame laid at another's door (cf. 1 Samuel 31; 2 Samuel 1–4).

> The king took the two sons of Rizpah daughter of Aiah, whom she bore to Saul, Armoni and Mephibosheth [i.e., not Jonathan's son] . . . and the five sons of Merab daughter of Saul whom she bore to Adriel son of Barzillai . . . and he gave them into the hands of the Gibeonites. And they impaled them on the mountain before YHWH, and the seven of them perished together. They were put to death in the first days of the harvest, the start of the barley harvest.
>
> But Rizpah daughter of Aiah took sackcloth and spread it for herself on a rock, and she stayed there from the start of the harvest until rain from the sky fell on [the bodies]. She did not allow the birds of the sky to settle upon them by day or the wild beasts by night.
>
> So when David was told what Rizpah daughter of Aiah, Saul's concubine, had done, David went and took the bones of Saul and the bones of his son Jonathan . . . and they gathered the bones of those who had been impaled, and they buried the bones of Saul and his son Jonathan in the land of Benjamin in Zela, in the tomb of Kish his father . . . (21:8-14)

Against Gibeonites and David (and YHWH?) is set Rizpah.

Against bloodguilt that traverses generations and swallows up the innocent is set a mother's care. Rizpah's loyalty traverses death as she fends off from her dead kin the ravening wildlife, the counterpart of the human world that consigned the sons to death. Her name captures, with some irony, something of her spirit: she is a "glowing coal," daughter of a bird of prey, "falcon."

At the beginning of the book Rizpah was the voiceless pawn in a man's quarrel (2 Sam 3:6-11). At the end she is still voiceless and still a pawn, as she watches her sons destroyed in another quarrel between other men. Yet this woman succeeds in exercising power through the only action open to her—her mourning and her defiance of men's politics of the body. (She has a classical sister, Antigone, who acts in similar fashion in Sophocles's play of the same name.) Her sons' bodies, her nephews' bodies, will not be torn and consumed by the birds and beasts. She joins her body to theirs in their exposure and faces out the months. She shames David into bringing the bones of Saul and his sons home, into their family tomb, in their own land.

Rizpah: glowing coal, falcon's daughter. Rizpah: Saul's concubine. Rizpah: mother of Armoni and Mephibosheth. Rizpah, who keeps the birds and beasts at bay. Rizpah, who forces a king to honor some bodies, albeit that they were corpses of his making.

When David's own body eventually turns cold it is covered with clothes (1 Kgs 1:1). Yet still he cannot get warm. So his servants seek a body to warm him (1:2-4):

"Let a young woman, ready for marriage, be sought for my lord the king; and let her stand before the king and be his nurse, and let her lie at your breast so that my lord the king will be warm." So they sought a beautiful young woman throughout the territory of Israel and found Abishag the Shunammite, and they brought her to the king. The young woman was very beautiful. So she became a nurse to the king and she attended upon him, but the king did not know her ["was not intimate with her"; TANAKH].

Another morsel is brought to the king, but this time he cannot eat, let alone devour. Ironically, the man's condition is marked out by this woman's difference. She is young (perhaps as young as thirteen or fourteen); he is "old, advanced in years." Her beauty is linked to her maidenhood; does that imply that his beauty is vanished? She is ready for sex ("of marriageable age"); he is unable to "know" her. She is warm; he is cold. She is his nurse; he is her patient. Perhaps, in that case, she is his mother; and he her child. The all-purpose woman of male fantasy. In the binary world of patriarchy, she is paradoxically the logical choice to give him life. Just because she is his opposite, his Other, she therefore, ironically, defines his identity, makes him again a Subject, gives him life. (As fast as the patriarchal Subject suppresses the Other, he must seek her out to stand before him or else he dies.)

But Abishag as the patriarchal antidote to death is a fiction. Death comes to all bodies, even that of this old patriarch. It only remains for him to come face to face with another woman for the last time. Bathsheba, conniving with Nathan, talks him into granting the kingdom to Bathsheba's son, Solomon (1 Kgs 1:11-53), so ousting his older half-brother, Adonijah son of Haggith. Does David know her when she comes to speak to him? We readers certainly do not know of the promise she claims he made to her, to put Solomon her son on the throne. But the old king, advanced in years, acts as if he knows it and grandly dethrones himself in favor of Bathsheba's son. And Bathsheba the wife of Uriah the Hittite becomes Bathsheba the queen mother.

And Abishag? What happens to her? In a bizarre turn of events, Adonijah goes to Bathsheba and asks, as though for a consolation prize, for Abishag. "You yourself know that the kingdom was mine, and that all Israel looked to me to reign . . . So now I have one request to make of you; do not refuse me . . . Please ask King Solomon—he will not refuse you—to give me Abishag the Shunammite for my wife" (1 Kgs 2:15-17). Without further comment Bathsheba agrees and goes to King Solomon "to speak to him concerning Adonijah." The narrator slows the pace, detailing the courtesies of the king rising and bowing and placing a seat for his mother at his right hand. "I have one small request to make of you. Do not refuse me," she says. "Make your request, my mother, for I will not refuse you," he replies. But then he does refuse her, with vehemence (2:22-25):

> "So why do you ask Abishag the Shunammite for Adonijah? Ask for him also the kingdom! For he is my older brother and Abiathar the priest and Joab son of Zeruiah are on his side . . . Now, as YHWH lives, who has established me, and place me on the throne of David my father, and who has made me a house, as he promised, Adonijah shall be put to death this day." So King Solomon sent Benaiah son of Jehoiada, who struck him down; so he died. (1 Kgs 2:22-25)

Abishag the Shunammite and the kingdom are a matching pair. Politics are written on women's bodies. Why is she a danger to Solomon? Some claim that to ask for the former king's concubine is tantamount to making a formal claim to the kingdom and that this is what Adonijah is doing here. But it is not clear that Abishag was ever David's concubine; and, more to the point, neither is it easy to imagine Adonijah being quite so brazenly stupid. The narrator provides us with one clue at least: in relating how Bathsheba went in to see David for the crucial interview she and Nathan had with David, it is observed, "now the king was very old, and Abishag the Shunammite was attending on the king" (1 Kgs 1:15). Abishag is witness to the subsequent conversations. Is that her problem? Does Abishag know too much? Does Solomon suspect that she knows more than she should, and that Adonijah is seeking that knowledge to his own political ends? Solomon fears the woman and kills the man.

Woman, knowledge, and death: so here we find yet another expression of that deepseated patriarchal anxiety about women who have the power of knowledge (and the knowledge of power). So women with knowledge, says the patriarchal undertone, spell death to men. The message is clear: the woman is dangerous. Abishag is to blame. It is the beautiful woman, ready for sex, who has brought death.[8]

And what of Abishag? What happens to her? The narrator says nothing. His interest is served by detailing the assassination of Adonijah, the establishment of Solomon's house, the apparent fulfillment of YHWH's promise to David. So Adonijah is struck down. And Abishag? Do we imagine that Solomon left her alone, intact—this beautiful young woman who knew enough to inspire the king to murder his brother? Did he shut her up under guard in a "house of keeping," a young virgin alone, or with the remnant of his father's violated concubines, now old and advanced in years? More likely, Benaiah slipped into her chamber one night and quietly slit her throat.

Chapter Eight

UNTIL NO BODY REMAINS

> All it takes is to push what you hate,
> what you fear onto the soft alien flesh.
> —Marge Piercy ("Rape poem")[1]

> In the Tao Te Ching, a victorious warrior is advised to dress for mourning . . . War is no victory parade. It must be seen for precisely what it is, a choice. A painful choice. A choice that calls for mourning . . .
>
> Greenpeace estimates that at least 120,000 Iraqi soldiers and 76,000 civilians were killed during the Persian Gulf War. Since then, the civilian death toll related to the war and its aftermath has reached perhaps a quarter of a million. According to the *New England Journal of Medicine*, between January and August 1991, 50,000 children died as a direct result of health problems brought on by the bombing of the Iraqi infrastructure. Total deaths among children are estimated to be 170,000.
>
> Can we mourn for 170,000 dead Iraqi children? I suspect the answer is "Hell No!" That answer is disturbing, because the opposite of mourning is not rejoicing; the opposite of mourning is being numb to suffering.
>
> —John Samuel Tieman (*Atlanta Constitution*, Memorial Day, 1993)

Death pervades the books of Kings, but it is rarely elaborated. It comes in generic form as the slaughter of some, the striking down of others. Occasionally a king dies a natural death and "sleeps with his fathers." More often when the killing is not part and parcel of war it is an integral part of the story's numerous accounts of royal coups. Noticeable, however, is the growth of detail as the narrator recounts the fall of the house of Ahab—detail regarding the context of the killing as well as its precise manner.

Death comes with challenging words in the sudden shock of betrayal.

> When Joram saw Jehu, he asked, "Is all well, Jehu?" But Jehu replied, "How can all be well as long as your mother Jezebel carries on her countless harlotries and sorceries?" Thereupon Joram turned his horses around and fled, crying out to Ahaziah, "Treason, Ahaziah!" But Jehu drew his bow and hit Joram between the shoulders, so that the arrow pierced his heart; and he collapsed in his chariot . . . On seeing this, King Ahaziah of Judah fled . . . Jehu pursued him and said, "Shoot him down too!" [And they shot him] in his chariot at the ascent of Gur . . . He fled to Megiddo and died there. (2 Kgs 9:22-28, TANAKH)

Or death comes as a silent ritual of victory, calculated, coldblooded, a demonstration of power for the benefit of victim, onlooker, and perhaps above all the victor himself. (And, of course, such manner of killing saves hauling the corpses to a grave when they can walk there themselves.)

> "Take them alive!" [Jehu] said [of King Ahaziah's kinsmen]. They took them alive and then slaughtered them at the pit of Beth-eked, forty two of them; and he did not spare a single one. (2 Kgs 10:14)

But perhaps the most graphic death of all is reserved for a woman, a foreigner, Jezebel the Phoenician, Ahab's queen.

> Jehu went on to Jezreel. When Jezebel heard of it, she painted her eyes with kohl and dressed her hair, and she looked out of the window. As Jehu entered the gate, she called out, "Is all well, Zimri, murderer of your master?" He looked up toward the window and said, "Who is on my side, who?" And two or three eunuchs leaned out toward him. "Throw her down," he said. They threw her down; and her blood spattered on the wall and on the horses, and they trampled her.
>
> Then he went inside and ate and drank. And he said, "Attend to that cursed woman and bury her, for she was a king's daughter." So they went to bury her; but all they found of her were the skull, the feet, and the hands. They came back and reported to him; and he said,"It is just as the LORD spoke through His servant Elijah the Tishbite: The dogs shall devour the flesh of Jezebel in the field of Jezreel; and the carcass of Jezebel shall be like dung on the ground, in the field of Jezreel, so that none will be able to say: 'This was Jezebel.'" (2 Kgs 9:30-37, TANAKH)

In all of Kings it is hard to find any deeper hostility than that expressed against this woman. In a story where bodies are little recounted, hers is hurled, splattered, crushed, dismembered, devoured, and turned thereby not to dust but to dung. Even her husband, Ahab, ostensibly the prime enemy of YHWH and the god's prophets, dies a more dignified death, propped up in his chariot as the battle rages and the sun sinks and the blood drains out of him (1 Kgs 22:29-38).

But while the vilest bile is brought up upon the woman, it is not altogether different from that spat upon Ahab. The two are linked in death by the devouring dogs and the apparently equally devouring word of YHWH.

> They buried the king in Samaria, and they flushed out the chariot at the pool of Samaria. Thus the dogs lapped up his blood and the whores bathed [in it], in accordance with the word that the LORD had spoken. (1 Kgs 22:37-38, TANAKH)

What is being said here, obscenely, is that if Jezebel is destined to be "'dog shit'" on the field of Jezreel, Ahab, for his part, will be "dog piss."[2] And there is more. In their deaths the two are also associated with prostitution. As the dogs lap, the prostitutes bathe in the blood of Ahab. As for Jezebel: "How can all be well as long as your mother Jezebel carries on her countless harlotries," Jehu hurls at Joram (2 Kgs 9:22) in justification of his imminent serial killing. Yet even in this linking, the primary object of enmity is made clear. It is not Joram's father Ahab who is invoked to justify killing the son (as, for example, "you continue to walk in the ways of your father, Ahab") but his mother.

Why has the narrator such visceral hostility toward this woman? After all, Ahab was the king, the man with authority, Jezebel merely his wife in a patriarchal monarchy; Joram was the king, Jezebel merely the queen mother. Although scholars have posited considerable institutional power for the queen mother in Israel, their main evidence is precisely this text in question.[3] Is Jezebel the primary object of vilification because she occupied a position of such institutional power, or because from the position that she did have, whether queen or queen mother, she was seen to be a woman of strength? Because she was seen to be a woman acting independently of the king? Because she was seen to be a woman exercising power over the king (21:25)? (In our time, the vilification by some of Hillary Rodham Clinton comes quickly to mind.)

The only other queen in the story to exercise similar power (2 Kgs 11) is Athaliah, daughter of Jezebel and Ahab, queen to King Joram of Judah (as distinct from her blood relative, Joram of Israel), and mother of King Ahaziah of Judah. Isolated as a northerner in Judah by the murders of her northern royal kin (Joram and Jezebel) and her Judean protector, her son (Ahaziah), she responds like her mother Jezebel "with power rather than surrender" (Camp 1992: 104).[4] Taking her cue from YHWH's agent Jehu, who massacres seventy princes in Israel, Athaliah wipes out the remaining males of the Judean royal house, leaving herself in control. Her extraordinary reign is tolerated by the patriarchy for only six years (though six years is at the same time a remarkable time).

Ironically, she is undone by another woman. Jehosheba, daughter of King Joram of Judah—presumably by another wife than Athaliah— and sister of the murdered Ahaziah, had rescued one of the king's sons, a baby called Joash, and had hidden him in the temple with the priest Jehoiada's connivance. At seven years old this male of the lineage of David is plucked out of hiding by Jehoiada and made the ostensible centerpiece of a counter coup. Taken by surprise and overwhelming armed force, Athaliah is promptly and meticulously murdered. ("Let her not be put to death in the House of YHWH," urges the scrupulous Jehoiada, in contrast to the rather less scrupulous

Solomon in a similar situation; 1 Kgs 1:50-53, 2:23-25, 28-34). The story celebrates the elimination of a usurping woman from the sphere of male power. Even the inclusion of Jehosheba's rescue of Joash plays into this patriarchal agenda. To be sure, the woman is presented as a rescuer, a latter-day Pharaoh's daughter. On the other hand, the story sets woman against woman, with the winner shown acting to elevate to power a seven year old boy controlled, as the narrator makes clear, not by his aunt, but by the male priest Jehoiada.

The narrator has previously expressed one reason why Athaliah was unacceptable. She was responsible, the narrator asserts, for Jehoram her husband's straying from the right path (namely, doing "what was evil in YHWH's sight"): "He walked in the ways of the kings of Israel, as the house of Ahab had done, for the daughter of Ahab was his wife" (2 Kgs 8:18). The parallel with Jezebel is striking. In each case the narrator holds the woman ultimately responsible for what her men do. In observing this propensity to shift the blame, Claudia Camp (1992:104-105) notes that Athaliah's rule, "set over against the legitimate succession of Davidic males, even those whose faithlessness would presumably deserve punishment," is rule "by a woman and an alien." Her point is well taken. Adam is busy justifying himself once more: the woman made him do it! And if Athaliah, the northerner, is an alien in the eyes of the (presumably Judean) narrator, how much more so is Jezebel, the Phoenician woman. Who should the narrator, the patriarchal Subject, blame for causing his fellow men to walk in the wrong path, if not that most disturbing of Others, the alien woman?[5]

So why the deep disgust poured out on Jezebel? Because as the quintessential foreign woman of power she is for the patriarchal Subject the quintessential Other, to be feared and blamed.

Our reader might retort that it is nothing so abstruse. Jezebel is despised because she is wicked. And that is how she has been characterized in subsequent interpretive tradition, not least in the Apocalypse of John (the Book of Revelation; see Pippin 1992). Not without reason has her name become a byword for an evil woman. But let us look a little more closely at her wickedness. What is so special about it?

The narrator, we might say, charges Jezebel basically on two counts. First, she is responsible for promoting the worship of Baal and Asherah (Astarte) and persecuting the prophets of YHWH (cf. 2 Kgs 18:3-5, 19; 19:1-2); second, she is responsible for taking Naboth's vineyard and having him judicially murdered (1 Kgs 21). Camp (1992:103), however, enters an interesting plea on her behalf:

It is unlikely that [Jezebel's] polytheistic religion would have motivated her to eliminate the prophets of Yahweh unless these presented a political threat. If anything, the reverse would have been the case: the exclusivistic nature of prophetic Yahwism might have induced some of its adherents to adopt a crusade mentality against worshipers of other deities. Given the activity of prophets of Yahweh in the political arena—anointing kings and promoting coups—Jezebel's concerns were probably not first and foremost religious. As a Phoenician princess, moreover, she was accustomed to royal prerogative and unused to the democratic impulse in Israelite culture that regarded land as a gift given to each Israelite family by Yahweh, rather than at the behest of the king. Thus her brutal response to Naboth's refusal to sell his vineyard [to the king] may be understood from her point of view as an appropriate royal response to insubordination, in contrast to Ahab's unconscionable weakness as a leader [—Ahab simply sulks when refused].

As concerns the vineyard episode, moreover, we might usefully compare it to an episode in the story of David, the narrator's model king, the king for whose sake YHWH is said repeatedly to have deferred punishment of his people and their kings (cf. 1 Kgs 11:12-13; 15:3-5; 2 Kgs 8:18-19; 18:3-4; 20:5-6). David takes for himself Bathsheba, the wife of Uriah the Hittite, while Uriah is out fighting David's wars. And when she is pregnant he arranges, by proxy, to have him murdered in a manner that disguises the murder. Jezebel, offended at Naboth's refusal to sell to the king a field adjacent to the palace, arranges, by proxy, to have him murdered in a manner that disguises the murder, and takes for her husband the field. YHWH's response to David's crime is to kill not David but Bathsheba's baby, to bequeath rape and murder on David's other children, but to bless the subsequent addition of Bathsheba to the king's harem by "loving" Solomon, her next child by David (2 Sam 12:24-25), and sustaining him as successor to the throne (cf. 1 Kgs 4:5-14). If YHWH's response to Jezebel's crime is to have her hurled from a window and torn to pieces by dogs, is that not a little disproportionate in relation to the divine response to David?

Why is King David's body held inviolate, the foreign queen's so obscenely violated? *Both* had violated the bodies of others. Or does the difference lie not in the murders but in the stealing? In patriarchal Israel, is the crime of taking a man's land greater than that of taking his wife? But that is a difficult question to answer. Perhaps it is safer to assume that the story of Naboth is really only a feint. The narrator's real concern is bound up with the question of religious apostasy.

When we back up and look at Kings as a whole, it would seem on the surface that the book is about the consolidation of monarchy and nation under David and Solomon, its division and divisions under subsequent kings, its coups, civil and external wars, and its destruction at the hands of the Assyrians and Babylonians. Ostensibly its theme could be said to be the political ramifications of religious apostasy: the people break their promise of allegiance to YHWH their god, so YHWH breaks his promise to sustain them as a nation and finally casts them off. This theological understanding of the nation's political story is based, as we have already seen earlier in the Exodus law, for example, on the root metaphor of covenant as marriage: the relationship between YHWH and Israel is understood as that between a patriarchal husband and his wife. The book's indictment of the people, as voiced by the narrator directly and by certain prophets as recounted by the narrator, is fundamentally that the people and their kings broke their marriage bond: like married women "whoring around" they worshipped gods other than their true god YHWH and at other places than the right one (cf. 1 Kgs 15:22-24; 21:25-26; 2 Kgs 17:7-17; 21:2-9). Perhaps the ultimate betrayal, on this view, is the worship of Baal (usually characterized by the narrator, probably falsely, as foreign), precisely because Baal means "husband/owner" and woman Israel can have only one husband/owner and that is YHWH, though for her to lust after female Asherah or other goddesses is probably almost as disturbing both for its sexual implications and for its ascription of authority to the female.

This construction of Yahwistic monotheism in terms of patriarchal marriage has profound social implications. Monotheism becomes the ultimate symbolic expression of and justification for men's control of women, women's bodies, and especially women's sexuality. By the same token, polytheism such as Jezebel's cannot be tolerated by the patriarchal Subject because it represents the ultimate symbolic threat to his exclusive control. In other words the narrator's theological assertions about the divine-human relationship are at the same time assertions about the social relationship between men and women. It is no accident that the climax of the story of Jezebel, the promoter of Baal worship, centers on the disposal of her body.

The introduction of the metaphor of whoring into the account, in Jehu's speech to Joram, adds credence to this understanding. "What peace can there be, so long as the many whoredoms and sorceries of your mother Jezebel continue?" (2 Kgs 9:22, NEB) The Hebrew root *znh* that appears in the word translated "whoredom" or "harlotry" also appears in the noun meaning "prostitute" or "whore," and in the verb meaning "to prostitute (oneself)," "play the harlot," "whore [after]." As Phyllis Bird (1989) has shown, these words are used broadly of illicit sexual activity, not simply of prostitution (sex for money) as such. Since nowhere in the story is there any suggestion that Jezebel was literally engaging in prostitution or illicit sex, and given the coupling of "harlotry" with "sorcery," it is clear that Jehu is speaking metaphorically of religious deviance. Yet there we have it: the strong, independent woman, worshipper of (male) Baal and (female) Asherah, the woman who is clearly her husband's master, the woman who is politically one of the two most powerful women and certainly the most powerful foreign woman in the whole of Israel's story from Genesis through Kings—this woman is labelled "whore." And patriarchal tradition has not been slow to understand the connection between the message of theological exclusivism and that of sexual control here. Jezebel in mainstream Jewish and Christian tradition *is* a whore (see Pippin 1992).

Of course there is a rather profound irony in the patriarchal espousal of the whoring metaphor to express religious apostasy. For female prostitutes as a class constitute a serious challenge to the patriarchal control of women's bodies. On the one hand, they embody the principle of control, since they exist to serve men's sexual needs. On the other hand, subversively, they represent the possibility of a woman controlling her own sexuality, her own body. Equally subversively, they also suggest the possibility of women having economic independence. Thus patriarchy must always remain ambivalent about prostitution, both tolerating it and at the same time delegitimizing it. Prostitutes are living witnesses to patriarchal hypocrisy.

Whoring, playing the harlot, is what women do. Therein, too, lies an irony. In a patriarchy like that of ancient Israel women had little opportunity, given the inclination, to initiate illicit sexual relationships. And if they were to do so and be discovered, the penalties were severe. The notion that Israel's proclivity to apostasy was somehow commensurate with Israelite women's proclivity to "whore around" is clearly a male fantasy, indulged in elsewhere by Jeremiah, Hosea and, in its sickest form, Ezekiel. The metaphor of whoring displaces onto women a male problem with the patriarchal system of sexual control. Put simply, it shifts the blame for men's desire for, and practice of, illicit sex (in a world where men define what is licit), including sex with prostitutes, onto women.

On the other hand, when the whoring metaphor is deployed in the rhetoric of religious apostasy, it is plainly Israel, as a nation of men, who are "playing the harlot" and so playing the woman. That rhetorical turn is unavoidable if the marriage metaphor is to be retained, and husband YHWH is not to be depicted as wife YHWH.

Thus the patriarchal propagandist turns Israel into a nation of whoring women. Again the absurdity of this picture is apparent. In a patriarchy it is not generally women who venture out, like ancestor Judah, in search of wayside sex. Nor in a patriarchy is it generally women who define a nation's religious practices. In both cases they are more likely to be found on the margins, waiting for the searching male or quietly observing the customs of their mothers and grandmothers.

In short, the whoring metaphor is a mechanism by which patriarchy attempts to shift blame and bolster male control—religious, political and sexual. Religious apostasy is really the fault of women. Disaster is the inevitable concomitant of women in political power. Women who exercise sexual freedom must be destroyed. Jezebel caused Ahab and Israel to desert YHWH. Chaos attended her reign. Her "whoring" ended in the only way possible, namely with the eradication of her wayward body (or, to be more exact, the sexually marked part of her).

We have come back to Jezebel's body. We can read it variously. Her body is apostate religion which will be consumed before YHWH's avenging agent and left with its symbols of power—head, hands, and feet—lying lifeless and disjointed. Her body is the body politic, Israel, before long to be devoured and almost wholly dissipated by an Assyrian Jehu. Her body is the body of a powerful and independent woman—which cannot be, so it must be unmade, in mocking fashion, leaving its symbols of power, in bizarre independence, without a woman's torso to signal unambiguously that they are a woman's.

Jezebel's body is broken and eaten. Ahab's blood is shed and drunk. A different kind of eucharist? Perhaps this affinity to Jesus is another reason why John in his Apocalypse found the whore Jezebel so disturbing. The dogs, in pursuance of YHWH's prophecy, eat and drink. But so does Jehu. After witnessing the queen's death, the narrator tells us, "he went in and ate and drank" (2 Kgs 9:34). Is Jehu any other than one of YHWH's dogs? Certainly he is no different than any other betrayer of his master, as Jezebel sarcastically observed: "Is all well, Zimri, murderer of your master!?" (9:31). What makes betrayal and murder palatable? That you do it in the name of God? Reading Jezebel's devoured body seems to disgorge much that we might imagine the narrator would rather have kept hidden.

When we conceive of Jehu as a devourer of human flesh we put him in the company of two women whose story is narrated only a few chapters earlier within a story of the king of Israel and the prophet Elisha (2 Kgs 6:24–7:2). Under siege, Samaria was suffering from a great famine. As the king was walking along the wall a woman cried to him for help. It transpires that another woman had said to her, "Give up your son and we will eat him today; and tomorrow we'll eat my son." "So we cooked my son," continues the women to the king, "and we ate him." The next day she had said to the other woman, "Give up your son and let's eat him," but the woman had hidden the boy.

At this point the narrator shifts focus to the king and his interaction with "the people" and with Elisha. The woman is left behind and her story hangs there on the surface as merely an illustration of the depth of the famine. Under the surface, however, is another message. Under pressure, women will even stoop to eating their children. This is indeed, like the story of Jezebel's death, a disgusting story. But what is most disgusting is not the recounting of cannibalism but the nonchalant way the narrator slips it in—no doubt to remind us of the Mosaic prophecy concerning what would befall a wayward people (Deut 28:53-57)—and moves to the *important* matter, the conflict between prophet and king. It is simply a rhetorical allusion, with more than a touch of graphic color, to be exploited and discarded. Yet the premise of this narrative element is not one so easily bypassed.

While Jehu is not in fact a cannibal, we have no difficulty in recognizing him in his crusading zeal as truly a consumer of human flesh. Such carnivores are all too common. What we do not recognize are the mothers who so matter-of-factly actually eat their children. Nor does the picture of a woman appealing to a king to help her force another woman to produce her son so they can eat him look anything but absurd. This narrator has again become seriously unreliable. It is hard to imagine any woman recounting this story in this way, let alone a mother. We are back in the realm of male fantasy and it is a deeply disturbing fantasy. What male anger against women lies behind this story? What is being displaced onto women here? Is it a patriarchal male's resentment of a mother's bond with her son? Or some deeper sickness?

The story has an analogue early in 1 Kgs 3:16-28, in the famous story known as "The Judgment of Solomon." Here the women are two prostitutes, both of whom come before the king to appeal for help. Both live together and have given birth to baby boys, one of whom has died. The one, however, claims that the other suffocated her own child and switched him for the live one. The other denies it. The king in his infinite wisdom proposes to divide the living boy between the two of them. The real mother pleads for the boy's life and tells the king to give him to her rival; the false mother urges the king to go ahead: "He shall be neither yours nor mine; cut him in two!" And so the king discerns the truth and awards the child to the true mother. It is a much feted story which, like that about the cannibal mothers, belies reality. The woman prostitute who cries, "Cut him in two!" is a no more credible creation than the mother who proposes, "Let's eat him!" There are remarkably few stories of women in the books of Kings. What trauma has its patriarchal Subject endured that he should find it necessary to bring these misogynist texts to expression?

Misogyny also characterizes another part of the Solomon story, namely its end, in 1 Kings 11, though in this case we are back with a more familiar theme, the apostate charms of foreign women. Solomon's marriage to Pharaoh's daughter receives brief attention from the narrator, who details the palace Solomon built for her and her entry into it (3:1; 7:8; 9:24). In the end, however, she joins the crowd:

> King Solomon loved many foreign women as well as Pharaoh's daughter—Moabite, Ammonite, Edomite, Phoenician, and Hittite women, from the nations of which YHWH had said . . . "You shall not be joined to them, nor they to you; for they will surely turn your heart away to follow their gods." Such Solomon clung to and loved. He had 700 royal wives and 300 concubines; and his wives turned his heart away. In his old age, his wives turned away Solomon's heart after other gods . . . Solomon followed Ashtoreth the goddess of the Phoenicians, and Milcom the abomination of the Ammonites. Solomon did what was evil in the sight of YHWH and was not wholly loyal to YHWH like his father David. At that time, Solomon built a shrine for Chemosh the abomination of Moab on the hill near Jerusalem, and one for Molech the abomination of the Ammonites. And he did the same for all his foreign wives who offered incense and sacrificed to their gods. (1 Kgs 11:1-8)

What extravagant apostasy! Beside this promulgation of foreign deities, Jezebel's effort looks meager indeed. A mere two "abominations" for her as opposed to the five named and perhaps hundreds more unnamed for Solomon. And all those shrines! It must have been hard for a faithful YHWH-only worshiper to take a walk without encountering one and being converted. And this is not to speak of that other small matter, the blatant breaking of the law against a king multiplying wives for himself, "lest his heart go astray" (Deut 17:17). Not that our narrator lets all this pass without relating some word of condemnation. On the contrary, we are informed in no uncertain terms of YHWH's anger at Solomon's turning away from him, from "YHWH, the god of Israel, who had appeared to him twice and had commanded him [i.e., personally] on this matter" (1 Kgs 11:9-10). And the punishment? Is Solomon to be hurled from the balcony of his fabulous palace of gold and silver ("nor shall he accumulate gold and silver to excess" [Deut 17:17; cf.1 Kings 10]), to be trampled by some of his 12,000 horses ("he shall not keep many horses or send to Egypt to multiply his horses" [Deut 17:16; cf. 1 Kgs 10:26-29]), and his body torn asunder by the dogs?[6] No, not exactly.

> And YHWH said to Solomon, "Because you are guilty of this—you have not kept my covenant and the laws which I enjoined upon you—I will tear the kingdom away from you and I will give it to one of your servants." (1 Kgs 11:11)

So there is to be some tearing, but not of Solomon's body. The body politic, his kingly possession, will be torn from him. Though not exactly. Unlike Jezebel, Solomon has a father to whom YHWH is partial.

> But, for the sake of your father David, I will not do it in your lifetime; I will tear it away from your son. (1 Kgs 11:12)

But then again, not exactly. There is David, and there is Jerusalem. Somehow Jezebel's Samaria could never quite measure up to Solomon's Jerusalem.

> However, I will not tear away the whole kingdom; I will give your son one tribe, for the sake of my servant David and for the sake of Jerusalem which I have chosen. (1 Kgs 11:13)

So Jezebel was torn apart, was devoured, was excrement on the field. And Solomon? He "slept with his fathers and was buried in the city of his father David" (1 Kgs 11:42). But then Jezebel had the wrong father and ruled in the wrong city. And she was a woman, a foreign woman.

As a woman, a foreign woman, Jezebel embodies apostasy. Blame comes to rest on her, has nowhere else to go. Solomon is a man, an Israelite man, son of a favorite man, David. In his case the narrator makes it clear where the true blame lies, with all those women, those foreign women, who caused him to go astray. The redundancy of this message in 1 Kgs 11:1-8 is striking. The point is reiterated with almost every verse, lest we miss it. Apostasy was not really Solomon's fault. The women made him do it.

The foreign woman is the quintessential Other, to be feared and blamed—or tamed. Jezebel is untameable. Hence her fate. Tamed, the foreign woman may bring not bane but blessing. Thus, Rahab. When the Other affirms the Subject's supremacy, when the Other subjugates herself to the Subject, that is affirmation and subjugation beyond measure. The Queen of Sheba plays out this role for Solomon, for YHWH his patron, and for the patriarchal reader (1 Kgs 10:1-13). The narrator tells us that when she heard of the fame of Solomon (fame due to YHWH) she came to test him with hard questions. To impress him with her own stature she brings not only her questions but a great retinue and a caravan laden with precious things. (It would appear that wealth and wisdom are correlates.)

> When the Queen of Sheba had observed all the wisdom of Solomon, the house that he had built, the food of his table, the seating of his officials, and the attendance of his servants, their clothing, his valets, and his burnt offering that he offered in the house of YHWH, there was no more spirit in her. (1 Kgs 10:4-5, cf. NRSV)

She was flabbergasted. "The spirit went out of her." All that remained to her was to confess her previous disbelief at the reports about Solomon, how totally impressed and overwhelmed she was now at seeing for herself the man's wisdom and prosperity, to extol the happiness of his wives (LXX) and servants, bless YHWH the god of Israel who had obviously delighted in Solomon, and give this already stupendously wealthy king even more gold, spices and precious stones. For his part, Solomon graciously condescends to grant the Queen of Sheba "her every expressed desire, apart from what he gave her according to Solomon's [regular] royal hospitality." Without further comment, we are told, she turned and went "to her own land" with her servants (1 Kgs 10:13).

Whether her every desire included sexual desires is hardly transparent, though Ethiopic and Rabbinic tradition is quite clear that it did. And of course that would round out the patriarchal picture splendidly. In his gracious response to her acknowledgment of his unsurpassability, the supremely wise and rich king granted her not only the regular royal bounty (*yad*, meaning "hand," "power/potency," and in at least one other case [Isa 57:8], "phallus"), such as he bestowed as a matter of course, no doubt, on his seven hundred wives and three hundred concubines, but he favored her in addition with meeting her every sexual desire. Naturally she had many, where he was concerned, and he, out of his supreme potency, ably met every one. Or so the narrator might wish to have us believe.

Read thus, in patriarchal fashion, this foreign queen serves to bolster the potency of the royal Israelite male over against the alien female who threatens to be his equal, or even overpower him. Suitably, she turns and goes to her own land, tamed, safely at a distance. In the vulgar male ritual of proving potency—"my little finger is thicker than my father's cock," as Rehoboam's young advisors crudely suggest he might put it to some insubordinate citizens (1 Kgs 12:10; English translations usually avoid the crudity) —the Queen of Sheba's function is to reassure the male Subject that his potency is like his great freestanding pillars rearing up in the

vestibule of the temple, their heads crowned with lilies and two
hundred pomegranates (1 Kgs 7:15-22; cf. the sexual symbolism of
Song of Songs).[7]

Another reading of the Queen of Sheba might see her, however,
as a woman of great intellect, remarkable independence, and liberal
wealth. Her very journey, a pursuit of wisdom, is a symbol of her
freedom in a world that we have seen to be so systemically controlling of women. She is a woman of power with her own place (land)
in the world. Intrigued by reports of Solomon's wisdom and splen-
dor, and perhaps shrewdly guessing what she might find, she makes
sure she brings not only her questions but an abundance of costly
gifts. And true to expectation she finds an incredibly pretentious
know-all: "Solomon answers for all her questions; there was nothing
that the king did not know, [nothing] to which he could not give her
an answer" (1 Kgs 10:3). Not only does he prove incapable of doubt-
ing his invincible intellect or imagining that his unfailing pontifica-
tion might be less than dazzling to his guest, he has a compulsive
need to show off (to an exceedingly wealthy woman) the trappings
of his own riches, right down to the brocade on the servants tunics
and the pattern of the golden goblets:

> . . . the palace he had built, the fare of his table, the seating of his
> courtiers, the service and attire of his attendants, and his wine service
> and . . . . (1 Kgs 10:4-5, TANAKH)

And just when she thinks she is about to be released from his interminable guided tour, he insists that she will absolutely want to see
something else—"the burnt offerings that he offered at the House of
YHWH" (vs. 5).

> And she was left breathless, winded! (cf. TANAKH)

Little wonder, we might think. And what remains to be done but for
her to tell the man what he wants to hear—that he is incredibly
brilliant, and amazingly wealthy, and that the wine goblets really
leave hers completely in the shade. (Oh, and the oxen for the burnt
offering would win a prize at any show; incomparable quality,
incomparable, no doubt about it.) Beaming, gratified, he responds by
giving her whatever she wants. And then she goes home.

What does she want? Certainly not sex with this bore. Perhaps
she asked for a little (or just enough to get the value of her gifts
back) and was content to enjoy the trip back home, swapping anec-
dotes of her visit with her companions to gusts of laughter or incredu-
lous snickers. Or perhaps she signed the lucrative trade deal she was
looking for, on the best possible terms for herself, of course, since
the great Solomon was so convinced of his mastery of this woman

that it never crossed his mind to give the trade matter a second thought, let alone read the fine print.

Our double reading suggests that this text, like so many others, sits on an interpretive knife edge. Whether it was intended to celebrate Solomon we cannot be certain. And if a patriarchal narrator so intended it, with a patriarchal reader in mind (terms he would doubtless not have recognized), he could not suppress the possibility of our reading counter-meanings—meanings perhaps precisely not intended, and precisely, therefore, of particular interest. For they represent in our time, for women and men struggling to reconceive our relationships in equity, the liberating meaning of the scripture.

We have not exhausted the ambiguity regarding foreign women in Kings. As the story of Solomon's reign comes to a close, in fact, immediately after the account of his many wives and apostasies, we learn of adversaries raised against him by YHWH, including a certain Hadad of the Edomite royal family (1 Kgs 11:14-22). Hadad and a few of his father's servants survived a genocidal expedition by Joab, David's general. As Joab and his army killed off all the males in Edom, these servants escaped with the boy to Egypt, where Pharaoh gave him a house, assigned him a food allowance, and granted him an estate. Taking a liking to him as he grew up, the king gave him the sister of his wife, Queen Tahpenes, to be his wife. In due course the queen's sister bore him a son who was weaned by Tahpenes in the palace and grew up among Pharaoh's sons. Yet eventually, on David's death, Hadad asked leave to return to his own country, where he became a thorn in the flesh for Solomon.

The parallels between this story and that of the raising of Moses are obvious. But how are we to understand the Egyptian queen and her sister? Are we to understand them to be further embodiments of the threat of foreign women to Israel's peace and well-being? Or should we view them with approbation, as saviors and nurturers like Pharaoh's daughter in Exodus? Pharaoh's daughter undermines any inclination by an interpreter to make absolute the significance of the foreign woman. Or, to put it another way, Pharaoh's daughter undermines the narrator's attempt to persuade us that the royal foreign woman is some kind of absolute threat. Patriarchal Israel could not have come into being without Pharaoh's daughter! So could it be that Jezebel, daughter of King Ethbaal of the Phoenicians, was not such a threat after all?

The narrator's anxiety about foreign women seems to dissipate somewhat with a change in social class. He seems readier to view with equanimity the widow of Sidonian Zarephath (1 Kgs 17:8-24).

In this story, the prophet Elijah is sent by YHWH to Zarephath during a famine to find food: "I have commanded a widow there to feed you." He meets a widow at the entrance gathering wood. He calls out to her, "Please bring me a little water in a pitcher to drink." As she goes to fetch it he calls out further: "Please bring along a piece of bread for me" (TANAKH). At this point the woman is moved to express her exasperation. Here is this man coming along and demanding "bring this" and "bring that," and has the gall to demand food in a famine! "As the Lord your God lives," she snaps back, "I have nothing baked, nothing but a handful of flour in a jar and a little oil in a jug. I am just gathering a couple of sticks, so that I can go home and prepare it for me and my son." And then with bitterness, or perhaps a sinking hopelessness: "We shall eat it and then we shall die!" No doubt it has dawned on Elijah by this point that YHWH has failed to make in advance the arrangements for his hospitality. Yet, nothing daunted, he immediately urges her to "fear not!" but to go ahead and do what he has demanded. His only compromise is to instruct her to make a small cake for him first, and afterwards to use what is left for her son and herself. It is easy to read a touch of deflating humor here aimed at the rather self-important prophet (the man who, for example, would later insist that he alone was left of the prophets of YHWH, when Obadiah for one had risked his life saving one hundred others [1 Kgs 18:1-19; 19:1-18]). On the other hand, he has another oracle to hand, promising that the jar of flour and jug of oil will never run out until the rains come. And so it proves. It is hard to shrug off this man.

After some time the woman's son falls ill and appears to expire. The woman confronts Elijah, accusing him of causing the calamity. She understands it to be punishment for some past sin of hers, "recalled" by the man of God's presence. Dismayed by the unexpected complication, Elijah presses YHWH to get him off the hook: "Will you bring calamity upon this widow—whose guest I am!—and let her son die?" (cf. TANAKH). And so Elijah is able to bring the child down to the woman and say, "See, your son is alive!" To which the woman responds by celebrating, not YHWH, but the prophet: "Now I know that you are a man of God and that the word of YHWH is truly in your mouth." In short, both characters seem to be presented with sympathy though not without a touch of irony and a sense of human limitations.

In a second account of a prophet being challenged to revive a young boy, Elijah's successor Elisha deals with a well-to-do woman of Shunem in Northern Israel (2 Kgs 4:8-38; 8:1-6). Here, too, a positive reading of the woman involved emerges relatively easily.

Noticeably more than in the account of the woman of Zarephath, this Israelite woman may be read as a woman of initiative and independence, more than a match for a sometimes inept prophet (cf. Shields 1993).

Passing through Shunem (north of Jezreel) one day, Elisha is invited in for a meal by a wealthy woman (*'ishshah g^{e}dolah*). And so, too, on subsequent occasions, to the point where the woman proposes to her husband that—since she is sure it is a holy man who is visiting—they should add a small upper chamber to their house and furnish it suitably so that he could stay there whenever he comes to them. One day, while lying down in the upper room, Elisha instructs his servant, Gehazi, to summon the Shunammite woman.

> He [Gehazi] called her and she stood before him [Gehazi or Elisha?]. He [Elisha] said to him [Gehazi], "Please say to her, 'Look, you have gone to all this trouble for us; what can be done for you? Would you like a word spoken on your behalf to the king or the army commander?'" But she said, "I live among my own people."
>
> He [Elisha] said, "Then what can be done for her?" So Gehazi said, "Well, she has no son, and her husband is old." "Call her," he [Elisha] said. So he [Gehazi] called her and she stood in the entrance. And Elisha said, "At this season next year you will be embracing a son." But she said, "Please, my lord, man of God, do not lie to your maidservant!"
>
> And the woman conceived and bore a son at the same season the next year, as Elisha had spoken to her. (4:12-17)

Apart from tantalizing ambiguities regarding who is the male subject, at least on a first reading, there is a curious gap in the text. After her first response, does she leave the men to their discussion, unremarked by either them or the narrator, in order then to be called back a second time? Or does she leave after their discussion? Matching the rhetorical gap is a physical gap between her and Elisha. Only with his last sentence predicting the child does he address her directly and even then he fails, as elsewhere, to use her name. She is only ever "the Shunammite woman" to Elisha and narrator alike. (By the same token Elisha is only ever the "man of God" to the woman.) Is the narrator anxious to signal distance between the Elisha and the woman, so as to disarm the inevitable gossips? So who *was* the father of this child? The old and "past it" husband? Or could it just be the itinerant holy man who came to stay so often, for whom she had set up, moreover, his own private room? Was the distance between them just a cover? Alternatively there was always Gehazi to consider. Just think about it, was he not the one who came up with the suggestion about the baby? Or maybe the husband was not past it after all, or perhaps it was simply a miracle. Undoubtedly it kept the neighbors talking for quite some time.

The woman's independence, if not pride, is marked in her first response. She does not need favors from high places, thank you. She can find what she needs among her own class. On the other hand, we may surely be forgiven if we suspect that Elisha is doing a little name dropping as the words "king" and "general" roll off his tongue. Perhaps it has the desired effect, since the woman addresses him as "my lord" and herself as "your maidservant." At the same time—unless the speech is a cover for Gehazi's benefit—her servility merely softens a strong retort: "Do not lie . . . !"

If Elisha's prediction is truly an inspired piece of miracle making, then it belongs with a genre. Even when babies (which is to say, sons) are the product of miraculous intervention, they are generally announced/bequeathed by a male who rarely asks the prospective mother if this is a condition she is actively seeking. Certainly Elisha never pauses to wonder whether the woman might want a child, let alone to ask her. Elisha knows, as all men know, that women want to be mothers of sons more than anything else in the world.

Like Elijah with the widow of Zarephath, however, Elisha is faced with an embarrassing complication. He may be in charge of the staff of life, but can he deal so facilely with death? One day the boy, grown now, goes out to his father (the woman's husband) in the field and cries out about his head. The father tells a servant to carry him to his mother. In her lap the boy dies. The woman puts him on the bed of "the man of God" (her point of view) and goes out, closing the door behind her. She summons her husband and insists that he send her a servant and an ass, so that she can "hurry to the man of God and be back." She says nothing about the boy—nor does the father ask about him. Rather he wants to know why she needs to be going to Elisha when it is not a holy day. (Is he just a little suspicious, too?) "Good-bye!" (*shalom*), she says.

She makes haste. "Urge [the beast] on!" she commands the servant. "Don't slow the pace for me unless I tell you." Spying her from a distance, the man of God recognizes her and sends Gehazi to ask how she, her husband, and her child are doing. Does she have *shalom*? Does her husband have *shalom*? Does her son have *shalom*? To which she replies, "*shalom*!"

But when she reaches the man of God and grasps his feet, he realizes belatedly that things are far from *shalom*. So when Gehazi tries to shake her loose (what does this woman think she's doing!?), the prophet tries to recover some lost ground. Indignantly he points out what ought to have been obvious to the oblivious Gehazi—the woman is in bitter distress—and then, perhaps in a peeved tone, mutters about why he did not know this fact in the first place: "and

YHWH has hidden it from me and not told me." This is too much for the woman. What gall for the man of God to complain in front of her about being kept in the dark. She is the one with a right to resent having things decided for her without her knowledge. She directs her remarks to Elisha but implicitly also to his master, YHWH. "Did I ask my lord for a son? Didn't I say, 'Don't lie to me!'"

Well Elisha may be a somewhat hit-or-miss prophet but, he is not always slow to draw the right conclusion. He realizes that the son is dead. Immediately he gives his staff to Gehazi and dispatches him as a matter of great urgency to set the matter right. Gehazi is to place Elisha's staff on the boy's face. Once again he is keeping his distance. Why? Does he think the matter is so trivial that his servant's services will suffice? Is he avoiding meeting the husband? Does he have no confidence in his own ability to do anything to help? Whatever the case, the woman will not accept being fobbed off by the master with the servant: "As YHWH lives and as you live, I will not leave you!" He is defeated. "So he arose and followed her."

Ahead of them, Gehazi achieves no results with the staff. Elisha shuts himself in with the boy, prays, and then gets to work (4:34-35):

> Then he got up [on the bed] and lay down on the child, mouth to mouth, eyes to eyes, palm to palm. And as he crouched upon him the child's flesh warmed. He got down and walked here and there in the room. Then he got up and crouched upon him. The boy sneezed seven times, and the boy opened his eyes.

Elisha calls Gehazi and, in a striking gesture of recovered authority, instructs him to "Call this Shunammite woman!" He does so (4:36-37).

> When she came to him, he said, "Pick up your son." She came and fell at his feet and bowed to the ground. Then she picked up her son and left.

Her silence is palpable.

There is a coda to this story (2 Kgs 8:1-6). It turns out that Elisha subsequently told the woman that she must go away with her household and sojourn wherever she could, because YHWH was starting a seven-year famine. So she did "according to the word of the man of God" and lived in Philistia for seven years. On her return, however, she discovered that her house and land had been taken, an eventuality obviously not anticipated by the holy man. The ironic upshot is that we next find her appealing to the king, of all people, for the return of her property. ("I live among my own people," is what she had proudly said before Elisha had started managing her life.) Now, as providence would have it, the king was having a conversation with Gehazi, wanting to know about "all the great things that Elisha has done." And, of course, Gehazi was majoring on the story of how

Elisha had brought a dead person to life, when lo and behold, along comes the very woman whose son Elisha had brought to life, appealing to the king for her house and land. Gehazi does not miss a beat. "My lord king," he announces, as though orchestrating his own modest little miracle, "here is the woman, and here is her son whom Elisha brought to life." Given the chance to confirm the story at first hand the king does just that and then appoints an official specially for the woman in order to see that her property is restored, plus "all the revenue of the fields from the day that she left the land until now."

This punch line may prompt ruminations. What revenue? Does the king not know there has been a famine? Or did the seven years see less of a famine than the man of God predicted? After all, he did not always get it right! Yet there he is, getting it right anyway—the woman ends up not losing her livelihood but gaining instead seven years income from someone else's work.

All she has lost is her proud independence. She has become the creature of the king, the holy man, and . . . Gehazi.

So here we have her, the "middle-class" woman, commanding her husband and household, sympathetically portrayed, yet gently but firmly put in her place—made into a mother who owes her continuing existence as a woman of means ultimately to the beneficence of men. Our narrator seems torn, attracted to her strength, yet unable to contemplate with equanimity female strength unfettered by male dispensation. Not that he promotes an especially flattering view of the holy man. On the contrary, we might reasonably suspect that he views prophets, like kings, with mixed feelings. Prophets are necessary checks to kings, and both are necessary for the maintenance of the people who really sustain the life of the nation, the landed gentry, the "people of the land" ('am ha'arets).

The Subject of the law, the male head of household, is the Subject of the narratives. With the woman of Shunem, he comes as close as anywhere in Genesis-Kings to risking his systemic boundaries. In celebrating her strength, however qualified, he risks celebrating the strength of the woman he knows best, namely his wife, and his neighbor's wife. In Jezebel's fall from the upper story, the bourgeois Subject celebrates metaphorically the fate of the powerful upper-class woman (cf. García-Treto 1992). Gazing through the lattice of an upper story window, Queen Michal, too, came before a fall, as did the mother of General Sisera. (How the mighty are fallen, indeed!) The woman of Shunem, in contrast, continues to build a life for the future. Still, while the woman of the gentry may be constructed in the narrative sympathetically as a woman of (limited) power, she hardly subverts the patriarchal paradigm. On the contrary, she represents the very compromise that allows patriarchy to maintain itself as the dominant system. Do women have no power in Israelite society? Are women *really* subordinate? Why, not at all, says the patriarchal Subject indignantly, they have all sorts of power. Just look at the Shunammite woman![8]

But the Shunammite woman is not our narrator's primary interest. Jezebel, the painted woman who looks through the window, is perhaps Ishtar-Astarte, who appears in Babylon as "Kilili of the window," or in Cyprus as Aphrodite *parakuptousa*, "who gazes through [the window]."[9] She is the lover goddess who seduces Israel to unfaithfulness. Her destruction looks forward to 2 Kings 17 and the account of (northern) Israel's deportation for the supreme sin of apostasy. Beyond that, the dispersal of her body portends the destruction of Judah in 2 Kings 24–25. YHWH, announces the narrator, brought disaster upon Israel and Judah (17:7-20).

> This came about because the people of Israel sinned against YHWH their god, who brought them up out of the land of Egypt from under the power of Pharaoh . . . They worshiped other gods and followed the customs of the nations whom YHWH drove out . . . and in the customs that the kings of Israel introduced. The people of Israel secretly did things that were not right against YHWH their god. They built for themselves shrines in all their cities . . . they set up for themselves pillars and Asherahs on every high hill and under every green tree; and they offered sacrifices there, at all the shrines . . . They did evil things, provoking YHWH to anger. They served idols, of which YHWH had said to them, "You shall not do this."
>
> Yet YHWH warned Israel and Judah by every prophet and every seer . . . But they rejected his customs and his covenant [*berit*] which he had made with their fathers, and the warnings which he gave them, and went after delusion and were deluded . . . They made for themselves cast images of two calves; they made an Asherah, worshiped all the host of heaven, and served Baal. They made their sons and daughters pass through fire [to Molech?], they practiced divination and augury. They sold themselves to do evil in the sight of YHWH, provoking him to anger. So YHWH became incensed with Israel and removed them from his presence; none was left but the tribe of Judah alone.
>
> Nor did Judah keep the commandments of YHWH their god; they walked in the customs that Israel had practiced. So YHWH rejected all the descendants of Israel. He afflicted them and gave them into the hand of plunderers, until he had cast them out from his presence.

Despite the repeated denunciation, specifics of the people's failure are few, and these relate almost exclusively to the general issue of apostasy. In that regard, this summary justification of the fate of the people is in line with what has preceded it and what will follow it. Where the narrator has paused to make judgment, it has not been to take exception to failures of personal or corporate morality, or to crimes of social oppression, or other such contraventions of the laws of Moses, but simply and consistently to denounce the breaking of YHWH's exclusive claim to the religious loyalty of the people and their kings. They prostituted themselves to other gods. And like an outraged husband punishing and divorcing his errant wives, YHWH removed them from his presence.

Even here, where the narrator appears to join his approval to the divine outrage, he cannot entirely refrain from suggesting that the iniquitous rejection of YHWH was in part the fault of others, those "nations" whom YHWH had cleansed from the land, who had infiltrated their seductive ways back among the susceptible people of Israel. Those insidious Jezebels.

And so we reach the inevitable conclusion of the story. The ingested Other must be cast out. Jezebel must be disgorged. But that has become impossible. She has fertilized the fields. Her body has been consumed by generations of Israelites. Her flesh is their flesh. To disgorge Jezebel, Israel must be disgorged. So the Subject narrates, with approval, his own dissipation. Only thus can the fearful, female, alien, Other be truly kept at bay.

The narrator's fascination with his theme of apostasy and divine judgment makes him numb to suffering. The interests of divine husband YHWH's exclusive claim to the women of his human harem ruthlessly overrides all considerations of particular responsibility. The closing pages of the story are full of suppressed voices, in particular the voices of women and children.

Who commits apostasy and who is punished? Jezebel's body is devoured, in graphic detail, before our eyes. Zedekiah's royal sons are put to death before his eyes, before his eyes are themselves put out. Children and wives are pawns in this game: "Your silver and gold are mine, and your most beautiful wives and children are mine," said Benhadad to Ahab (1 Kgs 20:2), articulating one of the regular gambits of the game. Even Elisha could not help weeping (2 Kgs 8:12):

> "Why does my lord weep?" asked Hazael. "Because," he answered, "I know what evil you will do to the people of Israel. You will set their fortresses on fire, you will put their young men to the sword, you will dash their little ones in pieces, and you will rip open their pregnant women."

These male gestures are reciprocal. Men write their politics (like they "cut" their covenants?) on the bodies of women according to a regular script.

> Menahem [king of Israel] subdued Tiphsah and all who were in it and
> its territory; and because it would not open to him, he massacred [its
> people] and ripped open all its pregnant women. (15:16)

In this story of patriarchy from Eden to Exile, who has been in
charge? Who has defined the nation? Who has controlled its institutions? When we can count on the fingers of one hand the royal
women who dare to exercise public political power in our story,
when the woman of Shunem stretches the limits of approved power
in the social world of the monarchy, what are we to say about the
responsibility of women for this apostasy that so stirs to vengeance
the narrator's god? When we search for the details of their crime in
the details of the narratives of Kings we are likely to be disappointed.
(Though some women apparently wove coverings for Asherah in
proximity to the cubicles of the sacred men [temple "prostitutes"?] in
the House of YHWH [23:7]!). And what of the responsibility of the
children? The babies whose blood, like Jezebel's, splattered walls; the
boys mutilated for service as eunuchs in the court of the Babylonian
king (cf. 20:18); the little girls raped and their throats slit, or sold as
slaves or concubines to have their bodies pillaged by strange men; or
even the lucky ones, torn from their parents, who found a life of
sorts in servitude to a hospitable family—like Naaman's wife's maid
(5:2-3), perhaps?

Perhaps the most vehemently denounced king of Judah, and
certainly the most abhorred in the closing chapters of 2 Kings, is
Manasseh, whose cultic deviations provoke YHWH finally to bring
matters to a head (21:11-15):

> Because King Manasseh has done these abhorrent things, has done
> things more evil than all that the Amorites did before his time, and
> because he led Judah to sin with his idols . . . I will bring upon Jerusa-
> lem and Judah such evil that the ears of everyone who hears of it will
> tingle . . . I will wipe Jerusalem clean as one wipes a dish, wiping it and
> turning it upside down. I will cast off the remnant of my heritage and
> give them into the power of their enemies. They shall be plunder and
> prey to all their enemies, because they have done what is evil in my
> sight and have provoked me to anger . . .

Then follows a final, damning comment, a rare condemnation of killing (21:16):

> Moreover, Manasseh shed very much innocent blood, until he had filled
> Jerusalem from one end to another—besides the sin that he committed
> in causing Judah to do what was evil in the sight of YHWH.

Manasseh put so many innocent persons to death that he filled
Jerusalem with blood from end to end. And what of YHWH? As he
turned Jerusalem upside down, who were dashed on the floor? Were

there no innocent ones left? Had Manasseh already wiped the plate of them? Or were the innocents there, like the children of Sodom, waiting for their teeth to be set on edge because their fathers had eaten sour grapes? Were they there, but like the women of Sodom, ignored by the narrator in his passion to justify a theology of retribution? How much innocent blood did this narrator's god shed, filling Jerusalem from end to end, as he vented his anger?

King Amaziah of Judah, our narrator tells us, once firmly in power, put to death the courtiers who had assassinated his father.

> But he did not put to death the children of the murderers, in accordance with what is written in the book of the Law of Moses, where YHWH commanded, "The fathers shall not be put to death for the children, nor the children be put to death for the fathers. But every man shall be put to death for his own sins." (14:6)

Is the YHWH of our narrator's story willing to be judged by this law? It would seem not. But we have been forewarned of this propensity to mock his own laws. We have watched Bathsheba's baby and David's daughter pay for their father's sins. We have seen the wife of Jeroboam bury her son in order that YHWH may make a scathing point about the iniquity of the boy's father (1 Kgs 14:1-18). The list goes on and on.

The books of Kings end with a brief cameo. In the thirty-seventh year of the exile, King Jehoiachin, of the house of David, is released from prison by King Evil-Merodach of Babylon.

> He spoke kindly to him, and gave him a throne above those of other kings who were with him in Babylon. His prison garments were removed, and [Jehoiachin] received regular rations by his favor for the rest of his life. A regular allotment of food was given him at the instance of the king—an allotment for each day—all the days of his life. (2 Kgs 25:28-30; TANAKH)

Scholars have long debated the significance of this ending. Does it signal pessimism or hope? As we contemplate the women and children of Sodom and Jerusalem we are inclined to respond, Why should we care? After all this violent death and dispersal, what has changed? Has the exiled narrator learned so little about exclusion that he can end his story soliciting our concern for a king living off the bounty of another king? This Jehoiachin, this king, this man, had his chance. What has the narrator to tell us of those others, who had no chance? The women who obeyed their husbands, the children who obeyed their fathers, as YHWH commanded, who watched Jerusalem burn. In the thirty-seventh year of the exile, where were they?

NOTES

Notes to Introduction

[1] Within the sacrificial system, the valuation of male over female is further extended (see Leviticus 1–7). Cultic regulations regarding animal sacrifice stipulate that only human males offer sacrifices and make clear that male animals are the most worthy offering to YHWH. Thus the sacrificial order, too, embodies a symbolic system reflecting society's attitudes toward gender. The irony is that a domesticated species can survive with relatively few males. Even a single female taken from the herd or flock diminishes its breeding potential; except for prized studs, on the other hand, most of the males have no such long term value and thus may be more readily slaughtered for food, hide, etc., and—very conveniently—sacrifice.

[2] In this present book, we have followed the arrangement of the Hebrew (or Jewish) Bible which, unlike Christian Bibles, does not place the Book of Ruth between Judges and 1 Samuel but locates it later among the "five scrolls"—Song of Songs, Ruth, Lamentations, Ecclesiastes and Esther. Our choice affects our reading of Genesis–Kings since Ruth contributes, when included, a celebration of women (and one of them a foreign woman, moreover) in marked contrast to much of its context. Yet the story is not unproblematic in terms of women in patriarchal society. Whether Naomi ever recognizes that her daughter-in-law who loves her is worth more than seven sons is doubtful. And Ruth, who more than anyone effects "redemption" in the story, disappears silently into the household of Boaz, the quintessential patriarchal Subject. The social system which jeopardizes Naomi, Ruth, and Orpah at the beginning is firmly in place at the end: men control the means of production and women are defined as childbearers. We have developed a reading along these lines elsewhere (Fewell and Gunn 1990).

[3] David Clines (1988) has written succinctly of the primary story as a whole literary work (he uses the term "Primary History," following David Noel Freedman). The work is postulated on the basis of its overall narrative form. It is a continuous story from Genesis through Kings; and while it includes substantial instructional material, these laws, as Clines observes, are *narrated* laws—that is, they are set in a narrative context (p. 81). Both Jewish and Christian interpretive traditions, on the other hand, have tended to view the books in question in terms of their content as either law *or* history. Jewish Bibles observe a division between the "Law" or Torah, Genesis–Deuteronomy, and the subsequent books, Joshua–Kings, which are considered part of the "Prophets" or Nebi'im. Christian scholarship adopts the same initial division by speaking of the "Pentateuch" as a distinct work.

A recent hypothesis emerging from this division postulates a separate "Deuteronomistic History," comprising Joshua–Kings with Deuteronomy as its opening. While popular for several decades, it is, like most current hypotheses regarding the compositional history of Genesis through Kings, tenuously based and coming under deserved criticism.

[4] For an extended introduction to our understanding of literary criticism, especially of biblical narrative, see Gunn and Fewell 1993.

[5] Such an understanding of power helps us in turn to understand culture (society's "domain of notions") as not a "set of rules of conduct followed blindly which [support] the organization of society, but a structure of conflicting premises within which struggle for domination [takes] place" (Peristiany and Pitt-Rivers 1992:4).

[6] A caveat must be entered here, however: the subjectivity of the text will always remain a construct of the subjectivity of the reader; there is no single fixed, objective meaning that can be guaranteed by either the text or the reader. In that sense, interpretation is always a "subjective" endeavor. Nevertheless, readers are not the same as the texts they read. Readers can attempt, and with good reason, to distinguish their subjectivity from what they construe to be that of the text, though the results will always be open to further question and interpretation.

Notes to Chapter One: Shifting the Blame

[1] Some scholars argue, with little immediate contextual evidence, that the plural reflects the god speaking on behalf of the "divine court."

[2] Critics seeking to uncover the sources from which Genesis 1–3 was composed usually find a "priestly" source (P) in Gen 1:1–2:4a which has been editorially connected to a "Yahwist" source (J) in the rest of Genesis 2–3.

[3] Francis Landy (1983:189) comments: "[God's] statement . . . ignores the one relationship that has mattered to [the human] up to this point, that with God himself; it may also be an indication of God's own need, his own loneliness, out of which he created the universe."

[4] This agenda, which implicitly makes genital difference a *sine qua non* of sexuality, has implications for any understanding of God and/or sexuality based on this text (see Eilberg-Schwartz 1992:32-33). Given that the human creature is made in God's image, the logic of the text suggests that sexuality is also a dimension of God and, like human sexuality, it must be specifically marked—in other words (since the narrator has consistently spoken of him in the masculine), that God has a penis. But if so, what does that imply for women? Are they not, then, made in the image of God? Or is sexuality not, after all, part of the image of God? Moreover, if sexuality is confined to reproduction, as has often (repressively) been claimed with reference to this text, the same issue arises. Since the monotheistic male God has no use for a reproductive organ, neither should male humans, if they are to be truly like God. "If God has no sex, then the reproductive organs of both males and females are rendered problematic. And if God does have a sex, whether male or female, God's reproductive organs are useless" (Eilberg-Schwartz 1992:33). In other words, in constructing heterosexuality as normative the narrator deconstructs the asexual masculine God of monotheism. This passage is another case of "the patriarchal mindset tying itself in knots" (Jobling 1986:43)—see below.

[5] Francis Landy (1983:215) sees prohibition introducing the idea of rebel-

lion and trespass into an otherwise harmonious world, because arbitrary or incomprehensible regulation "infallibly" ensures infringement. Even to eat from the other trees turns out to be a concession by God. The human suddenly discovers that "[he] has no independence, no rights, and that his harmonious enterprise in the garden, where he fulfils his purpose in creation by changing it, is part of a rigorous divine order."

[6] Later in Genesis–Kings, God, perhaps beginning to learn, will struggle to disturb assumptions of priority and hierarchy (e.g., regarding privileges of birth or occupation). In the very next episode, Cain, first-born and follower in his father's footsteps as tiller of the soil finds his sacrifice rejected. But God's peremptory rejection and ambiguous words prove stunningly disastrous. His provocation ends with Abel's blood. Does God, once more, tell only part of the story? Does Abel's blood cry out from the ground against both his brother and God? Does God, once more, shift the blame?

Notes to Chapter Two: Keeping the Promise

[1] As Peter Miscall (1983:12) has astutely noted, the text provides more than one motivation for Abram's behavior and refuses to settle the issue for us: "The syntax and the context prevent the definitive conclusion that Abraham went solely in response to the Lord's command; at the same time, the syntax and the context prevent the definitive conclusion that Abraham went for his own reasons and not in response to the Lord's command."

[2] Ilona Rashkow (1992:64-65) has also considered this possibility:

> Since discourse often reflects hidden desires, perhaps Abraham's real motive is a hope to receive gifts from the Egyptians, and his words "that it may go well with me because of you" are a euphemistic way of saying that by abandoning his wife to the lust of a foreign potentate, he might derive material advantage. Certainly Abraham shows no regard for Sarah's welfare, as his language demonstrates ("so that it may go well with *me* . . . that *my* soul may live . . ."). Perhaps Abraham sees Sarah as expendable because she has no child and wants to be rid of her as a wife.

[3] David Clines (1990:70) and Laurence Turner (1990:85-87) maintain that Abraham saw Lot as his heir, the "son" through which he would become a great nation. Abraham's insistent reminder to YHWH in chapter 15 that he has yet to have a son of his own makes this argument problematic.

[4] As Phyllis Trible (1984:10-11) notes: "Unlike the narrator, Sarai speaks of building up herself through Hagar rather than of bearing a child to Abram (cf. 16:1, 15). In a man's world, the woman's voice sounds a different emphasis."

[5] Howard Eilberg-Schwartz (1992:23-24; see also 1990:141-177) argues that the priests regarded circumcision

> as the physical inscription of God's promise of genealogical proliferation on the body of all Abraham's male descendants . . . [It is] a symbol that alludes directly to the substance of God's promise to Abraham, namely to multiply Abraham's seed . . . The penis is the male organ through which the genealogy is perpetuated. The removal of the foreskin has the effect of giving the penis the appearance it has when erect, thus symbolizing great things to come . . . [Also, like the pruning of an immature fruit tree] circumcision symbolically readies the stem for producing fruit

. . . Impressing a symbol of fertility on the male organ of reproduction establishes a connection between procreation and masculinity and creates a community of men who are linked to one another through a similar mark on their male members. By contrast, the potential connection between women and procreation is symbolically undermined: menstrual blood and blood of birth, which could easily symbolize procreative capacities, are instead associated with death.

[6] While Abraham's skepticism had expressed disbelief on the basis of his knowledge of life in general (Can a hundred year old man sire a child? Can a ninety year old woman give birth?), Sarah's disbelief centers on the particular (*She* is withered; *her husband* is old). It is self-knowledge and self-doubt that generates her incredulity.

Notes to Chapter Three: Assault at Sodom

[1] From "Lot's Wife" (written in 1924), in *The Complete Poems*, 273-74. It is moving to read this poem in conjunction with some she wrote during World War II (her home was Leningrad), such as the short poem beginning "And all those whom my heart won't forget," where she recalls the children she loved who will not get to grow up to be twenty, "But were eight, or nine, / But were . . . Enough, don't torture yourself" (*Complete Poems*, 671). Akhmatova also wrote on Rachel and Michal (pp. 272, 274-75).

[2] "Lot's Wife," in *Alive Now!* January/February 1988, p. 27.

Notes to Chapter Four: The Way of Women

[1] Naomi Steinberg (1988:6) discusses this distinction in trickster stories.

[2] We much prefer, however, a variation on Carol Meyers's (1988:95-121) translation and understanding: "I will greatly increase your toil and your pregnancies; (Along) with travail you shall bear children" (p. 118).

[3] Shechem's soul clung [*dabaq*] to Dinah—and clinging is what a man does to his woman when he leaves his father and mother (Gen 2:24, the only other use of the term describing human relationships in the book of Genesis). Shechem loved the young woman—and love is what Isaac felt for Rebekah (Gen 24:67), what Jacob felt for Rachel more than for Leah (Gen 29:18, 30) and what Jacob/Israel felt for Joseph (Gen 37:3, 4) and Benjamin (Gen 44:20). Shechem spoke to her heart—which is what Joseph did to his fearful brothers (Gen 50:21), and later Boaz did to Ruth (Ruth 2:13).

"To speak to the heart" appears to be a perlocutionary expression. This describes a speech act which produces consequential effects on the feelings, thoughts, or actions of its hearers—in other words, a successfully completed action (compare "convince" or "compel" with "urge" or "advise.") In both Gen 50:21 and Ruth 2:13 the phrase is paired with *niham* ("to comfort"). Hence RSV translates Gen 50:21, "Thus he reassured them (*wayyᵉnahem*) and comforted them (*wayyᵉdabber 'al-libbam*)." On perlocutionary language, see J. L. Austin, *How to do Things with Words* (Oxford: Oxford Univ. 1962) 99-103.

[4] Meir Sternberg (1986:445-81) consistently uses the word "looting" to describe what happens in the city, thereby masking the "defilement" of the Hivite women. For the modern reader of English, "looting" is unlikely to include women and children amongst its connoted objects. But the forcible

abduction—the rape—of women and children is an essential part of the narrator's depiction. By itself, the term "looting" downplays the extent of the brothers' violence, so that the reader may miss the disproportion of a single rape justifying mass rape. (This situation is parodied again in Judges 19-20.)

[5] A woman is defiled when she sleeps with anyone outside the proper boundaries of marriage; see Num 5:13-31, Lev 21:7, 13-14.

[6] As no few commentators have observed, even when not obviously conscious of the androcentric nature of this particular "honor" code. Gerhard von Rad (1972:334), for example, speaks of "the burning shame done to the brothers in the rape of Dinah"; Claus Westermann (1985:538) comments, "The brothers feel that their honor has been wounded." On honor and shame in the Mediterranean, see Pitt-Rivers (1977) and Gilmore (1987).

Walter Brueggemann (1982:278) moves the discussion to another significant aspect of the vengeance: "But the passionate vengeance is transparently self-serving. What they seized, they did not destroy as an act of faithfulness (cf. I Sm. 15:3, 14-19). Rather, they kept it for themselves so that their taking was not an act of righteous indignation, but an act of confiscation for self gain."

[7] Her fate is not unlike that of David's concubines, "defiled" by Absalom, and hence condemned to be shut up to the day of their death, living as widows in the king's house (2 Sam 20:3). See further below, Chapter Seven.

[8] There is also a subliminal message here about children leaving the father's house. For a son, separation is part of gaining identity as an adult. Misfortunes may befall him, but he learns from them (see Gen 38:26 and the way in which the character of Judah continues to develop in the Joseph story). For daughters, on the other hand, independence (however temporary) has grave consequences. Venturing out from under a father's protection and control can cost a young woman her future, maybe even her very life. These two stories send very different and gender-specific signals: one is a warning (Genesis 34); the other an invitation (Genesis 38).

[9] See, for example, our earlier reading in Gunn and Fewell 1993:34-45. The alternative we offer here was drawn to our attention by Lisa McKinney.

Notes to Chapter Five: The Subject of the Law

[1] For example, in the law pertaining to the menstruating woman in Lev 15:10-24, the woman is the grammatical subject of the injunction, but it is clearly not in her interests to be performing this ritual to mark her sexual otherness. She is Other to the discourse Subject who is the adult, property-owning ("middle-class"?), male head of household.

[2] Patrick Miller (1990:76), on the language of jealousy in the parallel passage in Deut 5:8-10, comments that "It is the kind of attribute that belongs to a marriage relationship, where there is a proper covenantal jealousy." He goes on to observe that "the Hebrew verb 'hate' is used to indicate divorce in Aramaic marriage contracts from Egypt."

[3] These marriage metaphors, both here and in the prophetic literature (especially Jeremiah, Ezekiel, and Hosea), often fail to be consistently sustained because they embody a fundamental tension. The metaphor places the male addressee (the one who is doing the "whoring") in the female position. But then the speaker frequently feels the need to break the meta-

phor in order to remind his audience that female really means male here. On the one hand, in accordance with patriarchal ideology, these metaphors are constructed to elevate the male and the husband by divinizing male and husband, but on the other hand, since their specific purpose is to castigate, they keep speaking of male as female. On balance, however, they might be viewed as successful in their larger purpose, since they always subordinate, and mostly negate (e.g., as prostitute, adulteress), female.

[4] The word '*onatah*, which occurs only here, is translated by some as "her marital rights" (RSV; cf. "conjugal rights," TANAKH—which offers as an alternative, "ointments" [!]), despite the glaring paucity of marital *rights* accorded to any woman in ancient Israel. Much more likely it connotes the basic provision of food, clothing and shelter [from the root, '*un*, "to dwell"].

[5] But, according to Exod 21:26-27, there are limits to what damage he may do with impunity, at least to his female slave.

[6] Another understanding of these laws would be that they ensure that, in a system where females are regularly subordinate to males, a mother can exercise, on the father's behalf, authority over sons.

[7] For an analysis of Leviticus 18 similar to the one following (which was formulated independently), particularly on the incest rules, see William Countryman's study of sexual ethics in the New Testament (1988). Of closely related interest, too, is Judith Romney Wegner's discussion of the status of women in the Mishnah (1988). Especially influential for the present discussion is David Greenberg's major comparative study of the construction of homosexuality (1985). (We note also that our analysis, though argued differently, is not incompatible with that of anthropologist Mary Douglas [1966]).

[8] We assume that the traditional view, that men alone have seed, prevails here, despite the recent argument by Pieter van der Horst (1992:35-39). His one piece of direct evidence that women in ancient Israel might have been thought to produce seed (literally, as distinct from offspring, descendant) is Lev 12:2, where the semantics are more complex than he acknowledges.

[9] In arguing that the expression *h'byr lmlk* means to transfer sons and daughters "to the authority of idolatry," Moshe Weinfeld notes an early rabbinic understanding of the "dedication" as involving passing the male Israelite's semen to a gentile woman (see Heider 1985:68).

[10] The category, "homosexuality," is generally unknown in the ancient world—probably because it implies a person necessarily having a fixed and exclusive same-sex orientation, something not obvious, it would seem, to many ancients. Furthermore, a strictly essentialist understanding of sexuality is deeply problematic—even though talk of genetic disposition may be helpful in confronting current bigotry. Sexual orientation might usefully (though not unproblematically) be thought of in terms of a spectrum where no person has necessarily a single fixed place, though genetic determination may constrain that person's range of options. For our present purposes, however, we are primarily concerned with the extent to which homosexual behavior between men is socially constructed as a negative in biblical literature.

[11] We seem to be dealing here with the notion of seed as a limited resource; there is only so much seed and its owner must not waste it. Hence Onan in Genesis 38 compounds his crime against his brother's name and inheritance with deliberate waste. Involuntary emissions in the night or

during sex with a woman (Lev 15:16-18) are understandably a different matter and can be dealt with less drastically.

[12] *Epistolam ad Romanos,* Homily 4; see George Edwards (1984:26), discussing the link between homosexuality, homophobia and patriarchy. Similarly Augustine is disgusted that a man should allow his body to be used like a woman's since "the body of a man is as superior to that of a woman as the soul is to the body" (*Contra mendacium* 7.10; see Boswell 1980:157-58).

[13] This is not to say that women have not been, and are not still being, oppressed for their sexual orientation. Nor is it to say that female-to-female sex does not itself pose a threat to men, especially when men perceive women in such relationships to be behaving and/or dressing "as men." Yet even when we take dress codes as a guide to the system, it would seem that resistance to women dressing "as men," though often fierce, will moderate long before men who dress "as women" are tolerated. That is certainly the case in North American society today, to the point where pants are in most—though significantly not all—contexts no longer considered "men's" clothes.

[14] On the comparative material in the preceding paragraphs, see further Greenberg 1985; also Eva Keuls 1985, on sexual politics in ancient Athens.

[15] With a slight shift of a vowel (which would, in any case, have been lacking in the earliest manuscripts written in consonantal script), from *yasaphu* to *yasuphu,* we could read "and they did not cease" (and indeed some versions read it that way)! Only a vowel separates failure from unceasing prophecy, threatening to subvert any certain reading.

Notes to Chapter Six: Possessed and Dispossessed

[1] Cf., e.g., Isa 30:7; 51:9; Job 9:13; 26:12; Ps 89:11.

[2] "Concubine" is an unsatisfactory translation of the woman's status. She is neither simply a mistress nor a servant, since the man is called "her husband" (19:3) and her father is identified as the man's "father-in-law" (19:4). She may be, as Koala Jones-Warsaw (1992) has argued, a secondary wife.

[3] The Hebrew here is ambiguous, but we choose to read, with recent translations, "one portion doubled." See McCarter 1980:51-52, 60.

[4] Cf. McCarter 1980:49; literally, "Why is your heart evil?"

Notes to Chapter Seven: In the Shadow of the King

[1] The word *yad* ("hand," "power") is a genital euphemism in Isa 57:8.

[2] On the address, "sister," in the Song of Songs and in the language of Egyptian love poetry, see further Fox 1985:xii-xii, 8 (etc.).

[3] See also Stefan Heym's novel on the politics of a totalitarian state, *The King David Report.*

[4] However, the LXX and Qumran (4QSamᵃ) texts of 2 Sam 13:21 read, "And King David heard all these things [i.e., the rape of Tamar] and was very angry [with him], and/but he did not trouble the spirit of Amnon his son, for he loved him, for he was his firstborn."

[5] The root *rgl* ("foot," "leg") occurs elsewhere as a euphemism for genitals (e.g., Ruth 3:4, 7; 2 Kgs 18:27 [*Qere*]; Isa 7:20; cf. Exod. 4:25).

[6] For development of the correlation and interconnection between "private" and "public" worlds in David's story—between the world of wives,

concubines, and daughters and the world of politics, warfare, and dynastic feuding—see further, Gunn 1978:88-94 and Schwartz 1991.

[7] Rizpah's story in 2 Samuel 21 belongs with a group of texts in chapters 21–24 which together form a kind of "coda" to the books of Samuel and may be read as a subtle (and sometimes not so subtle) deconstruction of the figure of David. It works through irony and by drawing attention to problematic aspects of the rhetoric of David (or the narrator on David's behalf). See further Gunn 1989, and, somewhat differently, Brueggemann 1988.

[8] This stereotype of the attractive woman who brings (sic) death is striking in Proverbs 1–9, particularly in terms of the "strange woman" ('ishshah zarah). See further, especially on Jezebel, in the next chapter.

Notes to Chapter Eight: Until No Body Remains

[1] In *Circles on the Water* (New York: Knopf, 1989), pp. 164-65.

[2] Francisco García-Treto (1992:165) notes that Jezebel's blood which splatters the wall is also turned to urine, through allusion to the crude idiom for males, "those who piss against the wall," used earlier in the prophecy against the house of Ahab (2 Kgs 9:8; censored in most English versions.)

[3] Solomon certainly rises and bows to his mother on her entrance, and seats her at his right hand. On the other hand, he denies her request despite having assured her he will grant it. Most queen mothers are named but, in terms of the narrative, they effect nothing.

[4] Claudia Camp's work is probably the most important single influence on this chapter. On Kings as a whole, her chapter in the *Women's Bible Commentary* is indispensable (Camp 1992).

[5] Highly germane to our book and especially to this discussion of Jezebel is Claudia Camp's lucid and nuanced analysis (1991) of the "strange [though not necessarily 'foreign'] woman" metaphor in Proverbs 1–9, though we have not attempted here to match the sophistication with which she traces the metaphor's variable meanings, particularly in respect of its rhetorical history and socio-historical setting. On the metaphorical relation between religious faithfulness and sexual deviance, see Camp's earlier work on wisdom and the feminine (1985:265-71). In this same connection—on the "strange woman"—note also Carol Newsom's important analysis (1989) of the construction of the patriarchal Subject in Proverbs 1–9.

[6] Or compare the hanged men whose crime was to eat and drink and "play the harlot" with the daughters of Moab; or Zimri son of Salu, speared to death at YHWH's behest for bringing home a Midianite woman (Num 25:1-15).

[7] "Your parted lips behind your veil are like a split pomegranate" (Songs 4:3; 6:7; cf. REB); "your channels are an orchard of pomegranates" (4:13); "I would give you spiced wine to drink, the juice of my pomegranate"(8:2).

[8] Something similar could be said of Huldah (2 Kgs 22:14-20) whom King Josiah consults about the law book found in the temple. She is undoubtedly a person of significance—whose prophecy, alas, is not quite accurate.

[9] She is perhaps most notably represented on some Phoenician ivories of the ninth or eighth centuries B.C.E. (Barnett and Wiseman 1969:56), though the iconography of "the woman at the window" is still a matter of some debate (cf. Winter 1983:296-301).

BIBLIOGRAPHY

Abbreviations

B&L   = Bible and Literature Series
CBQ   = *Catholic Biblical Quarterly*
ISBL = Indiana Studies in Biblical Literature
JBL   = *Journal of Biblical Literature*
JFSR = *Journal of Feminist Studies in Religion*
JSOT = *Journal for the Study of the Old Testament*
JSOTS = JSOT Supplement Series

Introduction

Bal, Mieke, ed. 1989. "Introduction," *Anti-Covenant: Counter-Reading Women's Lives in the Hebrew Bible.* B&L 22; Sheffield: Almond.

Beauvoir, Simone de. 1953. *The Second Sex.* New York: Knopf; repr. New York: Vintage Books, 1974.

Bem, Sandra Lipsitz. 1993. *The Lenses of Gender: Transforming the Debate on Sexual Inequality.* New Haven and London: Yale Univ.

Bird, Phyllis. 1974. "Images of Women in the Old Testament." In Rosemary Radford Ruether, ed., *Religion and Sexism: Images of Woman in the Jewish and Christian Traditions.* New York: Simon and Schuster. Pp. 41-88.

Clines, David J. 1988. "Introduction to the Biblical Story: Genesis–Esther." In James L. Mays, ed., *Harper's Bible Commentary.* Harper & Row: San Francisco. Pp. 74-84. Repr. as "The Old Testament Histories: A Reader's Guide," in *What Does Eve do to Help?* [See below, *Ch. One*] Pp. 85-105.

Fewell, Danna Nolan, ed. 1992. *Reading Between Texts: Intertextuality and the Hebrew Bible.* LCBI; Louisville: Westminster/John Knox.

Foucault, Michel. 1978. *The History of Sexuality. Volume 1: An Introduction.* New York: Vintage Books.

———. 1984. "Truth and Power." In Peter Rabinow, ed., *The Foucault Reader.* New York: Pantheon. Pp. 51-75. [Orig. 1977]

Gottwald, Norman K. 1993. "Social Class as an Analytic and Hermeneutical Category in Biblical Studies." *JBL* 112:3-22.

Gunn, David M. and Danna Nolan Fewell. 1993. *Narrative in the Hebrew Bible.* Oxford: Oxford Univ.

Humm, Maggie. 1990. *The Dictionary of Feminist Theory.* Columbus: Ohio State Univ.

Jeansonne, Sharon Pace. 1990. *The Women of Genesis: From Sarah to Potiphar's Wife.* Minneapolis: Fortress.

Jehlen, Myra. 1990. "Gender." In Frank Lentricchia and Thomas McLaughlin, eds., *Critical Terms for Literary Study.* Chicago and London: Univ. of Chicago. Pp. 263-73.

Lerner, Gerda. *The Creation of Patriarchy.* New York and Oxford: Oxford Univ.

Meese, Elizabeth A. 1986. *Crossing the Double-Cross: The Practice of Feminist Criticism.* Chapel Hill and London: Univ. of North Carolina. Pp. 133-50.

Meyers, Carol. 1988. *Discovering Eve: Ancient Israelite Women in Context*. New York and Oxford: Oxford Univ.

Newsom, Carol A. and Sharon H. Ringe, eds. 1992. *The Women's Bible Commentary*. Louisville: Westminster/John Knox.

Peristiany, J. G., and Julian Pitt-Rivers, eds. 1965. *Honor and Grace in Anthropology*. Cambridge: Cambridge Univ.

Plaskow, Judith. 1990. *Standing Again at Sinai: Judaism from a Feminist Perspective*. HarperSanFrancisco.

Showalter, Elaine. 1989. "The Rise of Gender." In *Speaking of Gender*. New York: Routlege, Chapman and Hall. Pp. 1-13.

Silverman, Kaja. 1983. *The Subject of Semiotics*. Oxford: Oxford Univ.

Weedon, Chris. 1987. *Feminist Practice and Poststructuralist Theory*. Oxford and New York: Blackwell.

Chapter One: Shifting the Blame

Aschkenasy, Nehama. 1986. *Eve's Journey: Feminine Images in Hebraic Literary Tradition*. Philadelphia: Univ. of Philadelphia.

Bal, Mieke. 1987. "Sexuality, Sin, and Sorrow: The Emergence of the Female Character." In *Lethal Love: Feminist Literary Readings of Biblical Love Stories*. ISBL; Bloomington: Indiana Univ. Pp. 104-32.

Bird, Phyllis. 1981. "'Male and Female He Created Them': Gen 1:27b in the Context of the Priestly Account of Creation." *Harvard Theol. Rev.* 74:129-59.

———. 1987. "Genesis 1-3 as a Source for a Contemporary Theology of Sexuality," *Ex Auditu* 3:31-44.

Bloom, Harold. 1986. "From J to K, or the Uncanniness of the Yahwist." In Frank McConnell, ed., *The Bible and the Narrative Tradition*. Oxford: Oxford Univ.

———. 1990. "The Representation of Yahweh" and "The Psychology of Yahweh." In David Rosenberg and Harold Bloom, *The Book of J*. New York: Grove Weidenfeld. Pp. 279-306.

Brueggemann, Walter. 1982. *Genesis*. Interpretation; Atlanta: John Knox.

Clines, David J. A. 1990. "What Does Eve Do to Help? and Other Irredeemably Androcentric Orientations in Genesis 1-3." In *What Does Eve do to Help? and Other Readerly Questions to the Old Testament*. JSOTS 94; Sheffield: JSOT. Pp. 25-48.

Dragga, Sam. 1992. "Genesis 2-3: A Story of Liberation," *JSOT* 55:3-13.

Eilberg-Schwartz, Howard. 1990. *The Savage in Judaism: An Anthropology of Israelite Religion and Ancient Judaism*. Bloomington: Indiana Univ.

———, ed. 1992. *People of the Body: Jews and Judaism from an Embodied Perspective*. Albany: State Univ. of New York.

Jobling, David. 1986. "Myth and its Limits in Genesis 2.4b-3.24." In *The Sense of Biblical Narrative: Structural Analyses in the Hebrew Bible, II*. JSOTS 39; Sheffield: JSOT. Pp. 17-43.

Kennedy, James M. 1990. "Peasants in Revolt: Political Allegory in Genesis 2-3." *JSOT* 47:3-14.

Landy, Francis. 1983. "Two Versions of Paradise." In *Paradoxes of Paradise: Identity and Difference in the Song of Songs*. B&L 7; Sheffield: Almond. Pp. 183-265.

Lanser, Susan. 1988. "(Feminist) Criticism in the Garden: Inferring Genesis 2-3," *Semeia* 41:67-84.

Meyers, Carol. 1988. *Discovering Eve*. [See above, *Intro*.]

Milne, Pamela J. 1989. "The Patriarchal Stamp of Scripture: The Implications of Structural Analyses for Feminist Hermeneutics." *JFSR* 5:17-34.

Miscall, Peter D. 1990. "Jacques Derrida in the Garden of Eden." *Union Seminary*

Quarterly Review 44:1-9.

Ramsey, George W. 1988. "Is Name-Giving an Act of Domination in Genesis 2:23 and Elsewhere?" *CBQ* 50:24-35.

Rashkow, Ilona N. 1990. "Adam and Eve." In *Upon the Dark Places: Anti-Semitism and Sexism in English Renaissance Biblical Translation.* B&L 28; Sheffield: Almond. Pp. 75-96.

Rosenberg, Joel. 1986. "The Garden Story Forward and Backward: The Non-Narrative Dimension of Gen. 2-3." In *King and Kin: Political Allegory in the Hebrew Bible.* ISBL; Bloomington: Indiana Univ. Pp. 48-68; 223-30.

Trible, Phyllis. 1978. "A Love Story Gone Awry." In *God and the Rhetoric of Sexuality.* Overtures to Biblical Theology; Philadelphia: Fortress. Pp. 72-143.

Von Rad, Gerhard. 1972. *Genesis.* Old Testament Library; Philadelphia: Westminster.

Chapter Two: Keeping the Promise

Brueggemann, Walter. 1982. *Genesis.* [See above, *Ch. One*]

Clines, David J. A. 1990. "What Happens in Genesis." In *What Does Eve Do to Help?* [See above, *Intro.*] Pp. 48-66.

Crenshaw, James L. 1984. "A Monstrous Test: Genesis 22." In *A Whirlpool of Torment: Israelite Traditions of God as an Oppressive Presence.* Overtures to Biblical Theology; Philadelphia: Fortress. Pp. 9-29.

Darr, Katheryn Pfisterer. 1991. "More than the Stars of the Heavens: Critical, Rabbinical, and Feminist Perspectives on Sarah" and "More than a Possession: Critical, Rabbinical, and Feminist Perspectives on Hagar." In *Far More Precious than Jewels: Perspectives on Biblical Women.* Louisville: Westminster/ John Knox. Pp. 85-131 and 132-63.

Delaney, Carol. 1989. "The Legacy of Abraham." In Bal, ed., *Anti-Covenant.* [See above, *Intro.*] Pp. 27-41.

Fewell, Danna Nolan. 1989. "Divine Calls, Human Responses: Another Look at Abraham and Sarah." *The Perkins School of Theology Journal.* Pp. 13-16.

Hackett, Jo Ann. 1989. "Rehabilitating Hagar: Fragments of an Epic Pattern." In Peggy L. Day, ed., *Gender and Difference in Ancient Israel.* Minneapolis: Fortress. Pp. 12-27.

Jeansonne, Sharon Pace. 1990. *The Women of Genesis.* [See above, *Intro.*]

Marmesh, Ann. 1989. "Anti-Covenant." In Bal, ed., *Anti-Covenant.* [See above, *Intro.*] Pp. 43-60.

Miscall, Peter D. 1983. "Genesis 12 and Related Texts." In *The Workings of Old Testament Narrative.* Chico: Scholars. Pp. 11-46.

Niditch, Susan. 1987. "The Three Wife-Sister Tales of Genesis." In *Underdogs and Tricksters: A Prelude to Biblical Folklore.* San Francisco: Harper & Row. Pp. 23-69.

Rashkow, Ilona N. "Intertextuality, Transference, and the Reader in/of Genesis 12 and 20." In Fewell, ed., *Reading Between Texts.* [See above, *Intro.*] Pp. 57-73.

Rosenberg, Joel. 1986. "Is There a Story of Abraham?" In *King and Kin.* [See above, *Ch. One*] Pp. 69-98.

Trible, Phyllis. 1984. "Hagar: The Desolation of Rejection." In *Texts of Terror: Literary-Feminist Readings of Biblical Narratives.* Overtures to Biblical Theology; Philadelphia: Fortress. Pp. 9-35.

———. 1991. "Genesis 22: The Sacrifice of Sarah." In Jason P. Rosenblatt and Joseph C. Sitterson, Jr., eds., *"Not in Heaven": Coherence and Complexity in Biblical Narrative.* ISBL; Bloomington: Indiana Univ. Pp. 170-91.

Turner, Laurence A. 1990. *Announcements of Plot in Genesis.* JSOTS 96; Sheffield: JSOT.

Von Rad, Gerhard. 1972. *Genesis.* (See above, *Ch. One*)

Waters, John. 1991. "Who Was Hagar?" In Felder, ed., *Stony the Road We Trod.* [See below, *Ch. Five*] Pp. 187-205.

Weems, Renita J. 1988. "A Mistress, a Maid, and No Mercy." In *Just a Sister Away: A Womanist Vision of Women's Relationships in the Bible.* San Diego: LuraMedia. Pp. 1-21.

Westermann, Claus. 1985. *Genesis 12–36. A Commentary.* Trans. John J. Scullion. Minneapolis: Augsburg. [Orig. 1981]

Wiesel, Elie. 1976. "The Sacrifice of Isaac: A Survivor's Story." In *Messengers of God: Biblical Portraits and Legends.* New York: Random House. Pp. 69-97.

Chapter Three: Assault at Sodom

Akhmatova, Anna. 1992. *The Complete Poems of Anna Akhmatova.* Trans. Judith Hemschemeyer; ed. Roberta Reeder. Boston: Zephyr; Edinburgh: Canongate.

Alter, Robert. 1990. "Sodom as Nexus: The Web of Design in Biblical Narrative." In Regina Schwartz, ed., *The Book and the Text: The Bible and Literary Theory.* Oxford: Blackwell. Pp. 146-60.

Jeansonne, Sharon Pace. 1988. "The Characterization of Lot in Genesis." *Biblical Theology Bulletin* 18:123-29.

Tapp, Anne Michele. 1989. "An Ideology of Expendability: Virgin Daughter Sacrifice in Genesis 19.1-11, Judges 11.30-39 and 19.22-26." In Bal, ed., *Anti-Covenant.* [See above, *Intro.*] Pp. 157-74.

Turner, Laurence A. 1990. "Lot as Jekyll and Hyde: A Reading of Genesis 18-19." In David J. A. Clines, Stephen E. Fowl, and Stanley E. Porter, eds., *The Bible in Three Dimensions.* JSOTS 87. Sheffield: JSOT. Pp. 85-101.

Chapter Four: The Way of Women

Alter, Robert, 1981. *The Art of Biblical Narrative.* New York: Basic Books. Pp. 5-12.

Exum, J. Cheryl. 1983. " 'You Shall Let Every Daughter Live': A Study of Exodus 1:8-2:10." *Semeia* 28:63-82.

Fewell, Danna Nolan and David M. Gunn. 1991. "Tipping the Balance: Sternberg's Reader and the Rape of Dinah." *JBL* 110:193-211.

Fishbane, Michael. 1979. "Genesis 25:19–35:22/The Jacob Cycle." In *Text and Texture: Close Readings of Selected Biblical Texts.* New York: Schocken. Pp. 40-52.

Fokkelman, J. P. 1975. *Narrative Art in Genesis: Specimens of Stylistic and Structural Analysis.* Assen/Amsterdam: Van Gorcum.

Fretheim, Terence. 1991. *Exodus.* Interpretation; Louisville: John Knox.

Fuchs, Esther. 1987. "Structure and Patriarchal Functions in the Biblical Betrothal Type-Scene." *JFSR* 3:7-13.

———. 1988. " 'For I Have the Way of Women': Deception, Gender, and Ideology in Biblical Narrative." *Semeia* 42:6.

Furman, Nelly. 1989. "His Story Versus Her Story: Male Genealogy and Female Strategy in the Jacob Cycle." *Semeia* 46:141-49.

Gilmore, David D., ed. 1987. *Honor and Shame and the Unity of the Mediterranean.* Washington, DC: American Anthropological Assoc.

Jeansonne, Sharon Pace. 1990. *The Women of Genesis.* Minneapolis: Fortress.

Niditch, Susan. 1992. "Genesis." In Newsom and Ringe, eds., *The Women's Bible Commentary.* [See above, *Intro.*] Pp. 10-25.

Pitt-Rivers, Julian. 1977. *The Fate of Shechem or The Politics of Sex: Essays in the Anthropology of the Mediterranean.* Cambridge: Cambridge Univ.

Rashkow, Ilona N. 1990. "The Rape of Dinah." In *Upon the Dark Places.* [See above, *Ch. One*] Pp. 97-118.

Setel, Drorah. 1992. "Exodus." In Newsom and Ringe, eds., *The Women's Bible Commentary.* [See above, *Intro.*] Pp. 26-35.

Steinberg, Naomi. 1988. "Israelite Tricksters, Their Analogues and Cross-cultural Study." *Semeia* 42:1-13.

———. 1989. "The Genealogical Framework of the Family Stories in Genesis." *Semeia* 46:41-50.

Steinmetz, Devora. 1991. *From Father to Son: Kinship, Conflict, and Continuity in Genesis.* LCBI; Louisville: Westminster/John Knox.

Sternberg, Meir. 1990. "The Wooing of Rebekah" and "Delicate Balance in the Rape of Dinah." In *The Poetics of Biblical Narrative: Ideological Literature and the Drama of Reading.* ISBL; Bloomington: Indiana Univ. Pp. 131-52 and 445-75.

Turner, Mary Donovan. 1985. "Rebekah: Ancestor of Faith." *Lexington Theological Quarterly* 20:42-50.

Weems, Renita J. 1992. "The Hebrew Women are not Like the Egyptian Women: The Ideology of Race, Gender and Sexual Reproduction in Exodus 1." *Semeia* 59:25-34.

White, Hugh C. 1991. *Narration and Discourse in the Book of Genesis.* Cambridge: Cambridge Univ.

Williams, James G. 1982. "The Arche-Mother: The Mother of Israel's Beginnings." In *Women Recounted: Narrative Thinking and the God of Israel.* B&L 6; Sheffield: Almond. Pp. 42-66.

Chapter Five: The Subject of the Law

Bailey, Randall C. 1991. "Beyond Identification: The Use of Africans in Old Testament Poetry and Narratives." In Felder, ed., *Stony the Road We Trod.* [See below, Felder] Pp. 165-84.

Boswell, John. 1980. *Christianity, Social Tolerance, and Homosexuality.* Chicago and London: Univ. of Chicago. See esp. 91-117: "The Scriptures."

Burns, Rita. 1987. *Has the Lord Indeed Spoken Only Through Moses? A Study of the Biblical Portrait of Miriam.* Atlanta: Scholars.

Carmichael, Calum M. 1992. *The Origins of Biblical Law: The Decalogues and the Book of the Covenant.* Ithaca and London: Cornell Univ.

Countryman, William. 1988. *Dirt, Greed, and Sex: Sexual Ethics in the New Testament and Their Implications for Today.* Philadelphia: Fortress.

Douglas, Mary. 1966. *Purity and Danger: An Analysis of the Concepts of Pollution and Taboo.* London: Routledge and Kegan Paul; New York: Praeger.

Edwards, George. 1984. *Gay/Lesbian Liberation: A Biblical Perspective.* Cleveland, Ohio: Pilgrim.

Felder, Cain Hope. 1991. "Race, Racism, and the Biblical Narratives." In Felder, ed., *Stony the Road We Trod: African American Biblical Interpretation.* Minneapolis: Fortress. Pp. 127-45.

Flesher, Paul Virgil McCracken. 1988. *Oxen, Women, or Citizens? Slaves in the System of the Mishnah.* Brown Judaic Studies; Atlanta: Scholars.

Fretheim, Terence. 1991. *Exodus.* Interpretation; Louisville: John Knox.

Frymer-Kensky, Tikva. 1984. "The Strange Case of the Suspected Sotah (Numbers V 11-31)." *Vetus Testamentum* 34:11-31.

———. 1989. "Law and Philosophy: The Case of Sex in the Bible." *Semeia* 45:89-102.

———. 1992. "Deuteronomy." In Newsom and Ringe, eds., *The Women's Bible Commentary.* [See above, *Intro.*] Pp. 52-62.

Greenberg, David. 1985. *The Construction of Homosexuality.* Chicago: Univ. of Chicago.

Heider, George. 1985. *The Cult of Molek: A Reassessment.* JSOTS 43; Sheffield: JSOT.

Hickcox, Alice McCracken. 1991. "Between Redemption and Promise: Literary-

Theological Readings in Numbers 11–21." Ph.D. Diss., Emory Univ.

Horst, Pieter Willem van der. 1992. "Did Sarah Have a Seminal Emission?" *Bible Review* 8:35-39.

Houten, Christiana van. 1991. *The Alien in Israelite Law.* JSOTS 107; Sheffield: JSOT.

Jobling, David. 1978. "A Structural Analysis of Numbers 11–12." In *The Sense of Biblical Narrative I.* JSOTS 7; Sheffield: JSOT. Pp. 26-62.

Keuls, Eva. 1985. *The Reign of the Phallus: Sexual Politics in Ancient Athens.* San Francisco: Harper and Row.

Miller, Patrick D. 1990. *Deuteronomy.* Interpretation; Louisville: John Knox.

Phillips, Anthony. 1984. "The Laws of Slavery: Exodus 21:2-11." *JSOT* 30:51-66.

Plaskow, Judith. 1990. "Toward a New Theology of Sexuality." In *Standing Again at Sinai.* [See above, *Intro.*] Ch. 5.

Sakenfeld, Katharine Doob. 1992. "Numbers." In Newsom and Ringe, eds., *The Women's Bible Commentary.* [See above, *Intro.*] Pp. 45-51.

Stulman, Louis. 1992. "Sex and Familial Crimes in the D Code: A Witness to Mores in Transition." *JSOT* 53:47-63.

Trible, Phyllis. 1989. "Bringing Miriam out of the Shadows." *Bible Review* 5:14-25, 34.

Waldavsky, Aaron. 1984. *The Nursing Father: Moses as a Political Leader.* Univ. of Alabama.

Wegner, Judith Romney. 1988. *Chattel or Person? The Status of Women in the Mishnah.* Oxford: Oxford Univ.

———. 1992. "Leviticus." In Newsom and Ringe, eds., *The Women's Bible Commentary.* [See above, *Intro.*] Pp. 36-44.

Wenham, G. J. 1972. "*Betûlāh*: 'A Girl of Marriageable Age'." *Vetus Testamentum* 22:326-48.

Westbrook, Raymond. 1991. *Property and the Family in Biblical Law.* JSOTS 113; Sheffield: JSOT.

Wilson, Robert R. 1983. "Enforcing the Covenant: The Mechanisms of Judicial Authority in Early Israel." In H. B. Huffmon, F. A. Spina, and A. R. W. Green, eds., *The Quest for the Kingdom of God.* Winona Lake, IN: Eisenbrauns. Pp. 59-75.

Chapter Six: Possessed and Dispossessed

Alter, Robert. 1981. *The Art of Biblical Narrative* [See above, *Ch. Four*].

———. 1983. "How Convention Helps Us Read: The Annunciation Type-Scene in the Bible." *Prooftexts* 3:115-30.

Amit, Yairah. 1987. "Judges 4: Its Contents and Form." *JSOT* 39:89-111.

Bal, Mieke. 1988. *Murder and Difference: Gender, Genre, and Scholarship on Sisera's Death.* Trans. Matthew Gumpert. ISBL; Bloomington: Indiana Univ.

———. 1988. *Death and Dissymmetry: The Politics of Coherence in the Book of Judges.* Chicago: Univ. of Chicago.

———. 1990. "Dealing/With/Women: Daughters in the Book of Judges" In Schwartz, ed., *The Book and the Text.* [See above, *Ch. Three*, under Alter] Pp. 16-39.

Beal, Timothy K. and David M. Gunn. 1993. "The Book of Judges." In John H. Hayes, ed., *A Dictionary of Biblical Interpretation.* Nashville: Abingdon.

Berquist, Jon. 1992. "Expectations and Repeated Climax in the Rahab Story." Unpub. paper, Society of Biblical Literature Annual Meeting, San Francisco.

Bird, Phyllis A. 1989. "The Harlot as Heroine: Narrative Art and Social Presupposition in Three Old Testament Texts." *Semeia* 46:119-39.

Culley, Robert C. 1984. "Stories of the Conquest: Joshua 2, 6, 7, and 8." *Hebrew Annual Review* 8:25-44.

Eslinger, Lyle M. 1989. "Those Nations that Remain." In *Into the Hands of the*

Living God. B&L 24; Sheffield: Almond. Pp. 25-54.

Exum, J. Cheryl. 1980. "Promise and Fulfillment: Narrative Art in Judges 13." *JBL* 99:39-59.

———. 1985. " 'Mother in Israel': A Familiar Figure Reconsidered." In Letty M. Russell, ed., *Feminist Interpretation of the Bible*. Philadelphia: Westminster. Pp. 73-85.

———. 1989. "The Tragic Vision and Biblical Narrative: The Case of Jephthah." In Exum, ed., *Signs and Wonders: Biblical Texts in Literary Focus*. Semeia Studies; Atlanta: Scholars. Pp. 59-83. Response by W. Lee Humphreys: 85-96.

———. 1990a. "The Centre Cannot Hold: Thematic and Textual Instabilities in Judges." *CBQ* 52:410-31.

———. 1990b. "Murder They Wrote: Ideology and the Manipulation of Female Presence in Biblical Narrative." In Bach, ed., *The Pleasure of Her Text*. [See below, *Ch. Seven*] Pp. 45-67. (On Jephthah's daughter.)

Fewell, Danna Nolan. 1992. "Joshua" and "Judges." In Newsom and Ringe, eds., *The Women's Bible Commentary*. [See above, *Intro.*] Pp. 63-66 and 67-77.

———, and David M. Gunn. 1990. "Controlling Perspectives: Women, Men, and the Authority of Violence in Judges 4 & 5." *Journal of the American Academy of Religion* 56:389-411.

Fuchs, Esther. 1985. "The Literary Characterization of Mothers and Sexual Politics in the Hebrew Bible." In Adele Yarbro Collins, ed., *Feminist Perspectives on Biblical Scholarship*. Chico, CA: Scholars. Pp. 117-36. Repr. in *Semeia* 46 (1989) 151-66.

———. 1989. "Marginalization, Ambiguity, Silencing: The Story of Jephthah's Daughter." *JFSR* 5:35-45.

Gunn, David M. 1987. "Joshua and Judges." In Robert Alter and Frank Kermode, eds., *The Literary Guide to the Bible*. Cambridge: Harvard Univ.; London: Collins. Pp. 102-21.

Hamlin, E. John. 1990. *Judges: At Risk in the Promised Land*. Grand Rapids: Eerdmans; Edinburgh: Handsel.

Hawk, L. Daniel. 1991. *Every Promise Fulfilled: Contesting Plots in Joshua*. LCBI; Louisville: Westminster/John Knox.

———. 1992. "Strange Houseguests: Rahab, Lot, and the Dynamics of Deliverance. In Fewell, ed., *Reading Between Texts*. [See above, *Intro.*] Pp. 89-98.

Jones-Warsaw, Koala. 1992. "Toward a Womanist Hermeneutic: Based Upon a Reading of Judges 19-21." Unpub. paper, Society of Biblical Literature Annual Meeting, San Francisco.

McCarter, P. Kyle, Jr. 1980. *I Samuel*. Anchor Bible; Garden City, NY: Doubleday.

Niditch, Susan. 1989. "Eroticism and Death in the Tale of Jael." In Day, ed., *Gender and Difference in Ancient Israel*. [See above, *Ch. Two*, Hackett] Pp. 43-57.

Penchansky, David. 1992. "Staying the Night: Intertextuality in Genesis and Judges." In Fewell, ed., *Reading Between Texts*. [See above, Intro.] Pp. 77-88.

Polzin, Robert. 1980. *Moses and the Deuteronomist: A Literary Study of the Deuteronomic History. Part One: Deuteronomy, Joshua, Judges*. New York: Seabury.

———. 1989. *Samuel and the Deuteronomist: A Literary Study of the Deuteronomic History. Part Two: 1 Samuel*. San Francisco: Harper and Row.

Sakenfeld, Katharine Doob. 1992. "Numbers." In Newsom and Ringe, eds., *The Women's Bible Commentary*. [See above, *Intro.*] Pp. 45-51.

Trible, Phyllis. 1984. "An Unnamed Woman: The Extravagance of Violence" and "The Daughter of Jephthah: An Inhuman Sacrifice." In *Texts of Terror*. [See above, *Ch. Two*] Pp. 65-91 and 93-116.

Warrior, Robert Allen. 1989. "Canaanites, cowboys, and Indians: Deliverance, conquest, and liberation theology today." *Christianity and Crisis* (Sept. 11) 261-65.

Chapter Seven: In the Shadow of the King

Ackerman, James S. 1990. "Knowing Good and Evil: A Literary Analysis of the Court History in 2 Samuel 9–20 and 1 Kings 1–2." *JBL* 109:41-60.

Alter, Robert. 1981. *The Art of Biblical Narrative.* [See above, *Ch. Four*] Pp. 114-30 (on Michal and David) and pp. 147-53 (on 1 Samuel 16-17).

Bach, Alice. 1990. "The Pleasure of Her Text." In Bach, ed., *The Pleasure of Her Text: Feminist Readings of Biblical and Historical Texts.* Philadelphia: Trinity Press International. Pp. 25-44. (On Abigail.)

Bailey, Randall C. 1990. *David in Love and War: The Pursuit of Power in 2 Samuel 10–12.* JSOTS 75; Sheffield: JSOT. Ch. 4, esp. pp. 83-90.

Bar-Efrat, Shimon. 1989. "The Narrative of Amnon and Tamar." In *Narrative Art in the Bible.* B&L 17; Sheffield: Almond. Pp. 239-82.

Berlin, Adele. 1982. "Characterization in Biblical Narrative: David's Wives." *JSOT* 23:69-85. Also in *Poetics and Interpretation of Biblical Narrative.* B&L 9; Sheffield: Almond. Pp. 23-33.

Brueggemann, Walter. 1985. *David's Truth in Israel's Imagination and Memory.* Philadelphia: Fortress.

———. 1988. "2 Samuel 21–24: An Appendix of Deconstruction?" *CBQ* 50:383-97.

Clines, David J. A. and Tamara C. Eskenazi, eds. 1991. *Telling Queen Michal's Story: An Experiment in Comparative Interpretation.* JSOTS 119; Sheffield: JSOT.

Dijk-Hemmes, Fokkelien van. 1989. "Tamar and the Limits of Patriarchy: Between Rape and Seduction (2 Samuel 13 and Genesis 38)." In Bal, ed., *Anti-Covenant.* [See above, *Intro.*] Pp. 135-56.

Exum, J. Cheryl. 1990. "Murder They Wrote: Ideology and the Manipulation of Female Presence in Biblical Narrative." (See above, *Ch. Six.*) (On Michal.)

———. 1992. *Tragedy and Biblical Narrative: Arrows of the Almighty.* Cambridge: Cambridge Univ.

Flanagan, James W. 1988. "Domain of Notions: Literary Images of the David Figure." In *David's Social Drama: A Hologram of Israel's Early Iron Age.* The Social World of Biblical Antiquity; Sheffield: Almond. Ch. 4, pp. 193-272.

Fokkelman, J. P. 1981. *Narrative Art and Poetry in the Books of Samuel, vol. 1, King David (2 Sam 9–20 and 1 Kg 1–2).* Amsterdam: Van Gorcum.

———. 1986. *Narrative Art and Poetry in the Books of Samuel, vol. 2, The Crossing Fates (I Sam 13–31 and II Sam 1).* Assen: Van Gorcum.

Fox, Michael V. 1985. *The Song of Songs and the Ancient Egyptian Love Songs.* Madison: Univ. of Wisconsin.

Gide, André. 1947. *Saül.* In *Le Théâtre complet d'André Gide.* 8 vols. Paris: Ides et Calendes. I, pp. 5-140. [Orig. 1904]

Gunn, David M. 1978. *The Story of King David: Genre and Interpretation.* JSOTS 6; Sheffield: JSOT. See esp. 87-111.

———. 1988. "2 Samuel." In James L. Mays, ed., *Harper's Bible Commentary.* San Francisco: Harper and Row. Pp. 287-304.

———. 1989. "In Security: The David of Biblical Narrative." In Exum, ed., *Signs and Wonders.* [See above, *Ch. Six*] Pp. 133-51. Response by Peter D. Miscall: 153-63.

Heym, Stefan. 1973. *The King David Report.* London: Hodder and Stoughton.

Horner, Tom. 1978. *Jonathan Loved David: Homosexuality in Biblical Times.* Philadelphia: Westminster.

Jobling, David. 1978. "Jonathan: A Structural Study in 1 Samuel." In *The Sense of Biblical Narrative I.* [See above, *Ch. Five*] Pp. 4-25.

Lerner, Anne Lapidus. 1980. *Passing the Love of Women: A Study of Gide's* Saül *and its Biblical Roots.* Lanham, MD: Univ. Press of America.

Linafelt, Tod. 1992. "Taking Women: Readers/Responses/Responsibility in Samuel." In Fewell, ed., *Reading Between Texts*. [See above, *Intro*.] Pp. 99-113.

McCarter, P. Kyle, Jr. 1980. *I Samuel*. [See above, *Ch. Six*].

———. 1984. *II Samuel*. Anchor Bible; Garden City, NY: Doubleday.

Miscall, Peter D. 1986. *1 Samuel: A Literary Reading*. ISBL; Bloomington: Indiana Univ.

Propp, William H. 1993. "Kinship in 2 Samuel 13." *CBQ* 55:39-53.

Schwartz, Regina M. 1991. "Adultery in the House of David: The Metanarrative of Biblical Scholarship and the Narratives of the Bible." *Semeia* 54:35-56. Also in Rosenblatt and Sitterson, eds., *"Not in Heaven."* [See above, *Ch. Two*, under Trible] Pp. 192-210, 253-54.

Trible, Phyllis. 1984. "Tamar: The Royal Rape of Wisdom." In *Texts of Terror*. [See above, *Ch. Two*] Pp. 37-63.

Yee, Gale. 1988. " 'Fraught With Background': Literary Ambiguity in II Samuel 11." *Interpretation* 42:240-53.

Chapter Eight: Until No Body Remains

Barnett, R. D. and D. J. Wiseman. 1969. *Fifty Masterpieces of Ancient Near Eastern Art*. London: The Trustees of the British Museum.

Bird, Phyllis. 1989. " 'To Play the Harlot': An Inquiry into an Old Testament Metaphor." In Day, ed., *Gender and Difference in Ancient Israel*. [See above, *Ch. Six*, under Niditch] Pp. 75-94.

Camp, Claudia V. 1985. *Wisdom and the Feminine*. B&L 11; Sheffield: Almond.

———. "What's So Strange About the Strange Woman?" In David Jobling, Peggy L. Day, and Gerald T. Sheppard, eds., *The Bible and the Politics of Exegesis*. Cleveland, Ohio: Pilgrim. Pp. 17-31, 301-304.

———. 1992. "1-2 Kings." In Newsom and Ringe, eds., *The Women's Bible Commentary*. [See above, *Intro*.] Pp. 96-109.

Fontaine, Carole R. 1990. "A Heifer from Thy Stable: On Goddesses and the Status of Women in the Ancient Near East." In Bach, ed., *The Pleasure of Her Text*. [See above, *Ch. Seven*] Pp. 69-95.

García-Treto, Francisco O. 1990. "The Fall of the House: A Carnivalesque Reading of 2 Kings 9 and 10." *JSOT* 46:47-65. Rev. and repr. in Fewell, ed., *Reading Between Texts*. [See above, *Intro*.] Pp. 153-172.

Kristeva, Julia. 1982. "Semiotics of Biblical Abomination." In *Powers of Horror: An Essay on Abjection*. Trans. Leon S. Roudiez. New York: Columbia Univ. Pp. 90-112. [Orig. 1982]

Lasine, Stuart. 1991. "Jehoram and the Cannibal Mothers (2 Kings 6.24-33): Solomon's Judgment in an Inverted World." *JSOT* 50:27-53.

Long, Burke O. 1984. *1 Kings with an Introduction to Historical Literature*. Forms of Old Testament Literature 9; Grand Rapids: Eerdmans.

———. 1991. *2 Kings*. Forms of Old Testament Literature 10; Grand Rapids: Eerdmans.

Miscall, Peter D. 1989. "Elijah, Ahab and Jehu: A Prophecy Fulfilled." *Prooftexts* 9:73-83.

Pippin, Tina. 1992a. *Death and Desire: The Rhetoric of Gender in the Apocalypse of John*. LCBI; Louisville: Westminster/John Knox.

———. 1992b. "Jezebel Re-Vamped." Unpub. paper, Society of Biblical Literature Annual Meeting, San Francisco.

Shields, Mary E. 1993. "Subverting a Man of God, Elevating a Woman: Role and Power Reversals in 2 Kings 4." *JSOT* forthcoming.

Winter, Urs. 1983. *Frau und Göttin*. Orbis Biblicus et Orientalis, 53. Freiburg: Universitätsverlag; Göttingen: Vandenhoeck & Ruprecht.

INDEXES

Authors

Biblical Names

Biblical References

David's Women

We are David's women
left to keep the house

Ten of David's women
abandoned by the king
to meet a marauding army
as if we could do anything
to keep the house

We are David's women
forsaken by the father
ravaged by the son
left without the spirit
to protest what was done
all because David
couldn't keep his house

We are David's women
widows so they say
locked in a house of keeping
until our dying day
all because we could not
keep the house

We are David's women
forever barred from view
our bodies marked like territory
(Give the dogs their due)
all because we could not
leave the house

We are Israel's women
few of us remain
all of us are marked
all of us constrained
by our sovereign's orders
to keep the house

We are Israel's women
time and text have veiled
bearing silent witness
to the fathers who have failed
to keep the house

—DNF